Introduction to intercultural studies

Introduction to intercultural studies

Outline of a project
for elucidating and promoting communication
between cultures
Unesco, 1976-1980

With the exception of the documents emanating directly from Unesco, the opinions expressed in the papers presented below do not necessarily reflect the Organization's views and commit only their authors.

1846

P(uve)

Published in 1983
by the United Nations Educational,
Scientific and Cultural Organization
7 place de Fontenoy, 75700 Paris
Printed by Imprimerie Floch, Mayenne

ISBN 92-3-101850-7
French edition 92-3-210850-0 (1980)

Foreword

The Unesco programme of cultural studies deliberately began to
tackle intercultural problems as from 1976 in order to give
effect to a resolution adopted by the Organization's General
Conference. Thenceforward, the prospecting of the transversal
axes and the areas where the major regional and sub-regional
cultures meet, and an analysis of the characteristics and
implications of such a meeting were to be added to research into,
and promotion and dissemination of these cultures, which had
for long constituted - and still do constitute - the basis of
this programme.

While the undertaking as such received general approval
from the beginning, the same cannot be said of the word used
to describe it: to be sure, from a vocabulary point of view,
"intercultural" is a convenient abbreviation, but it is not
found in the dictionaries. As a distant cousin of the more
widely accepted "cross-cultural", it is often considered ter-
minologically ambiguous. Before going further, it was necessary
to clear the air regarding this little controversy which,
incidentally, we only mention in the interests of intellectual
honesty, since it has little effect on the heart of the matter.
Furthermore, the term "intercultural" is flexible enough -
which is undoubtedly what causes these reservations - to be
applicable everywhere, since nothing and nobody in the world is
culturally all of one piece or is not the result of some degree
of contamination or mixture. Even if introspection reveals
nothing of this composite character to our individual consciousness, every person, by birth or by acquisition, is more or less
profoundly made up of extraneous cultural admixtures and successive influences; this is a commonplace, but one which might
help the progress of international understanding if it penetrated
people's minds more deeply.

At least, such discussions can help to clarify the distinction between the two approaches - the conventional study of a
given culture and inter-cultural research respectively. In the
first case, the researcher is confronted with a sufficiently
stable and homogeneous cultural reality - or one which is assumed
to be so as a working hypothesis - for its most constant features
to be distinguishable, having a geo-historical and human substratum sufficiently marked to conform to a distinctive name
and define a relatively circumscribed field of study. On the

other hand, the "intercultural" is everything not conforming to
this description: it is - to state it more simply - what brings
at least two cultures or two cultural components into play.

This elementary criterion could, obviously, be given an
infinite number of shades of meaning depending on the different
definitions of culture - but at least it has the merit of being
clear. It is the one selected, for example, for making a world
inventory of intercultural research, the principle of which has
just been adopted and the first - experimental - stage of which
will cover three pilot regions and three basic disciplines. The
investigation will subsequently be generalized only if this
first preliminary stage yields conclusive results. On the basis
of an inventory of the research work available at present, it
is supposed to bring to light what has been dealt with and what
has been neglected in the field under consideration: once this
is done, it will be easier to tackle the new programme on a sound
basis and along the most useful lines in furtherance of the
preliminary work carried on since 1976 relative to the definition
of its objectives and methodology.

Undoubtedly, in the minds of those who initiated the project,
there was more a vague feeling that there was a lacuna in
Unesco cultural programmes, in view of the development of human
society, rather than a well-defined programme. The first
directives of the Organization's deliberative assemblies, which
date back to 1974, were confined to mentioning "problems having
a common interest for various countries and cultures". It was
several years before the purport of the topic at hand was defined
exactly: in a world where barriers are falling, where the intensification of exchanges and communications is causing autarchies
to disintegrate and particularisms to become relative, it was
becoming insufficient to confine ourselves to a frontal approach
to the chief cultures which shared the world and which might be
described as more or less "established". The division of activities in relation to the analysis and promotion of cultural
values on the basis of major geographical areas was becoming too
rigid, and the research apparatus incomplete: a diagonal extension
was necessary.

Previously, Unesco had already taken a few initiatives in
this field. In particular, the "Major Project on Mutual Appreciation of Eastern and Western Cultural Values", essentially
aimed at educational and practical events and activities, had
helped to make the public - and undoubtedly the Organization
itself - aware of these problems between 1957 and 1966 and had
given some idea of their complexity. Also, certain projects
implemented within the context of the cultural studies programme
had begun to extend research to regions of the world (the
Caribbean, the Sahel, East Africa and Indian Ocean, etc.) where
movements of population and upheavals of history have caused
inter-ethnic mixtures which locally generated new cultural
features and values.

But the thinking which, in 1975-1976, preceded the establishment of the medium-term plan now being pursued (1) was to
extend Unesco responsability further in the direction of new
concerns, as witness the "principles of action" laid down by the
General Conference at its 19th Session (Nairobi, 1976):

"Intra-cultural authenticity must necessarily be supplemented
by inter-cultural dialogue. For unless one is to run the risk
of encouraging national compartmentalization and sectarianism in
one or other form, it is important to ensure that each culture
is open to the influence of all the others within a broad international framework. Specificity on the one hand and intercultural relations on the other are seen thus as two complementary
terms, giving poise and balance to this group of activities taken
as a whole (...)"

"It will, for example, be advisable to make the definition
of cultural regions fairly flexible. These rarely coincide with
political boundaries. The approach adopted must enable comparisons, exchanges and rapprochements to be made between sub-regions
and countries which share a common heritage, even if they differ
today in respect of economic or social circumstances or ideological standpoints. The programme will be planned more flexibly,
consideration being given to the individual sub-regions making
up the large geographical regions and special attention paid
to areas where different civilizations adjoin, such as the
Caribbean and South East Asia. In this way the programme will
make a greater contribution to promoting mutual inter-cultural
respect and international understanding".

These analyses and statements of intent are summarized in
the declaration of the objective relating to cultural studies:
"Appreciation and respect for the cultural identity". This
central theme can be considered from two complementary points
of view - that of the awareness of an individual, a group, a
nation or a region of its own identity - an awareness which
today is recognized as an essential factor in development - and
that of respect for the identity of others, which is related to
the questions of tolerance, recognition and ethnocentrism - and
communication problems generally. In fact, intercultural communication is merely a <u>complication</u> of communication in general -
since it makes such communication more complex by adding the
parameter of diversity of origin or adherence - but a complication which is being rendered less exceptional every day as a
result of world changes.

Thus it is that the word "intercultural" has gradually taken its
place in front of a series of general studies - nowadays grouped
in a new section of the Cultural Studies Division - aimed at

---

(1) Cf. Unesco: Medium-term plan (1977-1982), 1977. An abridged
     edition of this document was published by the Organization
     under the title: <u>Thinking Ahead: Unesco and the challenges</u>
     <u>of today and tomorrow.</u>

analysing the interplay of cultures at relational level - whether
such relation is historical and factual (phenomena of interaction
and acculturation) or created in the mind of the researcher (comparative approach).

To be sure, "intercultural" is now a by-word, and the field
of knowledge concerning it is spreading daily. I would therefore
not like to terminate this foreword without pointing out the spirit
in which the Organization decided to take a hand in it.

In the first place, Unesco is no more guided by a purely
speculative motive in this field than in any other. While it is
part of the Organization's task to promote the enrichment of
knowledge and scientific cooperation, its role is not so much to
undertake research itself as to stimulate it by relating it to
operational perspectives. Although Unesco is in some respects a
planning and advisory organization, it is not a university. It
would be hopeless to expect it to undertake analyses of pure elu-
cidation or to throw definitive light on the doubtful areas of
intercultural research which is still very fragmentary - an
almost unlimited field, even if we only consider one of the
highly diverse types or methods of intervention connected with
it; i.e. whether it is a matter of studying, from the socio-
cultural point of view, a region with a high rate of multi-ethnic
density or of detecting the trans-cultural migrations of an idea,
a typical object, or an artistic or ritual element which loses
certain features or acquires others according to the region where
it is propagated, or of comparing the similarities and dissimil-
arities of the relationship of certain myths, beliefs and values
to which the various cultures impart universal application, or
whether we take a more technical interest in difficulties of
translation and anything related to what is "foreign" or not
transmissible when an attempt is made to transpose the creative
values of one culture to another. Or again, whether we take an
interest in the mutations of a language from frontier to frontier
or an analysis of more generally applicable phenomena, such as
the psycho-social aspects of intercultural communication or the
patterns and processes of acculturation.

All this is the field of the scientist. But even if the
entire field were covered and all the gaps filled, it would still
be necessary to make sure, in order to bring the research validly
up to date, that certain existing studies were not affected by
the major shortcoming which has for too long handicapped cultural
anthropology - the one-sided point of view, or prejudice, to put
it simply. It is not merely that there are many gaps in the
list of studies; of those which do exist, many need to be re-
written. For no precaution is excessive when it is a question
of reducing the ethnocentric focusing and tendencies inherent
in the conceptual categories of even the most honest researcher
who takes it upon himself to make an objective exploration of
the interwoven influences of two cultures.

Undoubtedly, a scrupulous analysis of the problem would
result in our considering a number of cases, depending on whether
we were dealing with two very similar cultures or two cultures
which history has placed in a situation of rivalry or antagonism.

In the first case, everything leads us to suppose that the two
cultures concerned will be more profoundly and more objectively
discussed by a researcher belonging to the area of civilization
in which the relation takes place. In the second case, excessive
closeness to one of the two conflicting cultures may constitute
a handicap and engender prejudice.
There is, therefore, no question of invalidating all research
emanating from an outside view. It would also be unrealistic to
imagine that the method of multi-ethnic groups of specialists
(recommended during one of the meetings organized by Unesco to
lay the foundations of the project) can conveniently be applied
in all circumstances. What is most important to remember is
that the complicity which familiarization, as a result of lengthy
study, may have established between a researcher and the "foreign"
subject of his research - even when it results in heartfelt con-
version and a sort of intellectual and mental "naturalization" -
cannot be considered a full guarantee of neutrality.

This is why the conclusions of the Seminar which laid the
foundations of the new programme in Belgrade in 1976, the proceedings of which form part of this publication, laid such emphasis on the necessity of giving precedence, in the first stage,
to problems of methodology. Before tackling thematic research,
it was necessary - and this was the main task to which the past
three or four years have been devoted - to clarify the concepts
of method relating to "ways of acquiring knowledge" and to everything which comes into play and may contribute to distorting
the approach of specialists to forms of culture which are by
origin foreign to them; this, as the Report in question states,
would make it possible "to prevent this project, the aim of which
is greater respect for cultural relativism, from being itself
tainted with ethnocentrism".

To be sure, progress has been achieved in this direction
over the past few decades (as Professor Louis Bazin notes, in
a text reproduced here, in relation to Asiatic studies, now
relieved of a certain degree of "orientalism"). But the traps
set by ethnocentrism are so cunning and its reflexes in the subconscious mind of the researcher are so insidious, that they all
too often abuse his good faith. Too much emphasis cannot, therefore, be placed on the fact that impartiality in approach, based
on a consciousness sufficiently informed regarding the diversity
of attitudes and a feeling for the dignity attached to any culture, constitutes the essential prerequisite for an approach to
the "difference". This applies to everyday behaviour and to
research. It is difficult to see where such a principle could
be guaranteed apart from an organization such as Unesco.

In everyday life, wherever a good standard of intercultural
communication is a condition of success (diplomacy, technical
cooperation, prospecting of foreign markets, adaptation of advertising to suit the receiving culture, etc.), schemes designed
to train persons responsible in the ways of thinking, feeling,
acting and reacting of the opposite numbers to be convinced,
have increased in number. It is certain that in the hands of
diplomats, technicians and merchants, a more subtle knowledge of
the ways and means of gaining access to the person to be per-

suaded may be degraded into an instrument of cynicism and commer-
cialism and provide a new means of alienation, though in a more
roundabout way. The fact remains that international concern with
the intercultural is gaining ground every day and is being integrated into everyday life, come what may and in spite, undoubtedly, of many misgivings.

On the basis of widely varying motives, we thus note that Unesco
and the private sector unite in recognizing the necessity of
preparing the way for a more tolerant cohabitation among cultures:
a convergence - or rather a significant crosscheck - which would
confirm Unesco's officials, if such confirmation were necessary,
in the idea that a project likely to give us a better mastery
over the phenomena relating to the closeness, interaction and
integration of culture, and to provide an analysis of successes
and shortcomings in intercultural communication so as to appreciate its effect, has never been so necessary.
     At the beginning of this Foreword, we evoked, as the immediate
justifications of the project, the need to complement the studies
of regional cultures, and the necessity to respond to the international intensification of exchanges and communications. As
for its ultimate aims, we gave to understand that, so far as
Unesco was concerned, it was not merely a matter of taking part
in a particularly stimulating field of research: the statement of
a large part of the subjects for study and action given priority
by the various meetings whose proceedings are recorded in the
present publication, and the very title of one of them - devoted
to "Education for mutual understanding of cultures" - are a
sufficient indication of the action-oriented nature of Unesco's
objectives in this endeavour.
     Accepting the difference but also recognizing solidarities:
"It was recommended", we read in the Guidance Note on the objective "Cultural Identity" forming part of the Medium-Term Plan
already mentioned, "that...there should be still further expansion
of studies and operational activities which highlight the contributions, the manifold influences and particularly the forms of
intellectual and moral interdependence which exist between cultures so as to strengthen the bonds based on historical realities
and affinities of values between peoples, in conformity with
Unesco's universal calling". In short, behind this new activity
(and this is also applicable to the Organization's programme in
general), international understanding and peace are at stake,
no matter how indirect the approach may appear to be, no matter
how vast the task and how tenacious the resistance which has to
be overcome or corrected. Here, faith and patience are cardinal
virtues, as also is generosity of the sort which may result in
undertaking long-term projects without the certainty of being
present at their completion.

The papers presented below go back over the stages and con-
sultations through which the project has taken shape. They number
fifteen in all and represent the entire documentation provided for
the four meetings that have hitherto marked the exercise. Two of
them are briefing or guidance notes which, like this foreword,
were drafted by the Unesco Secretariat. The first document in the
collection : "Intercultural relations: schools, methods and research themes", was prepared by the Institut universitaire d'études
du développement, Geneva. Apart from the four final reports, the
other papers represent individual contributions signed by seven
authors who, by their nationality, origin, background or sphere of
competence, represent a panorama of regions and viewpoints
corresponding to a broad "geographical" and ideological coverage.
Their main titles and qualifications are given in the list of
participants at the end of the volume.

                                                          June 1980

Contents

I. Overview of the problem area

Meeting convened to study the preliminary aspects of the project: methodology, principal tendencies and state of research in intercultural studies (Belgrade, 1976)*

---

*   Organized by Unesco in cooperation with the Yugoslav National Commission for Unesco (Belgrade, 5-7 October 1976).

** Today: Institut universitaire d'études du développement.

1. *Preparatory document*

Intercultural relations:
schools, methods and subjects of research

*Institut universitaire
d'études du développement
Geneva*

VOCABULARY CONVENTIONS

Words are made to be understood or to confuse. Too many parallel
discussions are going on about the word "culture" for it to be
possible to introduce our subject without first indulging in a
few semantic clarifications (Cf. the file drawn up by Kroeber and
Kluckhohn, 1952). The purpose of these is not to give grounds
for thinking that the discussion regarding the notion of culture
is over so far as we are concerned. They merely indicate our
current conclusions and are offered as indispensable conventions
for our work, but they are provisional in the sense that our work
and our discussions will cause us to revise them - or at least
we hope so.

1. The most frequent use of this term limits its content to what
Violette Morin calls "Culture with a capital C", i.e. intellectual
and artistic production. This first acceptation (codified as C1)
seems to us to be a good description of a certain type of"produce
of civilization" (G. Gurvitch, 1957, 1960). But it is as well to
start from a wider perspective according to which all men and all
groups are the vehicles of culture, without which they could
not exist.

2. That being so, we shall adopt this second acceptation (C2)
inspired by Tylor (1871) and revived by G. Rocher (1968) -
a meaning which brings to light the systematic and total nature
inherent to any culture. "A related whole of more or less
formalized ways of thinking, feeling and acting which, learnt and
shared by a number of people, serve, both objectively and symbol-
ically, to make of those people a special, distinct collectivity".
This is the sense in which we shall henceforth use the word
"culture". Culture with a capital C (C1) and total culture (C2)
obviously designate two interrelated realities, the first being
a particular expression and degree of the second.

3. Culture and society should also be brought into relation with
one another. These two terms convey two ways of considering the
same reality. A society has a culture which is experienced by
men and by social groups, in a given territory. A culture only
lives when it is supported by living social groups. Society is

culture and men. By forgetting what may appear to be a truism, we
run the risk of forgetting to interpret the dynamism of a culture
by means of the dynamism of the human groups which experience it.
Preiswerk (1975) proposes the distinction, useful for analytical
purposes, between micro-culture, national culture, regional
culture and macro-culture. To emphasize the relation between
culture and the men who experience, assimilate, reproduce and
transform it, we would point out that a micro-culture corresponds
to a micro-society (or particular group), a national culture to
the nation-society (today marked by the universal presence of
the State), and regional culture to the regional society. Macro-
culture may be interpreted in two different ways. Either as the
dominant culture of a system of societies (system because it is
a number of societies linked by a unifying principle, such as
capitalism); or by placing emphasis on the diachrony. Macro-
culture therefore includes various national and regional
cultures forged during a long drawn out historical process which
has increased the number of contacts between them and the societies which support them. This process exceeds the lifetime of
a given society. That being so, this notion is very close to
that of civilization, at least in the sense in which Mauss and
Durkheim use it.

THE ENDOGENOUS AND THE EXOGENOUS

If the diachronic aspect of the social and historic sciences is
considered in perspective, two major currents affecting our
problem can be distinguished; these are absolute rivers, so
great is the extent to which each is fed by tributaries originatin
from the most varied sources:
- the first tends to grasp the dynamic principle of the history
of social change and cultural production and reproduction in the
encounters, exchanges and impacts between cultures. History consists of borrowings, rejections, mixtures, mergings and crushings.
This current, therefore, places emphasis on "external dynamisms"
(Balandier, 1971);
- the second, on the other hand, places emphasis on the notion of
society and its internal complexity which engenders the movement.
Here, history consists of antagonisms and/or collaborations
between the social groups of society, of tensions between their
economic and their social organization, etc. It is therefore the
production of "internal dynamism" and follows an endogenous course

1. External dynamisms
Let us first mention the school of anthropology known as "diffus-
ionist", which evolved chiefly in the United States and Germany
at the beginning of the century. Chiefly concerned with the
spatial dimension of cultural changes, it established geographical
maps making it possible to follow the diffusion of cultural
features (atomistic perspective!), such as the use of the horse
(Wissler, 1914) and painted pottery.

As a reaction against the evolutionism of the period, this approach is characteristic of North-American cultural anthropology right up to the present day. The first works on what is known as "acculturation" appeared in the United States in the thirties. According to the original usage, which is still in force, the term referred to "all inter-action phenomena resulting from the contact of two cultures" (Herskovits, M.J. 1938; Wachtel, N. 1974). Acculturation studies retain the atomistic perspective of diffusionism by breaking down cultures into a number of autonomous features, changes which can be followed in situations of contact. But they differ from diffusionism by concentrating on a precise geographical area.

Thus a study is made of the way in which the knowledge of Spanish, the use of shoes, literacy, etc., spread amongst the individuals of an Indian village in Mexico. Cultural change is considered purely as a process of communication (Redfield, 1950).

These studies have the defect of ignoring the fact that cultural features have no life of their own but depend on wider aggregates - the cultural systems and the societies into which they are integrated. The cultural features and their movements in space and time can only be understood when situated in the overall systems confronting one another. In spite of this fundamental shortcoming, however, these schools bequeath us their concern for phenomena of encounter and interesting typologies of cultural encounters. For example, the distinction between the processes of acculturation, which may be substitutive, additive, syncretic, deculturing, etc. and the results of acculturation (assimilation, incorporation, extinction, etc.).

It is worthwhile to mention other affluents, which also concentrate on encounter phenomena but with different purposes and in different styles: those military and diplomatic histories which deal with a country's external relations and their consequences; the histories of colonization written by the colonizer (cf. in this connection, the critical analysis of Preiswerk and Perrot, 1975). Such works usually have nationalist and ethnocentric overtones. For example, histories of colonization only see one-way traffic running from the colonizer to the colonized.

2. Internal dynamisms

In the second current - that which favours endogenous phenomena - the intercultural and the encounter of civilizations are given short shrift. And yet, this aspect should not be neglected, for two reasons:
(1) because "development sociology" is their offspring,
and because the latter, in its ignorance of external dynamism, led research into a cul-de-sac between 1945 and 1965. This error of guidance should therefore be taken into account;(2) the second reason is positive. This is the tradition in which we discover the thorough analysis of this totality made up of society and culture, whereas the first current had only a rough impression of it.

Into this river is integrated most of the sociological tradition, with which converges so-called evolutionist anthropology, for both are obnubilated by the problem of the origin and

evolution of humanity, so far as sociology is concerned, from
Comte to T. Parsons, and including Marx, Toennies (1887) and
Durkheim (1893), and so far as anthropology is concerned, from
Morgan (1877) and Tylor (1871) to L. White (1949) and J. Steward
(1955). The reply received always takes the form of a single (or
at least dominant) thread of evolution, always running from
"minus" to "plus". The driving force of this evolution should
be sought in the endogenous factors of the culture society. The
encounter between peoples and cultures, then, is interpreted as
an occasion given to backward peoples to catch up with the great
flow of history and speed up their progress towards it. An
ideal beloved of Hegel, evident in Marx (the expansion of
capitalism awakes the dormant peoples) and reasserted in Rostow's
"Non-communist manifesto" (1960). The negative repercussions of
this gigantic flood became manifest in the advent of a development sociology which deliberately ignored the fact that the socio-
cultural construction of the planet results from multiple inter-
crossings. Consequently, it does not show that the transformation of societies and cultures does not only depend on their
own resources but also on their insertion into the world-wide
system. To quote two examples, this is the major lure of the
schools presided over by Rostow (1960), who speaks of stages, and
by Eisenstadt (1965), who speaks of modernization.

Although marxism is in itself an evolutionism, it takes a
distinctive direction owing to the fact that it very soon develops
a theory of imperialism (Lenin, 1916), which may be considered
as the theory of forced acculturation caused by the capitalist
system.

On the other hand, by concentrating analysis on the society-
culture unit, this current - and each of the confluents in its
own way - has contributed to a knowledge of this unit as a
"total social phenomenon" (M. Mauss, 1930), or in other words
as a totality (predominance of the whole over the parts), which
is not compact and monolithic, but complex, plural and living,
and in which social types (from the micro-sociological to the
major groups) and cultural levels (from material culture to
collective mental states) are interwoven according to dialectics
of varying rhythms.

From what these authors tell us about the society-culture
unit, we deduce that intercultural relations cannot be reduced
to current cultural features, but constitute an encounter of
complex aggregates giving rise to a metasystem of interactions
with almost unlimited possibilities of exchange. Thus, the
principles governing exchanges must be deciphered in relation to
the internal dynamism of each unit concerned.

In our opinion it is to the outstanding credit of R. Bastide
that he always sought to put the sociological tradition and the
viewpoint of cultural anthropology in perspective - the "external"
and the "internal" factors in any encounter (Lalive D'Epinay,
1974).

BRINGING THE INTERNAL AND THE EXTERNAL INTO PERSPECTIVE

1. Apart from a few historical works, the necessity of bringing
the two viewpoints into perspective has only been recognized
since 1960. To be sure, attention should be drawn to an important line of thought in which the analysis has always depended
on patterns taking internal and external factors into account.
We are here concerned with B. Malinowski (1929, 1938) and,
subsequently, British social anthropology. To be sure, there has
been much criticism of Malinowski's functionalism and of his way
of subordinating anthropology to the requirements of the colonial
administration; but he did at least point out forcefully that
cultural novelties (external factors) could not be integrated
into, say, an African village, unless there was a "receptive
structure", i.e. except in relation to a certain state of
"internal factors". He also emphasized that culture was an integrated whole.

   Following in his tracks, British social anthropology produced
a plethora of monographs on the socio-cultural changes resulting
from Europe's irruption into the Third World. We would mention
Richards (1940), Mair (1939) and Gluckman (1960), to whom we owe
the expression "colonial situation" to designate the overall
insertion structure of Third World peoples.

   As from 1960, this complementarity of the two perspectives
was generally accepted, as it was in the majority of the social
sciences.

   In France, Bastide and Balandier set the fashion, the latter
reviving the notion of "colonial situation" and supplementing it
with the notion of "dependence situation" to describe the neo-
colonial context. Bastide's works on African religions in Brazil
demonstrate the force of collective memory, even in the most
dramatic social situations, and the dialectic between the infra-
structural movements of a host society (Brazil) and culture conveyed by memory, permanently creating and recreating religious
societies. In Bastide's footsteps, Lalive D'Epinay (1975) was
to cling to the ups and downs of a religious ideology of dominants - protestantism - in a dominated but post-colonial sub-
continent - that of Latin America. In Africa, under the stimul-
ation of Balandier, particular interest was to be taken in black
syncretic messianisms.

   Today, ethnic history is a necessity. In 1960, Bastide noted
the lack of any comparative study of the works of historians and
those of ethnologists. Since then, M.I. Pereira de Queiroz
of Brazil has carried out such a study in relation to messianisms. But others - the Mexican Leon Portilla (1964), J. Murra,
a United States Romanian (1974), the Frenchman N. Wachtel
(1973) and the Swiss L. Necker (1976) - integrated into their
approach to the matter the techniques of the historian and
those of the ethno-anthropologist.

   We owe to Soviet anthropology extensive work on acculturation known under the name of ethno-genesis.

   In Latin America, a school is emerging, in which anthropologists such as R. Stavenhagen (1969), sociologists like

F.H. Cardoso (1966) and economists such as O. Sunkel (1970) are
associating. These form the so-called "current of studies on
dependence"; they work out notions of "colonial socio-cultural
training" and concern themselves with analyzing concrete situations which result, historically, from the complex inter-
weaving of different cultures.

Not unlike the last-named, there is French economic anthropology, which incorporates elements of structuralism and
marxism : Godelier (1973) and Meillassoux (1969).

2. In spite of the vast progress achieved in the field of encounters between cultures over the last two decades, a long
road remains to be trod.

Firstly, entire sections of this problem have hardly been
tackled. Research is concentrated on acculturation resulting
from the expansion of the West into the Third World. What
about contacts between other cultures, the historic volume of
which is far greater than that constituted by the history of
Europe? Moreover, our knowledge of the influence of other
cultures on the West is very patchy.

Next it should be noted that the vast majority of research
on encounters between cultures is the work of Westerners. The
work of the Latin Americans is beginning to establish itself,
while that coming from Africa and Asia is more often individual
than emanating from currents and schools of thought. It is to
be hoped - and the trend is already becoming evident - that
such work will be carried out to an increasing extent by non-
Westerners, not only as regards their own cultures but also
as regards those of the West, which has everything to gain by
seeing itself as others see it.

Finally, theoretical and systematic structures relating
to intercultural encounters have scarcely been started. Two
works only have established themselves owing to their system-
atics: that of Bastide, whose Anthropologie appliquée (1971)
perhaps constitutes the best summing up, and that of the Brazilian D. Ribeiro (1968) who propounds, in a work which is
still too little known, a theory of world history bringing the
exogenous and the endogenous, continuities and interruptions,
unification and fragmentation processes into perspective.

THE COGNITIVE DIMENSION OF INTERCULTURAL RELATIONS

The very fact of more or less consciously sharing the cultural
heritage of a given society or social group places a restriction
on knowledge of other cultures and societies and of relations
with them. In order to grasp the extent of possible distortions,
it is necessary to resort to certain fundamental concepts.

1. Cultural identity
If we wish to study the way in which different cultures encounter,
fertilize and destroy one another, we ought in principle to have
the means of marking off cultural "frontiers". This gives rise

to the question of selecting criteria by means of which a
typology of cultures can be established. For the purpose of
simplicity, two approaches are possible. Firstly, we can consider marking off geo-cultural units (societies or ethnic groups)
which have characteristic features enabling us to distinguish
them. This approach leads to the establishment of a cultural
atlas of the world. Attempts along these lines, particularly in
the field of German ethnology and American anthropology, have
not met with unmixed enthusiasm or approval. This is partly
because the idea of "cultural purity" (as is clearly expressed in the German term 'Reinkultur") is extremely problematic.
Too often has there been a tendency to attribute to a society
the exclusive originality of its identity, even when it was
historically impossible to prove the absence of interaction
with different societies. It should also be remembered that
cultural identity is often asserted in relation to a political
movement. For example, we have, at the level of micro-cultures,
separatist or irredentist movements or, at the level of regional
cultures, movements of unification (pan-Africanism) or expansion
(pan-Germanism).

Secondly, we can determine non-spatial units, in order to
establish, on the basis of an analysis of values, behaviours and
institutions in the various societies, an inventory of similar or
dissimilar characteristics. According to the criterion selected,
a distinction would be made between materialistic and spiritual-
istic cultures, market-economy and planned-economy cultures,
cultures favouring the large family or the small family, etc.
(Such opposites should in no case be understood to be dichotomies
attributing a cultural feature exclusively to one type of society).
The advantage of this approach is that the researcher is not
confined to a viewpoint obliging him to present the diversity of
cultures in the form of a "geographical" type of document, for
such a document has the disadvantage of presenting a static view
of cultures, unless the atlas is revised at fairly frequent
intervals. No matter what the approach chosen, it is essential
that it should be able to show cultural exchanges and influences
and that it results in a comparative study of cultures. This,
obviously, gives rise to serious epistemological and methodological problems (Rokkan, 1968).

We must therefore review the problems confronting a researcher
investigating a culture which is not his own.

But beforehand, determining cultural identity still gives
rise to the problem of cultural representativity. Who, in a given
society, is qualified and able to define what makes it specific
in relation to others? What does a prime minister represent as
compared with a villager? Or a university graduate as compared
with a manual worker ? Two elements should be taken into account
when we try to assess the information provided by one or the other
of these social groups regarding their identity. On the one hand,
researchers tend to attribute more weight to information provided
by an educated élite. As a result, there is a risk of total
culture (C2) being reduced to culture with a capital C (C1), considered by the dominant class as being representative of the
whole. On the other hand, by favouring the élite as valid sub-

jects for interrogation, we enter the segment of society which is
most subject to or accepts external cultural influence, although,
on the contrary, it may fight with determination against all
foreign penetration. The concept of cultural identity has a
heuristic value in research and is even indispensable for an
understanding of intercultural phenomena, but it is difficult
to impart a precise content to it and to attribute scientific
value to the results obtained in the context of research based
on it (Erikson, 1968; Zavalloni, 1973; Berthoud, 1976).

2. Cognitive ethnocentrism
Ethnocentrism is not, as has sometimes been said, an evil which
must be extirpated at all costs (ethnocentrism is often confused
with racism). In fact, we are concerned with a human attitude
inextricably bound up with the very existence of cultural diversity. To accept diversity is to accept ethnocentrism, for social-
ized man in the context of a given culture is usually unconscious
of the cognitive processes by means of which he reproduces false
images of other cultures. Should he be obliged to sacrifice his
identity in order to limit the extent of the cognitive distortions
he is liable to produce? The problem, incidentally, is not confined to intercultural relations. All knowledge is a social
structure (Berger and Luckmann, 1966).

Having said as much, we can study ethnocentrism in the cognitive behaviour. Such research is liable to provide openings
towards the correction of an obviously too restricted knowledge.
There is an abundant, though somewhat heteroclite, literature on
this subject (see bibliography in Preiswerk and Perrot, 1975;
and particularly, Brown, 1963; Klineberg, 1966; Leiris, 1960;
Levi-Strauss, 1960 and 1971; Northrop, 1946, Northrop and
Livingstone, 1964 and Sachs, 1971).

The chief concern of most ethnologists and anthropologists
who have studied this problem is that of the cognitive distortions, at micro-culture level, capable of explaining an aggressive attitude towards other groups (Levine and Campbell, 1972).
At present the tendency is rather to analyse the phenomenon at
the macro-culture level. In the literature quoted in the above
paragraph, the types of question asked are as follows : where
are the obstacles to mutual understanding between East and
West situated? What are the epistemological reasons limiting
the accessibility of different societies to the sciences of
Western man? What is the relation between culture and the development strategy which different countries suggest at international
level? What are the cognitive mechanisms ensuring the establishment of an intercultural hierarchy - or a "peoples' honours-list"
as Levi-Strauss said - ?

The conceptual instruments at present available are sufficient
for research into cognitive ethnocentrism at macro-culture level
to be pursued further. Among the many analytical categories,
that of the intercultural transfer of concepts is worth mentioning.
Such a transfer takes place when a concept worked out and defined
in the context of the observer's culture of origin is used to describe a phenomenon of the culture of destination. This process
exists in all fields of knowledge, from religion to political

science, from the arts to the economics of development. Only
quite recently has there been an awareness of the possible danger
of distortion arising from the unconscious use of concepts, for
it is usual to describe societies different from that of the
researcher by what they are not (societies without markets; pre-
industrial, illiterate, etc.) without saying at the same time
what they are. The concepts emerging from the different cultural
contexts and applied in all directions out of their context are
innumerable. A few research projects are under way (e.g. Unesco,
1975) but we are only at the beginning.

RESEARCH SUBJECTS

As we have just seen, there is a vast field of research to be
covered in the category of intercultural transfers of concepts
alone, in view of the multiplicity of concepts suitable for study
and the variety of cultural contexts (from a point of view both
of origin and destination) that can be included in a sample. But
the transfer of concepts is only one of many categories of cognitive ethnocentrism. These categories differ according to
culture, and it is precisely by means of research that they can
be listed.

Before tackling a few particularly important research subjects, it should be specified that cultural research is a form in
intercultural relations. To enter into contact with another
culture in order to study it is to set up an interaction with it.
The questions that the researcher may put stimulate curiosity or
awake mistrust. They may, to take extreme situations, induce in
the person or group interrogated either an open-mouthed admiration
of the culture or the interrogator or a radical withdrawal. The
objects accompanying the researcher, his attitude and his way of
life, which is more or less obvious, are all factors which may
be considered as being integrated into an overall cultural
penetration process. At the same time, it may happen that the
researcher changes during his own investigation and finishes by
regarding his culture of origin in a different way. There is,
therefore, actually a relation - a phenomenon which is inadequate-
ly expressed by the term study alone.

1. Categories of cognitive ethnocentrism in various cultural
   contexts
There is a comparatively large number of studies on the way in
which Westerners approach the study of other macro-cultures. The
study of this ethnocentric knowledge, however, is incomplete. At
the same time, only a few studies are available on the cognitive
ethnocentrism which characterizes other macro-cultures (Fitzgerald,
1964). Catalogues of cognitive categories applied in various
cultural contexts could be drawn up. The indicators differentiating the cognitive behaviour of one macro-culture from that of
another should be discovered by means of empirical research, the
exact sources and method being chosen in accordance with the con-

text. For example, to what extent does a non-Western ethnocentrism manifest itself through the same mental categories as
those which were noted in the case of Western ethnocentrism -
cultural evolutionism, literacy, entry into contact as a condition of historicity, projection of values, unilateral legiti-
mation of action, transfer of concepts, stereotypes, enhancing
terminology, self-centred selection of data, ignoring the existence of others, dichotomization, naturalization of cultural
phenomena? (Preiswerk and Perrot, 1975). Is it possible to establish a typology of ethnocentrisms - for example, introverted
and expansionist, self-glorifying and self-denigrating?

2. Cultural dimension of national behaviour patterns

Apart from the macro-cultural level, it is important to carry out
more detailed studies at national level. To what extent is the
interaction between the nationals of different countries, whether
they represent official bodies or are businessmen, tourists or
university graduates, conditioned by cultural traditions? Here,
we find ourselves on the threshold of political science, the
study of international relations and social psychology. We should
have to go further than the numerous studies on national stereotypes (Buchanan and Cantrill, 1953; Klineberg, 1966). Any
valorization, belief, type of behaviour or institutions interiorized by the subject of one culture should be measured in relation
to the data which the subject of another culture considers as
being his own norm. Subsequently, it is a matter of relating
these considerations to the behaviour of the negotiator, the
diplomat, the technical cooperation expert or the businessman. An
effort in this direction, certain epistemological and cultural
assumptions of which call for some revision, is to be found in a
study of Americano-Greek and Americano-Japanese relations (Triandis
et al., 1972).

3. Diversity of cultures or cultural levelling

In this day and age, government activities relating to economic
development are concerted at world level. Whether it is a matter
of the present economic order or of a new order suggested by the
Third World to the United Nations, it would appear that a process
of unification of development patterns is taking place. In descriptive terms, this process can be examined at various levels:
at the summit, the question can be asked to what extent existing
and new development strategies convey a certain pattern of society,
the industrial society for example, which determines the options
of national decision-makers regarding the use of their resources.
At the base, the mere transmission of objects and gadgets produced
by the industrial society and consumed by another society ensures
that a social change has taken place. Between these two extremes,
there are other levels, but the question still remains: towards
what pattern of society is present development leading? Are we
actually in the presence of a standardization of values, institutions, types of behaviour, of a levelling of cultures to a world
standard?

Here again, the possibilities of empirical research are unlimited. But in addition, this problem is so important that we

must accompany it with a speculative dimension directed towards
the future. This consists of two lines of thought: what will happen
(forecast) and what sort of society do people want (normative)?
For the time being, we are uncertain, but recent experiments give
grounds for thought that a systematization of speculation should
be considered a valid aim of research. To give a few examples:
the number of geo-cultural units selected as fundamental for a
future world order varies from five (Mazrui, 1975) to ten (Rome
Club 1974) and even twenty-four (Kothari, 1974, Appendix). The
more the number increases, the nearer we get to a system based
on the existing nation-State. Only the Mazrui proposal is based
entirely on an organizational criterion favouring cultural
elements. We should also bear in mind another document, the significance of which has still to be assessed: the Declaration of
the International Federation of Institutes of Advanced Studies,
according to which cultural diversity is an essential condition
for the survival of the human species (IFIAS, 1976).

4. Cultural permanence in encounter processes

Ex. 1 : Colonization (the organization of the colony) succeeds
in large empires because the Spanish fit into a principle of
continuity and reinterpretation of these empires.
Ex. 2 : Colonization fails in the frontier zone and then succeeds through the mediation of the religious orders, since the
latter reintroduce the principle of continuity and reinterpretation.
Ex. 3 : Traditional Protestantism fails because it is a clean
break with Latin American culture. On the other hand, Pente-
costism succeeds because it displays this principle of continuity
and reinterpretation.
Ex. 4 : The Afro-American religions. This, in fact, would be a
matter of analysing encounter situations on the basis of notions
of:

- cultural reproduction;
- alogy/analogy of the cultural systems encountering one
  another - notions which, in the encounter process, have
  the equivalent in those of continuity/interruption;
- types of reinterpretation - types of syncretism.

5. Rates of change out of step

Looking for consistancies in cultural encounter phenomena, Bastide
(1971) put forward a theory according to which the rate of change
resulting from such encounters varied according to the level of
culture. The most rapid change occurred in the case of material
culture, the slowest in the mental and symbolical field; between
the two were situated transformations of social relations.

It would be interesting to develop this theme and try to find
out more precisely the reasons and mechanisms governing this time-
lag.

While this theory appears to be confirmed in the case of Third
World cultures affected by Western expansion, it is by no means
sure that it is so in the case of other encounters (e.g., during
the expansion of great religions such as Islam). It would be necessary to study the variations in these time lags in terms of the

contact situations and to find out to what extent it is possible
to discover universals.

6. Theories of world history explaining cultural unifications
    and dispersals

One way of understanding and explaining cultural encounters is
to transfer them into the more general context of great historical movements which have alternately produced cultural unifications
and cultural diffusions or dispersals.

The theme suggested here is to study the phenomena by the
light of the major theories of world history, particularly those
related to the study of the growth and decline of empires (e.g.,
Toynbee, 1934-54, Spengler, 1922-23 and Ribeiro, 1968).

For the reasons given above, particular attention would be
paid to theories taking both the exogenous and endogenous aspects
of the development of peoples into account. An attempt would be
made to discover the stage at which mankind is at present and
particularly whether, as certain people have asserted, it is in
a process of cultural dispersal owing to the decline of the "Western Empire".

BIBLIOGRAPHY

(List of authors quoted)

Balandier, Georges, Sens et Puissance, 1971, Paris.

Bastide, Roger, "La causalité externe et la causalité interne dans l'explication sociologique" in Cahiers internationaux de sociologie, XXI, 1956. "Problèmes de l'entrecroisement des civilisations et de leurs oeuvres" in G. Gurvitch, Traité de sociologie, Vol. 2, 1960, Paris. Les religions africaines au Brésil, Brésil, 1960, Paris. Anthropologie appliquée, 1971, Paris.

Berger, Peter and Luckmann, Thomas, The Social Construction of Reality, 1966, New York.

Berthoud, Gérald, "L'Identité et l'Altérité : pour une confrontation de l'épistémologie génétique et de l'anthropologie critique" in Les Sciences sociales avec et après Jean Piaget, 1976, Geneva.

Brown, Ina C., Understanding Other Cultures, 1963, Englewood Cliffs.

Buchanan, W. and Cantrill H., How Nations See Each Other, 1953, Urbana.

Cardoso, F.H. and Faleto, E., Dependencia y Desarrollo en América Latina, 1966, México.

Club de Rome, Stratégie pour demain (2nd report), 1974, Paris.

Comte, A., Cours de philosophie positive, 1830-1842, Paris.

Durkheim, E., La division du travail social, 1893, Paris.

Durkheim E. and Mauss, M., "Note sur la notion de civilisation" in l'Année sociologique, 1909-1912.

Eisenstadt, S.N., Protest and Change Modernization of Traditional Societies, 1965.

Erikson, Erik, Identity : Youth and Crisis, 1968, New York.

Fitzgerald, C.P., The Chinese View of Their Place in the World, 1964, London.

Gluckman, M., Custom and conflict in Africa, 1960, Oxford.

Godelier, Maurice, Horizon, trajets marxistes en anthropologie, 1973, Paris.

Gurvitch, G., La vocation actuelle de la sociologie, 1960, Paris.

Herskovits, M.-J., Acculturation, the Study of Culture Contact, 1938, New York.

Ifias, Le développement global : fin de la diversité culturelle, 1976, Stockholm.

Klineberg, Otto, The Human Dimension in International Relations, 1966, New York.

Kothari, Rajni, Footsteps into the Future, 1974, New York.

Kroeber, A.L., and Kluckhohn, C., "Culture : a critical review of concepts and definitions", in Papers of Peabody Museum of American Archaelogy and Ethnology, 1952, Harvard.

Lalive d'Epinay, Christian, "R. Bastide ou la sociologie des confins", in l'Année sociologique, 1974. Religion, dépendance et dynamique sociale, 1975, Paris.

Leiris, Michel, "Race et civilisation", in Le racisme devant la science, 1960, Unesco, Paris.

Leon-Portilla, A., El Reverso de la conquista, 1964, Mexico.

Lénine, V., L'impérialisme, stade suprême du capitalisme, 1916.

Levine, Robert and Campbell, Donald, Ethnocentrism : Theories of Conflict, Ethnic Attitudes and Group Behaviour, 1972, New York.

Lévi-Strauss, Claude, "Race et Histoire", in Le racisme devant la science, 1960, Paris. "Race et Culture", Revue internationale des sciences sociales, 1971, 4, pp. 657-658.

Mair, L., An African People in the Twentieth Century, 1939, London.

Malinowski, B., Practical Anthropology, 1929, Africa, II, 1. The Scientific Basis of Applied Anthropology, 1938, VIII, Convegno Reale Accademia d'Italia, Rome.

Marx, Karl, Oeuvres complètes.

Mauss, Marcel, "Civilisation, le mot et l'idée", 1930, Semaine du Centre international du synthèse, Paris.

Mazrui, Ali, "World Culture and the Search for Human Consensus", in On the Creation of a Just World Order, 1975, S.Mendlovitz, Ed.N.Y.

Meillassoux, Claude, L'anthropologie économique des Gouro de Côte d'Ivoire, 1964, Paris.

Morgan, Lewis H., Ancient Society, 1877, New York.

Morin, Violette, "La culture majuscule", in Communications, No. 6.

Murra, J., Formaciones económicas y sociales andinas, 1974, Lima.

Necker, Louis, Indiens Guarani et Chamanes franciscains, 1976, Geneva, 1979, Paris.

Northrop, F.S.C., The Meeting of East and West, 1946, New York.

Northrop, F.S.C., and Livingstone, Helen (Eds), Cross Cultural Understanding : Epistemology in Anthropology, 1964, New York.

Pereira de Queiroz, Maria-Isaura, Etnologia e historia de los movimentos mesianicos, 1969, Mexico

Preiswerk A. Roy, "Relations interculturelles et développement", in Le Savoir et le Faire, 1975, Cahiers de l'Institut d'Etudes du développement, No. 2, Geneva.

Preiswerk A. Roy, and Perrot, Dominique, Ethnocentrisme et Histoire: l'Afrique, l'Amérique indienne et l'Asie dans les manuels occidentaux, 1975, Paris.

Redfield, G.R., The Village That Chose Progress, 1950, Chicago.

Ribeiro, D., O Proceso civilizatario, 1968, Rio de Janeiro.

Richards, A.I., Land, Labour and Diet in Northern Rhodesia, 1940, Oxford.

Rocher, Guy, Introduction à la sociologie générale, 1968, Paris.

Rostow, W.W., The Stages of Economic Growth, 1960, Cambridge.

Rokkan, Stein (Ed.), Comparative Research Across Cultures and Nations, 1968, Paris.

Sachs, Ignacy, La découverte du Tiers Monde, 1971, Paris.

Spengler, O., Der Untergang des Abendlandes, 1922-1923, Berlin.

Stavenhagen, Rodolfo, Les classes sociales dans les sociétés agraires, 1969, Paris.

Steward, J., Theory of Culture Change, 1955, Urbana.

Sunkel, Osvaldo and Paz, Pedro, El subdesarrollo latinoamericano y la teoría del desarrollo, 1970, Mexico.

Toennies, F., Gemeinschaft und Gesellschaft, 1887.

Toynbee, A.O., A Study of History, 1934-1954, London.

Triandis, Harry et al., The Analysis of Subjective Culture, 1972, New York.

Tylor, E.B., Primitive Culture, 1871, London.

Unesco, Les cultures et le temps, 1975, Paris.

Wachtel, N., La vision des vaincus, 1973, Paris. "L'acculturation" in : Le Goff, J. and Nora, Pierre, Faire l'histoire, 1974, Paris.

White, L.A., The Science of Culture, 1949, New York.

Wissler, C., "Influence of the Horse in the Development of Plain Culture", American Anthropologist, XVI, 1914.

Zavalloni, Marisa, "L'identité psychosociale, un concept à la recherche d'une science", in Introduction à la psychologie sociale, Vol. II, 1973, Paris. Serge Moscovici (Ed.).

2. *Final report*[1]

1. The meeting was jointly convened by the Yugoslav Commission for Cooperation with Unesco and Unesco itself. It was organized by the Serbian Cultural Development Research Institute (Belgrade) and the Croatian Cultural Research Institute (Zagreb). It was held at the Headquarters of the Serbian Community for Culture and Education. There were twenty participants and a number of observers (2).

2. The first day was devoted to a general discussion in plenary session on the subject "intercultural". After an address of welcome by Mrs. Olga Nikolic, member of the Executive Board of the Serbian S.R., Mr. Stevan Majstorovic, Chairman of the Cultural Committee of the Yugoslav Commission for Cooperation with Unesco, described the complexity and range of the subject before the meeting, in a world where the solidarity of men of diverse cultures was becoming increasingly vital with every day that passed. Mr. Majstorovic emphasized the extent of the project of intercultural studies and its significance for a country like Yugoslavia, in which cultural pluralism was characteristic.

3. He was followed by Michel Conil Lacoste, representing Unesco, who said how glad he was that Yugoslavia, where the cohabitation of cultures was a daily experience, was the host country for a consultation of this sort. The speaker gave a history of the project, described the "diagonal" dimension which it was to add to studies of "cultural areas" already undertaken by Unesco, and specified the objectives of the meeting from the Unesco point of view and in accordance with the directives of Member States.

---

(1) Drawn up by Louis Necker (I.U.E.D., Geneva), Rapporteur, in cooperation with the Unesco Secretariat.
(2) The names of experts who participed in the different meetings reported on in the present brochure are grouped in a single alphabetical list showing region of origin, to be found at the end of the present publication.

4. The Bureau of the meeting was composed as follows:

Chairman :   Professor H. Kirkinen (Finland)

Vice-Chairmen :   "   M.T. Osman (Malaysia)
                          "   S. Arutiunov (USSR)
                          "   B. Gagro (Yugoslavia)

Rapporteur :   "   L. Necker (I.E.D., Geneva)

5. The discussion which ensued centred mainly on the working document drawn up by the Development Institute of Geneva. Participants attempted to elucidate a few basic ideas regarding the methodology and conception of the intercultural studies project.

The term "culture" was the subject of a wide-ranging exchange of views. The majority of participants felt that, where intercultural studies were concerned, the term should be understood in its widest sense as including all fields of human behaviour such as technology, the arts, philosophy, social organization and the economy. There was also discussion on such concepts such as acculturation, cultural identity and the relation between cultural plurality and biological polymorphism, both of wich are a means of better adaptation to a changing milieu.

During this exchange of views, the Unesco representative had the opportunity of specifying the delimitation and aim of the new studies project in relation to the Unesco cultural policies programme and to the studies in which the Organization was associated regarding cultural pluralism.

6. The discussion centred on the areas of investigation and on possible subjects for the studies project. So far as the principles governing their selection were concerned, the debate dealt mainly with the aims of the research and the way in which it could contribute to promoting respect for cultural plurality. Two participants considered that research should concentrate in the first stage on epistemological problems, which would make it possible to prevent the project, the aim of which was a greater respect for cultural relativism, from being itself tainted with ethnocentrism. Four subject areas were defined, and more detailed subjects, which could be integrated into them, were suggested (Cf. final recommendations). It was agreed that, although one of the subject areas was related specifically to epistemological problems and the theory of intercultural encounters, the other areas should also include empirical studies and methodology, whether the latter was empirical or conceptual. Finally, it was considered extremely advantageous to the progress of the project that a study was shortly to be carried out with two purposes :
(a) improving the methodological context by comparing analyses entrusted to researchers from various origins and horizons regarding the various theoretical and conceptual approaches in use;
(b) providing a bibliography.

7. Recommendations adopted
The meeting recommended:
(a)   that Unesco should set up an intercultural studies programme
       with the aim of increasing knowledge of the phenomena
       associated with encounters between different cultures.This
       project, while making as wide as possible a use of empirical
       research, should be chiefly designed to provide the con-
       ceptual and methodological context for thinking and research
(b)   that Unesco should shortly prepare a document containing
       analyses, by researchers from different horizons, of the
       various theoretical and conceptual approaches to the problem
       of cultural encounters (reference context, hypotheses,
       methods of research), with a commented bibliography;
(c)   that the project should take four directions, to each of
       which would correspond one of the four main "areas of
       research" or "subject areas". Particular attention should
       be paid to the necessity of subjects being studied not only
       from the point of view of cultural mixture but also from
       that of a multi-dimensional social space (i.e., both variety
       of cultures and variety of socio-professional situations).
       The four areas of research suggested were as follows:
-   research involving a territorial approach;
-   theoretical research (epistemology, methodology, selection of
    patterns);
-   thematic research centred on a material or immaterial trans-
    cultural object;
-   research centred on the phenomenon: industrial societies/
    traditional cultures.
       These four subject areas are described below.

8. Research involving a territorial approach should cover geographical areas which are rich in cultural phenomena (e.g., the
Caribbean, Sahel region, Balkans, South-East Asia, East Africa/
Madagascar/ Indian Ocean, etc.).
       Special subject suggested:
-   study of folklore and oral traditions in South-East Asia.

9. Theoretical research (epistemology, methodology, selection
of patterns) would be divided into two categories: the first,
epistemological in character, could deal with subjects such as
the diversity of modes of knowledge, ethnocentrism in the study
of intercultural relations, and possibilities of transcending
such ethnocentrism; the second could cover the entire range of
phenomena of cultural encounters in an attempt to classify them,
determine their typology and patterns and work out theories
regarding the method.
       Special subjects suggested:
-   studies indicated in the working document;
-   comparative studies of classifications of discourse.

10. <u>Thematic research would be centred on a material or immaterial
    transcultural object</u>, the variants and mutations of which
through various cultures would be traced.
    Subjects suggested:
- pharmacopoeias and traditional medicines;
- style of modern and traditional dress (relations between
  traditional tastes on the one hand and fashion and industrial
  aesthetics on the other);
- subjects related to the transcultural migration of symbols,
  myths, ritual, and ceremonial or artistic elements;
- the subject of the "foreigner" in the theatre;
- musical instruments improvised from everyday materials and
  objects;
- other subjects within the context of the general phenomenon
  of "improvisation".

11. The research to be considered under the subject "industrial
societies and traditional cultures" would revolve round the
phenomenon of the impact of "modernity" on traditional cultures:
urbanization, "technification", mass-media, industrialization,
standardization, etc.
    Subject suggested:
- Comparative study of the effects of urbanization on four
  villages situated in Finland, Western Europe, North Africa
  and in another continent (1).

---

(1) The meeting also considered the problems involved in the
     establishment of cultural and intercultural atlases. It
     was not considered necessary to report here on the highly
     technical conclusions regarding this subsidiary problem.

II. Outline of a programme

Consultative meeting to draw up a programme of intercultural studies
(Unesco, Paris, March 1978)*

---

* Convened at the initiative of Unesco jointly with the International Council for Philosophy and Humanistic Studies (Unesco Headquarters, Paris, 21-22 March 1978).

*This second part presents the proceedings of the international
meeting held under the joint auspices of Unesco and the
International Council for Philosophy and Humanistic Studies at
Unesco Headquarters on 21 and 22 March 1978, for the purpose of
analyzing the conditions for developing intercultural studies and
of putting forward a plan and indeed a comprehensive policy
directed at the parallel implementation of a study programme and
of action designed to elicit interest in the progress of intercultural knowledge or to foster education for that purpose.*

The proceedings consist of the following:
*1. The preparatory documents drawn up by Unesco or at its
instigation, comprising six papers;*
*2. The summary report on the work of the group, together with its
principal recommendations in respect of the definition of
continuous action to develop intercultural knowledge.*

*The report is supplemented by a recapitulation of all the
proposals put forward at the meetings.*

*In order to enable a comprehensive picture to be obtained of the
contents of this compilation, the individual papers are briefly
analyzed below. The headings have been devised by the Editor and
do not constitute their original titles.*

The parameters of the intercultural issue

*Taking the science of ethnic processes and linguistics primarily
as his starting-point, S. Arutiunov sets out to define the scope
of comparative cultural studies, examines various methodological
schools, and goes on to stress the usefulness of cultural atlases.
His paper offers an initial evaluation of the accomplishments and
shortcomings of research and underscores the piecemeal character
of certain approaches, such as when he states, for example, that
it is virtually impossible to point to a single case where models
of cultures can be said to have been studied and described in terms
of all their parameters. After assessing the scientific quality
of the work already done, the author concludes by putting forward
a programme, the first part of which would consist of the preparation of a body of source materials and the elaboration of
methodological concepts, and the second would comprise a number
of pilot studies designed to give substance to the intercultural
problem area. In the final pages of his paper, he suggests a*

*number of themes coming within that context. A short bibliography
is appended.*

The retreat of ethnocentrism
*Two particular developments that are general in scope can be
singled out from the paper presented by L. Bazin. The first of
these consists of a useful compilation of the different features
defining cultural identity and thereby forms a sort of model
cultural profile that can be applied to different cultures. The
second observes the salutary change in attitude that has taken
place over the past few generations among Western researchers
specializing in cultural studies, and has resulted in the gradual
but undeniable demise of ethnocentrism.*

The semantic field of the poet
*By contrast, Cheikh Anta Diop focuses his enquiry on a very
specific aspect of the intercultural phenomenon, namely the communicability of poetic language from one geo-cultural environment
to another or, in other terms, the ability to superimpose semantic
fields in poetry. He bases his arguments on examples involving
literary expression in French-speaking Africa in its relationship
with the French language.*

A programme comprising three approaches
*In a form which he sees as being essentially an "interrogation",
A. Dupront suggests three approaches in a bid to narrow down a
problem whose magnitude he very pertinently underscores. The first
could be said to consist in establishing the "instruments of knowledge and communication", namely the corpus of such key concepts
as culture and civilization, universal archetypes and branches of
knowledge, tradition and modernism, the sense of time in different
cultures, and so on. The second would be given over to compiling
and analysing "factual data", such as cultural destruction and
acculturation, the "melting-pot" syndrome, the intercultural
response to "universal" forms, the impact of an "outlook of
homogeneity" on the economies and equilibria of autochthonous
cultures – all of which are aspects that could give rise to a
series of tangible case studies concerning the "technicity" of the
homogeneous, such as concrete architecture, "turnkey" projects, and
"differential or thematic" elucidations: such as the "imago urbis",
a sense of history and its breakdown by periods, awareness of
things sacred, studies of stereotypes (the language of adversity,
the theme of the foreigner and the barbarian, the processes by
which stereotypes are crystallized, and so on). The third approach
would entail carrying out long-range studies with a view to developing intercultural exchanges, in which the analysts would not re-
frain from setting themselves up, no matter to how small a degree,
as guides to the future. Here again, there is no shortage of
research themes, regardless of whether they stem from a fundamental
approach (the methodology and pedagogy of the intercultural issue)
or from an experimental approach (study of the "trade" phenomenon
in the broad sense or of mass tourism, or the study of the psycho-
social forces activating intercultural exchanges).*

The need for a "moral basis"

V. Elisseeff, who has long been associated with Unesco's activities and who was, in particular, the rapporteur of the Major "East-West" Project, brings into play the historical background of the Organization's studies of cultures in determining the "moral basis" which derives its inspiration from the "joint Declaration" adopted when the Major Project was launched and which could serve to underpin the intercultural programme that it is planned to conceive and direct. He recalls that any cultural or intercultural study makes reference to value judgements and can arouse emotional reactions that are liable to affect the objectivity and serenity of the researches carried out, and he accordingly proposes that these be forestalled by setting the facts in a threefold chronological, geographical and socio-economic perspective in order to reduce the glare of the "spotlight". He goes on to say that if, in some instances, the synchronic approach is tempered by the diachronic, many present-day contrasts that are a source of mitigated evaluations will fade away. Lastly, any cultural phenomenon that is at first sight surprising enables everybody to give an unreserved assessment, since it is liable to be reversible for some people and capable of imitation for others. The author takes these principles as a basis for establishing an order of priority for the themes to be studied and concludes by suggesting a variety of conditions on which a co-ordinating committee or group could be set up.

1. *Briefing note*

The purpose of the present document is to state the objective
of the Working Group set up jointly by the International Council
for Philosophy and Humanistic Studies (ICPHS) and Unesco and to
show why the Organization is today faced with urgent recommendations from Member States for intercultural studies. It provides
information on the contribution hitherto made by Unesco to the
"intercultural" within the programme of cultural studies and
certain associated activities, and reports on the preliminary work
carried out by the Secretariat since 1976 in connection with
launching the Project.

Referring to the documents governing the activities of the
Organization for the preceding two-year period and the current
one, it underlines the evolution of the directives of the General
Conference and lays down the context of the present programme,
which is to be extended by the Programme and Budget for 1979-1980
(1), and which is to be defined and supplemented by the Working
Group. Lastly, it deals with future prospects in the context of
the medium-term programme by objectives (1977-1982) adopted during
the nineteenth Session of the Unesco General Conference, particularly as regards the guidance and coordination of a concerted
system of intercultural studies.

INTRODUCTION

The intercultural: implicit and explicit

It is difficult to deny at a time of intensified exchanges, when
the mobility of persons is increasing and communications are constantly proliferating, that all cultures - unless one were sur-
prised today at birth - are subject to successive admixtures and
extraneous influences (extraneous constitutionally to their
original sources and geographically to their initial, more or
less stabilized, areas of expansion). Consequently, any cultural
study is already stamped with the "intercultural" seal.

---

(1) Then in the draft stage.

The studies in which Unesco has been engaged for several decades are no exception: the "geo-cultural" areas, to which the various sections of the cultural studies programme pursued by the Secretariat are assigned, correspond only to cultural homogeneity which is obviously relative, although acceptable and even necessary as a working hypothesis.

Beyond this "interculturality" which might be described as constitutional - inherent to the very texture of any culture and, practically, at the individual level, to the heart of every personality - the intercultural establishes itself at a more obvious level as soon as an attempt is made to describe and inventory objectively - i.e. in all its aspects, components and prolongations - a culture which is sufficiently homogeneous and characteristic to have a distinctive name.

It would be possible to give many examples of cultural explosions which show that the definition of a culture is related not only to its consisting of a sufficient number of characteristic features together present in a territory (whether all of one piece or dispersed) of a sufficient extent for it to be possible to distinguish it from others, but also to the dynamism by which it expands from its cradle to the limits of a zone of expansion - in short to its potential for propagation and acculturation of a positive kind (and even, it might be added, of a negative - or rather receiving - kind).

I. THE DIFFERENT LEVELS AT WHICH THE INTERCULTURAL APPEARS IN UNESCO PROGRAMMES

The intercultural feature of cultural studies and the "Major Project"

It goes without saying that Unesco is particularly attentive to this second aspect, as is borne out by those studies, included in its programmes for a long time, which bear on geo-cultural zones that are particularly significant from the point of view of cultural interpenetration.

The Organization also deals with the "intercultural" in certain projects for the study of cultures not limited to a specific geo-cultural area. For example, the one recently started which considers the impact of the technological society on culture implies a certain "degree" of an intercultural comparative approach since, while it mainly concerns highly industrialized countries (at least in the first stage), research is pursued concurrently into different cultures. By definition, it also implies the "intercultural" since it studies the implications, for the original culture of developing regions, of a technical and industrial culture of outside origin.

Lastly, this list would be incomplete if no mention were made of the "Major project relating to the mutual appreciation of the cultural values of East and West" (1957-1966), regarding which one of those most closely associated with it provides more detailed information in another document submitted to this conference

(Cf. V. Elisseeff: Extending cultural studies to cover intercultural studies).

It will, however, be pointed out that the study and research
activity undertaken in connection with this "transversal" project
constituted not only one of the three parts of its programme,
while the two others were concerned (a) with educational activities which aimed rather at the pure and simple dissemination of
cultures little known among the general public of the West than
at a real educational promotion of the intercultural relationship and (b) with activities related to information and publicity
for the project itself.

The intercultural impact of dissemination

But Unesco also engages in the intercultural field when it takes
an active and not merely speculative part in promoting the mutual
appreciation of cultures by methods of cultural dissemination.
This dissemination takes place:
a)   firstly, through the geo-cultural sections of cultural studies,
as a result of the publication of reports, studies, language textbooks, collections of general works, albums summarizing the results
of research work, seminars, conferences and symposia covering all
aspects of the culture under consideration. Such works are
intended either for the actual populations covered by the culture
under consideration or for the public extraneous to such culture,
though the one does not exclude the other.
b)   Secondly and mainly, by means of a unit specially devoted to
cultural dissemination. The two major activities of this unit
are the Programme of translation of literary works known as the
"Unesco Collection of Representative Works" (the chief purpose of
which is the publication in widely used languages of works written in little used languages) and various projects for the dissemination of the arts, the most systematic of which is a programme of travelling exhibitions summarizing the chief contributions
of a specific culture to civilization and the arts. The Unesco
Collection of Representative Works, inaugurated in 1948 and
based on cooperation between the Organization and publishers, today includes nearly six hundred titles covering about sixty different literatures. The programme of travelling exhibitions is
at its twelfth exhibition (1).
c)   Additionally, by means of periodicals, the most specialized
of which is the Journal Cultures, while the most accessible to
the general public is the Unesco Courier .

Operational aspects

At multi-lateral level, this dissemination assumes the task of
exchanging and "presenting" cultures, which is not always assumed
under the same conditions at national or bi-lateral level. In
the interests of completeness it will also be remembered that
projects with an intercultural dimension may exist in other
sectors of the Secretariat, particularly education. Lastly, and

---

(1) Today at its thirteenth.

even further removed from the intellectual and cognitive approach
to cultural studies, the intercultural objective is implemented
in programmes of a more deliberately operational and promotional
character, such as in that of fellowships or the two-yearly
publication of Studies Abroad which gives a list of fellowships
available on the one hand and reception facilities offered to
foreign students in all countries on the other, together with the
courses and seminars open to multi-national participation in
many countries. It may even be claimed that Unesco's very purpose
coincides with the concept of an interculturality which is active
in all spheres.

II. NEW DIRECTIVES FOR A NEW APPROACH

This recapitulation was necessary in order to define clearly the
position from which we must now advance. But if a concern for
the "intercultural" has actuated for so long so many parts of
the programme, from research activities to semi-operational and
operational intervention, what are the new prospects which have
caused this working Group to be convened? Here we must go back
to the actual text of the provisions adopted four years ago by
the General Conference on the subject of intercultural studies.

The development of the Project through the biennial programmes
These provisions are to be found in the "work plans" of the
Programme and Budget for 1975-1976 (18 C/5 approved) and of the
corresponding document for 1977-1978 (19 C/5 approved), and in
the Medium-Term Plan (1977-1982) adopted in Nairobi at the 19th
Session of the General Conference under Objective 1.2: "Appreciation and respect for the cultural identity of individuals, groups,
nations or regions", together with its accompanying guidance
note.
       The essence of this is reproduced below, the quotation of
the appropriate paragraphs of the document concerned being followed in each case by a short analysis (in which the directives and
concepts appearing for the first time are underlined).

                    18 C/5 approved (1975 - 1976)
                        (para. 3172):

              Cross-cultural studies. -"Besides individual
              area-studies, some interdisciplinary projects
              in the humanities will be developed on pro-
              blems of common interest to a diversity of
              countries and cultures. As a first step, a
              methodology of cross-cultural studies will be
              elaborated and some significant themes of
              international relevances selected. For this
              purpose, ICPHS (1) will be entrusted with the
              preparation of a plan of action. Questions of

_____

(1) International Council for Philosophy and Humanistic Studies.

interdisciplinary methodology related to the
preparation of "cultural atlases" will be
examined jointly by ICPHS and the Secretariat".

The only paragraph of the Work Plan, adopted at the end of 1974,
is more the outline of an intention than a programme. Its draft-
ing reflects an approach to the problem by Member States, which
is still exploratory, and a degree of ambiguity regarding the
level of intervention under consideration, particularly when it
refers to "problems of common interest", the exact range of which
is not stated.

However, as from this first text there appears a concern for
methodology, which is indissociable from long-term intercultural
activity.

19 C/5 approved (1977 - 1978)
(paras. 4041 and 4042) :

Promotion of intercultural studies. "In accordance with the orientation given by the General
Conference, stressing the intercultural di
mension and the need to establish a body for
international co-ordination to that effect, a
study of the scope and nature of this coordination will be carried out and a working
group of representative scholars from all the
main regions will be convened in co-operation
with ICPHS, for the purpose of establishing a
plan aimed at promoting, systematizing and
evaluating the activities in the field of
intercultural studies.(...) Favourable consideration will be given to requests from
member States for aid under the Participation
Programme for the preparation of cultural
atlases".

This text, which was adopted at the end of 1976, takes note more
clearly of a directive by the General Conference to emphasize the
intercultural, and the problem of coordinating intercultural
studies is raised for the first time. Here we find mentioned for
the first time the project which, owing to a joint effort of the
ICPHS and Unesco, led to the meeting of this Working Group, which
had to be postponed, for a number of reasons, until the first
quarter of 1978.

The "Programme Activity Details" for 1978 (PAD 1978) specified
more clearly the nature of the studies to be undertaken. It
consists partly of studies on the methodology and epistemology
of the intercultural and partly of comparative thematic studies.
(No subject was decided upon for these studies, and the Working
Group might be asked to make suggestions.)

Prospects through the Medium-Term Programme

19 C/4 Approved (1977 - 1982)
(paras. 1222 (3) and 1224 (b) and (c)):

A) Principles of action
"In their rich variety and diversity, and in
the reciprocal influences they exert on one
another, all cultures form part of the common
heritage belonging to all mankind.(...)
"Intra-cultural authenticity must necessarily be supplemented by inter-cultural
dialogue. For unless one is to run the risk
of encouraging national compartmentalization
and sectarianism in one or other form, it is
important to ensure that each culture is open
to the influence of all the others within a
broad international framework. Specificity
on the one hand and inter-cultural relations
on the other are thus seen as two complementary terms, giving poise and balance to this
group of activities taken as a whole.
"The principles thus laid down will have
a direct effect on the programme organization.
It will, for example, be advisable to make
the definition of cultural regions fairly
flexible. These rarely coincide with
political boundaries. The approach adopted
must enable comparisons, exchanges and rapprochements to be made between sub-regions
and countries which share a common heritage,
even if they differ today in respect of economic or social circumstances or ideological
standpoints. The programme will be planned
more flexibly, consideration being given to
the individual sub-regions making up the
large geographical regions and special attention paid to areas where different civilizations adjoin, such as the Caribbean and
South East Asia. In this way the programme
will make a greater contribution to promoting
mutual inter-cultural respect and international understanding".
B) In the Guidance Note related to Objective
1.2 on cultural identity
(Annex II, pp. 357-358, paras. 3 to 6):
"It was felt to be necessary to bring two complementary aspects to the fore for future
guidance: firstly, the specific features which
constitute the originality of the various
cultures, their authenticity and their historical roots as well as the values specific to them
as they are experienced today by different
peoples and communities; and, secondly, the

exchanges and interpenetration between
cultures. The programme for the study of
different cultures has been concerned essentially with this first aspect of cultural
identity.

"At the same time, however, and while
still intensifying the study of specific areas,
importance should be attached far more than in
the past to the second aspect, i.e. to activities to encourage the mutual appreciation
of cultures. The principle of cultural identity should serve not only the promotion of
human rights, but also the aim of strengthen-
ing peace since, as was stated many times
during the discussion, the reciprocal understanding of cultures fosters international
co-operation, expressed in terms of equality
and mutual respect among peoples. This is
why it was recommended that in future programmes there should be still further expansion
of studies and operational activities which
highlight the contributions, the manifold influences and particularly the forms of intellectual and moral interdependence which exist
between cultures so as to strengthen the bonds
based on historical realities and affinities
of values between peoples, in conformity with
Unesco's universal calling. In terms of programme priorities, this approach will call for
greater attention to be paid to regions which,
whatever their geographical size, are places
where cultures meet and merge.

"Various practical measures were proposed
in order to implement these recommendations,
including the establishment of an intercultural committee composed of representatives
of various regions who would evaluate ongoing
experiments, identify subjects for comparative
studies and plan joint projects."

The Medium-Term Plan (1977-1982) is the first document in the
programme to bring the intercultural problem expressly into
relation with the necessity for a dialogue between cultures and
the duty of making each culture accessible to all others; it
suggests "comparisons (...) between sub-regions and countries
which share a common heritage" transcending the disparity between
cultural frontiers and ideological and social and economic frontiers.

For the first time, too, the terms of the "guidance note"
related to Objective 1.2 and adopted in Nairobi emphasizes the
articulation of cultural studies into two branches of activity,
both designed to promote cultural identity, but one considering
it from the point of view of awakening of consciousness (studies
by geo-cultural areas) and the other from that of mutual appre-

ciation (intercultural studies), it being specified that "importance should be attached far more than in the past to the second
aspect".

In particular, priority should be given to the study of regions constituting "places where cultures meet and merge", such
as the Antilles or South East Asia, "whatever their geographical
size".

Lastly, mention is made, among "measures suggested with a
view to the implementation of these recommendations", of the
establishment of an intercultural committee or coordinating group
including personalities representing various regions, which
would be responsible for assessing current experiments and proposing subjects and projects.

In short, as compared with the previous situation, four new
elements emerge from the preceding texts and comments:

1. greater articulation between the study of "homogeneous"
cultures according to geo-cultural areas on the one hand, and
studies of the intercrossing of cultures on the other, with
priority given to an investigation of zones particularly rich in
cultural mixtures, at the meeting point of these two fields;

2. emphasis on the intercultural so as to impart to the Unesco
cultural studies programme the invigorating diagonal axis which
was missing from it;

3. a definition of the policy to be followed in this field, based
on a number of concepts and suggestions gradually evolved over
the four-year period (particularly, the necessity for a methodology; thematic and comparative approach and any system of coordination required for guiding, proposing and assessing);

4. a much closer integration of the promotional into the intercultural.

This is perhaps the most important innovation. It has been
noted that in the past the link was much looser, and the intercultural dimension was either implemented in research and
clarification activities or directly practised in relation to
activities of the operational or semi-operational type. The new
method of planning by objectives now deliberately brings these
two terms together, as is indicated by the very wording of the
two distinct but complementary sub-objectives to which correspond studies by geo-cultural areas on the one hand ("Promotion
of the cultural identity as a factor for independence and
solidarity") and intercultural studies on the other ("Promotion
of appreciation and respect for the cultural identity of individuals, groups, nations or regions").

The first of these sub-objectives implies that the awareness
of and respect for cultural identity and specific cultural
character constitute an essential feature of the promotion of
human rights as well as a stimulant for development; the second
that international understanding and peace can be achieved through
the mutual appreciation of cultures.

III. THE PRELIMINARY STAGE OF BELGRADE

The preceding indications explain why it is only since quite
recent times that the Secretariat has had a corpus of well-
defined systems and guiding principles at its disposal.
The meeting held in Belgrade in September 1976 could not thus
have been anything more than a preliminary consultation. Nonetheless, it provided useful clarification, particularly by insisting on the priority to be given to devising the methodology
and by enumerating a number of areas of research for a long-term
programme.

As regards the first item, the Belgrade Final Report recommended launching a research project "with the aim of increasing
knowledge of the phenomena associated with encounters between
different cultures" which "while making as wide as possible a use
of empirical research, should be chiefly designed to provide the
conceptual and methodological context for thinking and research".
The report expressed the hope that Unesco would ask researchers
from a wide variety of horizons for a number of analyses covering
"the various theoretical and conceptual approaches to the problem
of cultural encounters (reference context, hypotheses, methods
of research), with a commented bibliography" and that these
studies should be grouped in a brochure (1).

The working document drawn up for the Belgrade meeting by
the Geneva Institut universitaire d'études du développement at
the request of Unesco provides a useful instrument to contem-
plate the problem of methodology and the different theoretical
and conceptual approaches, while dealing with "cognitive ethnocentrism", acculturation and the "intercultural transfer of
concepts".

The three "areas of research"
Regarding the second item concerning the subjects which could
form the substance of a programme, the Belgrade Report recom-
mends the study of the subjects selected "not only from the
point of view of the intermingling of cultures, but also from
that of a multi-dimensional social space (i.e. both variety of
cultures and variety of socio-professional situations)."

It suggested dividing the subjects for study into three
main "areas of research" or "subject zones":
a)   theoretical research (epistemology, methodology, searching
     for models);
b)   research involving a "territorial" - or in a wider sense,
     geographical - approach;
c)   thematic research centred on a material or immaterial
     "transcultural" object.

---

(1) A number of studies of this type, in addition to those in-
     cluded in this brochure, have been carried out since or
     are now being completed. They will be the subject of a
     subsequent publication.

(A fourth category of subjects - not depending on the same criterion as the three preceding ones - had been added:"research centred on the phenomenon: industrial societies and traditional cultures").

The theoretical research would itself be sub-divided into two categories:
a)   studies of an epistemological nature covering subjects such as the diversity of modes of knowledge, ethnocentrism in the approach to the "other" culture and cultural relations, and possibilities of overcoming such ethnocentrism;
b)   studies dealing with cultural encounter phenomena generally, in an attempt to "classify them, determine their type and pattern and work out theories regarding the method".

Studies related to a territorial or geographical approach would deal with areas particularly rich in intercultural phenomena (the Caribbean, the Sahel, East-African borders, Madagascar, Indian Ocean, South East Asia, Balkans, etc.).

The aim of thematic studies would be to follow certain material and immaterial objects, particularly charged with cultural significance, in their migrations and mutations through different cultures; such objects, elements or concepts could belong to the field of art or customs, or that of religion, conception of the world, metaphysics, etc.
    In the Belgrade Report, each of these areas of research was followed by a number of proposals for concrete subjects.
    The Belgrade Meeting also dealt with the problem of a cultural atlas, considered as a work instrument in the service of intercultural studies.

IV.   DOCUMENTARY FILE OF THE WORKING GROUP

Some of the ideas which emerged from the Belgrade exchange of views can thus be added to the file of the project. But the discussions of the Working Group can be based more directly on five documents:
- Problems of intercultural studies, by Serghei Arutiunov
- A method of approaching intercultural relations, by Cheikh Anta Diop
- Thoughts on intercultural research policy, by Alphonse Dupront
- Extending cultural studies to cover intercultural studies and the role of an international organization in coordinating, promoting and assessing such studies, by Vadime Elisseeff
    In addition to these four documents drawn up especially for the Working Group, there is a fifth which was chiefly intended for another meeting (the Bureau of the International Union for Oriental and Asian Studies) but which the ICPHS and Unesco were authorized by the author to include in the file of the present meeting:

- Ways and means of a systematic contribution by Oriental and
  Asian Studies to achieving Unesco objectives in relation to
  cultural identity, by Louis Bazin.

A valuable aspect of these documents is that they approach the
problem from different angles. Several of them include concrete
proposals for study subjects which the Working Group will be
able to consider.

V. TASK SUGGESTED FOR WORKING GROUP

An analysis of the phenomena and problems related to the intercultural, working out a conceptual and methodological apparatus,
defining the field of studies: these are the three points of view
from which the Working Group is invited to advise the ICPHS and
Unesco in drawing up a coherent research programme.
     The purpose of this consultation is thus defined. More pre-
cisely, discussions and recommendations could cover the following items:
- long-term orientation, objectives and priorities;
- methodological aspects;
- general organization of project - particularly as regards any
   coordinating system;
- substance of a short and medium-term programme (choice of
   study subjects).
     As regards the last item, the representatives of Unesco will
provide participants during the meeting with all necessary additional information:
1. on the context of the programme drawn up for the next two-year
period in the Draft programme and budget for 1979-1980, which has
been prepared in accordance with the general directives of the
Medium-Term Plan (1977-1982) set forth above;
2. more immediately, on projected activities in 1978 within the
terms of the Programme and approved Budget 1977-1978, but the
content and ways and means of which may have to be specified.

2. *Preparatory documents*

Intercultural study problems

Serghei Arutiunov

The present article was intended as a possible basis for a discussion at Unesco of a problem the very formulation of which
would appear to cover a wide field. After all, what are we
to understand by the expression "intercultural study" (1)? In the
widest sense it means all studies devoted to the history, the
functions and the conditions of life of any isolated element of a
cultural whole, of a sphere of culture or an entire local culture, providing that the examples and materials are taken from
more than one local culture. Such an interpretation would include
in the context of "intercultural" studies, all comparative, culturological and ethnographical studies and much more besides.

Seen from this angle, the works of Thucydides and Herodotus,
Pliny and Strabo, and even some of Plato's dialogues, must necessarily be classified as intercultural studies.

In ethnographical and culturological research circles in
the English-speaking countries, what are usually known as "cross-
cultural studies" (2) include comparative cultural studies the
subject of which deals with the transmission and function of some
isolated element or cultural system into a number of local cultures. At present, studies of this type are already so numerous
and cover such a wide variety of cultures that even a general
outline of them would appear to be absolutely impossible. All we
can do is quote a few isolated examples of work of this nature
which have played an important part in the development of science
in general.

Among the most striking examples are the Mythologiques by
Cl. Lévi-Strauss (3) and, among the works of older writers the
Three Chapters in the History of Poetry by A.N. Viesselovski
(St. Petersburg 1899). A. Lomax's work (4) also constitutes a good
example of an all-round "cross-cultural study". Other research of
this type deals with isolated continents or historical ethnogra-
phical regions - such as the book by J.S. Kotliar (Myths and
Legends of Africa, Moscow, 1975). In the fields of mythology,

---

(1) "Intercultural Studies" in English-speaking publications.
(2) The term was introduced by American researchers.
(3) Cl. Lévi-Strauss, Mythologiques, I-IV, 1964-1970, Paris.
(4) A. Lomax, Folk Song Style and Culture, 1968, Washington, D.C.

folklore and religious studies, the number of such publications is particularly large and is only exceeded by the total number of publications on comparative linguistics. This is understandable, seeing that with our subject, as in linguistic studies, the material analysed takes a verbal form, expressing thought immediately and adequately in a discrete form which is easily divided up into emic units (lexemes, phraseologemes, etc.)(1). However the number of studies of the "cross-cultural" type - which we shall henceforth refer to as "comparative cultural studies" - of a universal or regional nature is much more limited, since such studies have been devoted to non-verbal phenomena of spiritual culture. This is all the more valid as regards works on material culture. A few studies on these subjects written at the beginning of the century are already out of date now (2). Among the most recent, one of the best is that by A. Leroi-Gourhan (3). However, this same work brings out the fact that very little study has yet been devoted to the typological principles and methodological bases, although such principles and bases are necessary for a large scale comparative cultural study of material culture as well as spiritual culture. Obviously, we are not dealing here with the phenomena of artistic culture of a professional nature, such as architecture, sculpture, painting, etc. While plenty of treatises and comparative studies on professional architecture are available, as much cannot be said for those dealing with traditional popular architecture, for example.

As regards the comparative study of complete systems of traditional culture, (including its manifestations in social and economic fields), the very character of the predominant publications devoted to these questions gives striking evidence of the elementary levels of such research. Generally speaking, they are collections of articles or of symposia material in which each text is devoted to the culture of an isolated society, whereas the generalization is carried out by the editors-publishers in the introductory and final chapters.

Good examples of collective studies of this nature are to be found in the collections dealing with hunters (4) and band societies (5). There is an example in Soviet literature - the book entitled: Hunters, Collectors and Fishers (published by A.M. Riechetov, Leningrad, 1972). It is characteristic that such summaries tend to deal with primitive societies with a predominantly appropriation economy. Works of a similar nature dealing with nomadic graziers are usually much less extensive and are generally confined to an analysis of the social structure. Studies of this type dealing with agricultural rural societies are practically non-existent.

---

(1) Cf. K.L. Pike, "Etic and Emic Standpoints for the Description of Behaviour" in Communication and Culture, pages 152-163, A.G. Smith, N.Y.
(2) F. Groebner, Kulturkreise in Melanesien.
(3) A. Leroi-Gourhan, Evolution et techniques, 1943-1945, Paris.
(4) Man the Hunter, edited by B.B. Lee and I. De-Vore,1968, Chicago.
(5) Band Societies, edited by D. Damas, 1969, Ottawa.

To be sure, comparative cultural studies constitute an important element in the intercultural problem, although they do not cover the whole field of the "intercultural" exhaustively. The present predominance of studies devoted to such and such an isolated cultural element and only covering a limited number of local cultures, is easy to explain. A research worker may have a perfect knowledge of a certain aspect of the culture of a people, but it is almost impossible to have a perfect knowledge of all the spheres of a people's culture, even if only one people is concerned. In the same way it is possible to know the functions of such and such an element of culture such as the bow or the plough, but it is impossible to cover the entire diversity of their functions and technical design at a universal scale. In order to do so it would be necessary to have comparable material collected according to a standard method. Generally, however, this material is far from being adequate.

The subsequent development and perfecting of comparative cultural studies, therefore, are conditioned by the establishment of a corpus of sources for this type of studies. As secondary sources historico-cultural and ethnographical atlases can be used. In this sphere, G.P. Murdock Ethnographic Atlas (1) provides the widest experience. By means of this atlas a number of universal "cross-cultural" comparisons have already been carried out. Nevertheless, experience has shown the shortcomings of this work based on a pluralist approach in interpretation and on the classification of cultural phenomena, frequently generalizing from fortuitous data.

In the U.S.S.R. an extensive project for the publication of ethnographical and historico-cultural atlases is being implemented. Some have already been published while others are in preparation.

Soviet science is actively engaged on formulating the concept of economico-cultural types and historico-ethnographical regions (cf. M.G. Levine, N.N. Cheboksarov: "Economico-cultural types and Historico-ethnographical Regions", Sovietskaĭa Etnografiya, 1955, No. 4; B.V. Andrianov, N.N. Cheboksarov: "Economico-cultural Types and the Problems of their Cartography", ibid, 1972, No. 2). This concept is of considerable importance for the logical and systematic classification of cultural phenomena and for an "arealization" of them. It appears to be necessary to pursue and promote the study of the theory of economico-cultural types and historico-ethnographical regions, to standardize programmes and the principles governing the publication of atlases and to give every possible assistance in extending the work of publishing such atlases to various countries in accordance with a standardized programme. In the same way, too much attention cannot be paid to the formulation and standardization of a taxonomic scale of cultural elements, or in other words the working out of emic units for the analysis of cultures (culturemes, behaviouremes). It is only on this condition that a quantitative, formalized approach to cultural comparisons is possible, which

_____

(1) G.P. Murdock, Ethnographic Atlas - a summary - Ethnology, 6 (2), pages 107-236.

has already been noted in scientific literature (cf. the article
by K. Kwasniewski: "The structural-statistical method applied
to the study of contemporary popular culture", Sovietskaĭa
Etnografiya, 1964, No. 3, p. 110).

The accumulation of standardized material of the atlas type
is of vital importance for any comparative cultural study. But
it is supremely necessary for comparative cultural studies of
the "areal" type, i.e. those in which an attempt is made to bring
to light not only the functioning of similar elements in various
local cultures but also their distribution in space. It is not a
matter of chance that, in spite of the vast quantity of individual
comparative cultural studies, the number of studies based on an
"areal" approach, even without any clear distinction as to iso-
pragmata - although such a distinction is ideally most desirable -
is very small nowadays. On the other hand, the number of comparative cultural studies of various particular cases has become
enormous. On the contrary, among the area studies, which are relatively numerous in the field of culture, with or without distinction as to isopragms, the search dealing with a local culture
predominates, whereas comparative cultural studies or even those
using the comparative material of other cultures, constitute
only a rare exception. For example, if we consult the collection
entitled "Area studies in linguistics and ethnology" (published
by M.A. Borodina, Leningrad, 1977), which is one of the most
recent Soviet publications in this field, we shall find no comparative research proper, but only a few studies using comparative
material (cf. the article by A.V. Gour: "Linguistic and Ethnographic Differences and Community in the marginal zone of Russian
North" from the same collection).

Whatever the importance which should be attached to comparative cultural studies within the general problem of intercultural
contacts, it should be recognized that not only comparative cultural studies but also those covering two or more local cultures
are even more important. The former are devoted to similar phenomena belonging to cultures widely apart from one another and
having no relation; in the latter, the cultures studied are in
contact or are interacting, and it is the specific character of
this interaction process which concerns the researcher.

Here again, the works which are most numerous and most
successful are those on folklore, literary and artistic studies.
Here again, no doubt, there are specific problems, particularly
Eurocentrism, gradually and paradoxically overcome in the course
of a movement which started with the work by O. Spengler, The
Decline of. the West a few decades ago and which has not yet been
completed. From this point of view, the importance of N.I. Konrad's
book entitled The West and the East (Moscow 1972) should be
underlined.

In general, the cultural interaction of different populations
in the field of spiritual culture, and above all professional
artistic culture, is being intensely and successfully studied in
the modern world.

But in the majority of cases this study is pursued by isolated
elements in the narrow context of a few scientific disciplines
or their sub-divisions. We are speaking of the interaction of

literatures, schools of architecture or music, the history of the
diffusion and development of knowledge in the fields of astrono-
my, etc. However, generally speaking, no comparative study of
this type deals with cultural interactions (between populations
used as the basis for a comparison) in other fields, even conti-
guous ones, or even takes them into consideration, to say nothing
of attempts to retrace the results of reciprocal cultural influences.

A particular problem connected with the study of the interaction of local cultures of a specifically ethnic character (i.e.
cultures of particular populations or ethnic groups), is the one
considered in research into this interaction generally. Processes
of this type are known as ethno-cultural or ethnic. When speaking
of ethnic cultures, Western specialists understand those appropriate to relatively limited groups and minorities. And out of
the entire variety of ethnic processes, it is chiefly the process
of acculturation which is studied. Soviet ethnographic studies,
like those carried out in the academies of other socialist countries, give priority to examining ethnic processes in their entire
complexity, i.e. not only processes of acculturation and assimilation but also those of ethno-national consolidation, integration,
inter-ethnic understanding, and those of ethnic divergence, which
is less frequent nowadays. There is an extensive literature dealing with this problem in the U.S.S.R.: it is worth mentioning, in
view of its theoretical importance, the chapter on "The Ethnic
Processes" in the work by Yu.V. Bromley (cf. Yu.V. Bromley
Ethnos and Ethnography, Moscow 1973); the collective studies:
Modern Ethnic Processes in the U.S.S.R., Moscow 1975; Ethnic
Processes in the countries of Southern Asia, Moscow 1976 and a
few others. Among Western publications devoted to various aspects
of ethno-cultural relations, mention should be made of the book
by F. Barth (1).

Incidentally, it should be noted that the studies of ethnic
processes chiefly emphasize the decisive factor of ethnic background, or in other words ethnic consciousness. All the other
cultural indications - language, usual habitat, favourite food,
rites performed on such and such occasions, etc., - are considered
in relation to this principal factor which, however, is only a
derived indication resulting in any individual, social group or
collectivity from all the other cultural factors, such as language
profession, religious belief, oral tradition and many other of
the same nature. All these components of culture have their own
communicative function. And it is from all these communicative
functions from the information network, at a given frequency and
intensity born of this universality that finally emerges the ethnic consciousness displaying such and such a gradation according
to the configuration of the system (cf. S.A. Arutiunov,
N.N. Cheboksarov: "The Transmission of Information as the means
of existence of the ethno-social and biological groups of mankind"
in Races and Peoples, Volume 2, Moscow 1972).

---

(1) Fr. Barth, Ethnic Groups and Boundaries, 1969, Boston.

Undoubtedly, each ethnic group, i.e. local culture, has some specific feature in the configuration of its information system. The different parts of the latter, the various components of the culture develop differently and unevenly in the various cultures. Certainly the natures of ethnic and intercultural contacts bear the mark of this difference. For example, there is the fact that, in contacts between Tibetan and Mongolian cultures, the Tibetan religious worship and ritual aspect has been much more developed than in the pre-Buddhist Mongol culture, which caused the intensive penetration of Lamaism in the Mongol environment and the Lamaization of local Shamanist religions. On the other hand, the technology of building the nomad dwelling and its symbolism appeared among the Mongols in a much more elaborate form than in Tibet; this is why no influence can be detected. It would be easy to quote many examples of this type. But it is almost impossible nowadays to point out even one case in which cultural patterns in contact have been studied and described more or less adequately with all their parameters and relations with the special features of the cultural contact process under consideration. It is, however, necessary to do this if we wish to raise the study of intercultural contacts to a satisfactory scientific level.

In the same way the studies of the actual systems with their varied combinations governing contacts between the various types of culture entering into communication with one another, the selective reaction of the host culture to the various elements of the guest culture, the destiny of innovations within the culture which adopts, the mechanism of assimilation of these innovations and other problems of this nature are all quite inadequate. Obviously, different mechanisms come into play in cases of the mutual influence of two traditional cultures (for example, the historical Greco-Persian and Indo-Persian contacts), as in the situation predominating in the present-day world where we see a universal, industrial non-ethnic culture of the urban Western type predominating traditional local cultures. At present we are only witnessing the beginning of attempts to elucidate the regularity of the action of such mechanisms (1).

The method of extrapolating the study of intercultural contacts by means of considerable achievements in the field of contacts between various languages may be considered very promising since very careful study is being made of these contacts. At the same time, there is no doubt that if, by culture in the widest sense of the word, we mean a specifically human activity transmitted from one generation to another by the non-biological channel (cf. E.S. Markarian: Essais sur la théorie de la culture, 1969 Erevan; and De la genèse de l'activité humaine et de la culture, 1973 Erevan), language must be considered as the specific element of culture, although generally subordinate to regularities of the functioning of culture alone. It follows that, generally speaking, the description and analysis of intercultural contacts can be

---

(1) S. Arutiunov, "Original Elements and Foreign Contributions to the Material Culture of Japan", Problems of the Contemporary World, No. 3 (10), 1971, Moscow.

effected within the context of the same conceptual apparatus as those of studies and analyses of linguistic contacts. A few attempts have already been made in this direction, but unfortunately'they have been little more than attempts (cf. V.Yu. Rosentsveig, "Approche linguistique appliquée à la description des contacts culturels", Travaux du VII CISAE, Volume 5, page 629, 1970, Moscow).

The study of intercultural contacts is organically and indissolubly bound up with the study of contacts between languages. This has already been brought to light by the fact that language, more than any other cultural factor, generally appears in the part of the primordial factor in ethnic formation and division. It is one of the most important bases for the formation and conservation of the ethnic consciousness. It is true that, "In view of the relative rigidity of each linguistic system, all that is necessary to define the ethnic relationship of people speaking a given language is to know a few words of it. That is why, general speaking, in cases of this sort it is not necessary to make an exhaustive analysis of such a system" (Yu.V. Bromley, op. cit. page 222). However, exceptions to this rule (necessity for analyzing the system in general) often arise in areas of contact: in areas where transitory dialects exist, during the course of clarification of the correlation (coincidence or non-coincidence) of the frontiers of dialects with those of sub-ethnic groups (ethnographical sub-groups) within the context of an ethnic group, in delimiting closely related ethnic groups and, above all, in the formation of mixed languages of the creole type and zones of overwhelming bilingualism. This latter problem is particularly acute today, and it is not by accident that a considerable number of publications have been devoted to it (cf. S.I. Brouk, N.N. Gouboglo, "Bilingualism and the Reconciliation of Nations in the U.S.S.R.", Sovietskaïa Etnografiya, 1975, No. 4; and by the same authors: "The Factors Affecting the Diffusion of Bilingualism among the peoples of the U.S.S.R.", ibid, 1975, No. 5).

It should be remembered that bilingualism is only one of the elements making up the vast, complex problem of studying the linguistic situation. This problem includes the study of the correlation in functions and trends in the evolution of literary languages, spoken dialects and slang in homogeneous ethno-social organizations, and different languages in multinational, poly-ethnic and ethno-political countries. This is a problem on the borderline between ethnography and linguistics, and is being actively studied by both.

Linguistics as the study of spoken languages may be considered as a part - the one which has been formulated in the most detailed way - of semiotics in general, i.e. the theory of symboli systems. The symbolical index is more or less appropriate to all the integral parts of the extra-linguistic culture; certain aspects of it may also be dealt with in the context of the concepts of a symbolic system. That is why regularities, concepts and principles common to such systems in general, but studied most completely and in the greatest detail in connection with spoken languages, can also be applied, to a certain extent, to the study

of other aspects of culture if they are considered in the context
of symbolic systems.

This is the opinion which seems to have been expressed in
its most extreme form in the well-known theory of Sapir and
Warf, known as the theory of linguistic relativity, according to
which the mentality and entire structure of the culture of each
people depend to a large extent on the specific nature of the
language which is theirs. This hypothesis has been criticized in
Soviet linguistic literature as making the part played by language
as a link between reality and thought absolute. From the ethnographical point of view it would appear even more justifiable to
speak of a dictatorial part played by the linguistic component of
a culture in relation to its non-linguistic elements. Empirically,
a number of examples can be quoted in which a comparatively rapid
change of language by an ethnic group (the Turkification of
numerous Farsi-speaking groups in Central Asia and the Caucasus,
the Arynification of the languages of numerous small populations
of India) has not led to an equally profound transformation in
the field of extralinguistic culture. It would therefore appear
fairer to presume that different symbolical systems, including
language, are found in the mutual relations of influence and
dependence in any specifically ethnic culture without their being
necessarily hierarchically subordinate. But this is only a sup-
position which needs to be checked on the basis of concrete facts;
the question of the correlation between the linguistic reciprocal
influence and the cultural reciprocal influence therefore needs
to be studied in depth.

There is no doubt that vocabulary as a whole constitutes a
sub-division of linguistics with much closer links with the study
of extra-linguistic cultural realities. Certain isolated sectors
of the vocabulary of each language are, in turn, integral cultural
systems so far as their denotata and specificata are concerned;
they form an integral part of the entire spiritual culture of a
people speaking the language. The study of such cultural systems,
as well as the denominating lexical systems corresponding to the
said systems presupposes in principle a complex linguistic and
ethnographical study carried out on the borderline of the two
disciplines. Among systems of this sort a distinction can be made
between various onomastic ones - toponymy, anthroponymy, zoonymy,
etc. Of recent years there has been a considerable increase in
the U.S.S.R. in the scope of studies of these problems (cf.
E.M. Mourzaïev: Essays on Toponymics, 1974 Moscow; V.A.Nikonov:
Introduction to toponymics, 1965 Moscow; and by the same author:
Name and Society, 1974, Moscow.

In linguistics, the distinction of special onomastic problems
among linguistic problems as a whole is justified by the position
of proper nouns in the language. Proper nouns constitute the part
of the language which offers us the most paradoxical situations,
an analysis of which should contribute to the emergence of new
and more profound conceptions of linguistics in general (cf.
A.V. Souperanskaïa: General Theory on Proper Nouns, page 5, 1973
Moscow). So far as the ethnographer is concerned, these problems
interest him owing to their relation with the highly specific
elements of culture which are, in some cases, of an ethno-

differential character and in others bring to light the ethnic
history of the people. What has just been said may be illustrated
by examples which are far from exhausting the range of the problems involved. It is undoubtedly ethnomony which has the most
direct relation to ethnographical problems, for it reflects the
ethnic awareness and the perception of other ethnic groups,
stereotypes and autostereotypes, and ethnic structure and sub-
structure. The anthroponymic model serves as an important ethno-
differential index; its conservation or transformation may constitute one of the highly reliable indices of trends towards trans
formation or change of ethnic consciousness and relationship. On
the other hand, indices such as the special features of the
cosmonymy make it possible to trace wide areas coinciding with
former ethnographic and historical regions of the same nature,
while toponymical data make it possible to trace the areas of
former ethnic groups of the substratum, which enables us to perfect our ideas on the ethnogenesis of contemporary populations.
Such are the fields of culture whose material provides the best
opportunities for studying cultural contacts and mutual influences, and modern processes of cultural interaction, to say nothing
of the far-reaching prospects of comparative cultural research
which opens up in this field.

Terms of family relationship constitute a specific system
of lexical form with the significance of a cultural component.
They constitute a system which tends to be formed at cultural -
i.e. ethnographical - level rather than at linguistic level.
Systems of family relationship are therefore studied more as a
part of ethnography than as a part of linguistics, although the
links between these disciplines are extremely important and
polyvalent. They cannot be confined to the fact that the subject
of study is simultaneously an ethnocultural and a linguistic one.
These links also manifest themselves owing to the fact that at
present systems of family relationship are studied by means of
a series of new methods, particularly by component analysis.
"The principles at the base of this method and the main concepts
which it uses (these are the concepts of denotat and designat,
component and differential variables, S. Aroutiunov), are taken
from a new current of linguistic thought which studies semantics
by the light of the theory of symbols". (M.V. Kriukov: The System
of Family Relationship among the Chinese, page 24, 1972, Moscow).

In addition, special "languages" or codes are created in
order to avoid the subjectivity which may arise when it is required to express terms of family relationship of the language
and collectivity studied by means of terms in the language of the
community to which the researcher belongs. Some of these codes
are well-known, but the most scientifically based, which are used
in Soviet research circles have been formulated on the basis of
the concepts and methods of mathematical semiotics (cf. Yu.I.Levir
"Regarding the Description of a System of Terms of Family Relatior
ship", Sovietskaïa Etnografiya 1970, No. 4). This coding system
promises well for the study of systems of family relationship
from both the comparative cultural study and the inter-ethnic
relationship point of view. The systems of family relationship
have for a long time been the subject of comparative cultural

studies, but the most recent achievements of Soviet scientists make it possible to improve the methodological level.

To sum up, it may be concluded that further work of intercultural studies should be divided into two sectors. One of these may be further sub-divided into two main directions. The first is the preparation of the corpus of sources which could provide really comparable material in a standardized form - standardized for use in intercultural comparisons and continuous opinion surveys. The second direction within the same sector consists of formulating methodological conceptions to be used as the basis for intercultural studies. The second sector consists of carrying out a few concrete pilot studies on intercultural problems.

The first of these sectors includes assistance in the work of editing historico-cultural and historico-ethnographical atlases which is proceeding in various countries.

This work would appear to be urgent, for in many regions of the world the phenomena of traditional, specifically ethnic culture, both material (habitat, clothing, working tools) and spiritual (life cycle rites, songs, popular theatre) are rapidly disappearing. At the same time it is essential to take measures to standardize methods of collecting cartographic material and its graphical presentation, so that the material collected will be easily comparable.

The problem of formulating a clear taxonomy of the objects studied is closely bound up with the above; it is essential that the standards brought to light in giving details of the analysis of a dwelling or other building, a costume or a ceremony can be used as units of emic character.

In this connection the extrapolation of the conceptual apparatus used in the study of linguistic contacts and comparative linguistics to the method of intercultural studies may be viable.

A possible subject for the pilot study could be societies which were already at the level of a productive economy (agriculture and livestock raising) at the time of the great geographical discoveries and which began after European penetration to have close contacts with European culture in some form or another and continued to develop as peasant societies. Such are the native populations of the South-West of the United States, Mexico, the Andean Plateau, the coastal plantation regions of West Africa and the Philippines, a few regions of Eastern Africa, Southern Siberia and so on. From the point of view of comparative cultural studies, this would make it possible to bring out the institutions of peasant society developing convergently, at a subsequent stage to be involved in the orbit of the modern economy of supply and demand. From the point of view of cultural interaction, the constant features of contacts between European and traditional cultures (a contact which is still going on today) could be revealed. Such studies could be carried out in cooperation by the researchers of different countries in accordance with a coordinated programme aimed at providing comparable data.

The above-mentioned societies being used as an example, a comparative study could be made of the problem of the divorce of "professional" artistic culture (i.e. that of the individual artist)

and the current of anonymous traditional culture, as also the
relations between the "professional" culture of the countryside
and the imported culture of the industrial and urban type. This
makes it possible to follow the mechanism of the diffusion of
mass culture in a formerly traditional society, the part played
by the mass media, the predominance of "professional" culture
over the way of life, every day conduct, and the transformation
of systems of values.

The study of the anthroponymic model of microtoponymy,
systems of family relationship and their development in societies could become a specialized field of research.

Another field of research, on the basis of this same or
any other material, consists of studying the development of
bilingualism and the degree of association between such development and the process of biculturalism. Under certain conditions,
the latter could take the form of a tendency towards assimilation, acculturation without assimilation, intercultural reconciliation, etc.

Among the subjects on a more modest scale which can be
studied almost anywhere, it is worth mentioning the transformation of local artistic crafts under the impact of commercial demand and marketing ideas, patterns and mass production world
images, together with the reverse process, i.e. the reflection
of local artistic traditions in that production.

Such a study, also carried out in accordance with a comparable
programme in various regions of the world, can immediately be put
into practice in the form of recommendations dealing with the development of popular industries and the introduction of the best
achievements of craftsmen in mass-production.

A few meetings and consultative symposia could be held under
the auspices of Unesco in the next six years. It would be as well
to organize two symposia for each of the fields of study selected:
the first in one or two years to draw up a working programme; the
second in four or five years (i.e. two or three years after the
first) to examine the results obtained within the context of this
programme. The subjects of the meetings in question could be laid
down as follows:

1. Problems of international harmonization and cooperation in
publishing historico-cultural and ethno-graphic atlases;
2. Problems of taxonomy and the selection of basic emic units
for the comparative study of material and spiritual cultural
elements;
3. Prospects for the study of traditional peasant societies coming
into contact with urbanized culture of the Western type;
4. The tasks of international cooperation in the fields of
anthroponymy;
5. Problems of bilingualism in the contemporary world and the
predominance of bilingualism over the development of mutual intercultural influences.

The conditions for objectivity in approaching the intercultural: the case of oriental and asian studies

Louis Bazin

The following text constitutes the essence of a report drafted by Professor Louis Bazin, Secretary General of the International Union of Oriental and Asian Studies (IUOAS), for a meeting of the Bureau of that organization, but contributed by the author to the file of the March 1978 Study Group. In agreement with him, we have omitted certain technical arguments specific to Oriental and Asian studies and retained the considerations applicable to the dialogue between cultures in general. It also contains a useful analysis of what makes up the concept of cultural identity. The last part of this text also complies with the requirements inherent to the project by presenting a strict statement of the conditions for adequate and sincere international cooperation in humanistic studies and for the deontological guarantees with which the anthropologist - more than any other researcher - should equip himself in dealing with his subject (man - his likeness), i.e., usually, in an ideal intercultural situation.

PREAMBLE

Although the expression "cultural identity" only recently became part of international terminology (with justified success), the conceptual whole which it covers proceeds from a tradition which, partially at least, has its roots in the ancient history of the scientific study of languages and civilizations and which enriched itself considerably from the time when, owing to the introduction of comparative methods, there gradually emerged the notions of specificity and relativity of cultural values, which have contributed to the disparagement of the former dogmatisms (obviously self contradictory) presupposing absolute cultural values which were the exclusive property of the "civilized".

Now, research devoted to the Near East and Asia have played a capital part in this gradual revelation of the relative values and plurality of cultures (considered, not as a shortcoming but as a wealth of mankind). It was thanks mainly to such research that the West gradually became aware (although to an extent which is still insufficient) of the Oriental and Asian origins of many basic elements constituting its own culture and of the remarkable

achievements of various civilizations which followed different
roads of development. These first acquisitions, which were essentially due to Western "Orientalism" (fed, it should not be forgotten, by the cultural wealth accumulated by the people and scholars
of the Orient) have mainly been a source of profit to the West,
particularly to the élite of its intellectual class, which, thus,
in the interests of a more or less egotistic delectation, widened
the horizons of its humanism - which, incidentally, had remained
centred on Europe.

At this stage there was still no question of a real intercultural dialogue, for a number of inter-related reasons: first,
because the scientific acquisitions of western Orientalism
accompanied - and in fact reinforced, whether consciously or not -
the great movement of colonial or semi-colonial exploitation of
the peoples of the Orient by those of the West; and secondly
because, under such conditions, the equality and mutual respect
presupposed by any real dialogue were far from existing or even
possible, since the superiority and inferiority complexes created
by the factual encounter of rulers and ruled basically distorted
any profound and sincere attempts at exchange.

To be sure, a few broad-minded and far-seeing people on both
sides, rising above historical situations which they knew to be
precarious, attempted to conquer such complexes and overcome such
opposition, but their attempts, though shedding precious light for
the future, clashed in the immediate with obstacles created by
history. In the West, classical Orientalism continued to be dominated, even though unconsciously, by Europeocentrism: the very
successes that it had achieved in the study of the languages,
religions, history and archaeology of the East by scientific
methods perfected in Europe (but which, in fact, owed much to many
Oriental scholars) lent comfort to its faith in the superiority of
Western values, even though it recognized that the great cultures
of the Orient had some merit. Oriental scholars for their part,
usually well aware of the dangers incurred by their national
cultures at the hands of the different forms (military, political,
economic, social, religious and ideological) of Western expan-
sionism, were on the defensive. Some withdrew to their ancestral
traditions, rejecting a modernity which they felt to be a form of
Western aggression; for them there could be no question of carrying on a dialogue with the West. Others, more daring and often
younger, reacted by attempting to take over the very weapons of
the adversary, by acquiring a knowledge of his methods, technology, science and language with the aim of better defending the
national values to which they were so profoundly attached. The
duality of their culture made them potential men of dialogue for
the future but conferred on them for the time being a conflictual
character (and sometimes a divisive one) which deferred to the
coveted time of independence and rewon equality a calm encounter -
and even an enriching exchange - between the two systems of values
Obviously, those who were induced by various circumstances - or
their personal interests - to repudiate their national culture
and adopt that of the colonial or semi-colonial dominator forfeit-
ed all credibility as participants in an intercultural dialogue.

For this dialogue to start and be pursued constructively and fruitfully on a real equal footing and in an atmosphere of sincerity, dignity and mutual good will, it was necessary to await the end of the colonial epoch.

The period of decolonialization which followed on the end of the second World War therefore marked the opening, at international scale, of the great cultural dialogue which Unesco, from the time of its foundation, promoted vigorously and since that date has unceasingly encouraged, reinforced and guided by the light of principles which have been to a large extent adopted internationally by States with widely differing ideologies, including both those which were former colonizers and those which recently acceded to independence at the end of the colonial period.

Among the activities undertaken by Unesco in order to promote this dialogue it is as well to quote the launching, as a result of the ninth General Conference held in New Delhi in 1956, of the "Major Project related to the mutual appreciation of the cultural values of the East and West".

The impulse thus imparted by Unesco to the dialogue, on an equal footing, between eastern and western cultures had repercussions in the non-governmental international cultural organizations directly concerned by this supremely important question, such as the International Council for Philosophy and Humanistic Studies. Of the member organizations of this Council, one of the most directly concerned by its very nature in the development of the intercultural dialogue between the East and the West was, of course, the International Union of Orientalists, which was shortly afterwards to become, through a change in its title to give substance to its internal mutation (characterized by the rejection of the Europeanized conception of classical "Orientalism"), the International Union of Oriental and Asian Studies.

This Union, the organizations composing it, and the individual scholars who devote themselves to these same disciplines cannot fail to be concerned by the intercultural dialogue and, in particular, to attempt to contribute to the definition, safeguarding and appreciation at international level of the values which characterize the cultural identity of the Oriental and Asian peoples, while taking their internal point of view more fully into account.

I propose, in the following pages, to explore the ways and means of achieving such a contribution.

ORIENTAL AND ASIAN STUDIES

Geographical area
The obviously conventional phrase "Oriental and Asian Studies" finally adopted in 1973 by the International Union of Oriental and Asian Studies to replace the disputed term "Orientalism",

covers a group of studies concerned, on the one hand, with the
whole of Asia (including the Asian islands) and on the other, the
northern part of Africa (area of Arabic Islam and the Hamito-
Semitic languages). This continuous geographical area does not
include Black Africa, for reasons connected exclusively with the
history of the development of humanistic studies, since Africanist
sciences have developed autonomously, with their own traditions
and organizations (which, incidentally, does not exclude cooperation with "Oriental" studies, since the two fields are inter-
dependant in North Africa and African Islam).

The area defined above cannot be considered as finite, since
cultural expansion has extended it (for example into Eastern
Europe, for the study of the Turkish-speaking peoples of the USSR
or of the Islam of south-eastern Europe). Its limits are ambiguous where australasia is concerned, where the Oceanists have
their own traditions. It does not include the American Indian
world or the "Western" world, studies of which have been developed
and organized independently although there is no absolute separation, in view of migrations, cultural interpenetration and the
advantages of comparative or interdisciplinary studies.

Thematic field

The thematic field of "Oriental and Asian Studies" is that of
humanistic studies in general (the IUOAS is a member organization of the International Council for Philosophy and Humanistic
Studies).

So far as the regions under consideration are concerned, it
includes linguistics and philology, cultural anthropology, the
history of societies, cultures, religions, philosophies, science
and technology, letters and the arts.

This list, which is not exhaustive, may well give an impression of confusion and laxity to an intellectual accustomed to a
systematic classification of the sciences, such as is in force in
the Western tradition. This would imply a hasty and superficial
interpretation and a lack of understanding of the underlying
realities.

For the fact is that what makes for the value, originality
and cohesion - in spite of appearances - of the scientific whole
consisting of "Oriental and Asian Studies" is its very basic
inter-disciplinary nature, its character of overall exploration
of the cultural field, in a universalist spirit which allows
neither of barriers between peoples nor of partitions between the
sciences.

This inter-disciplinary character, the merits and fruitful-
ness of which the West is rediscovering, was the rule in Western
science until the advent of the industrial era (which it helped
to produce) and has never ceased to be the rule of the Oriental
and Asian scientists. This last fact explains to a very large extent the fact that it has been forcefully maintained in Oriental
and Asiatic studies.

While it is true that Western Orientalists have greatly
benefited from the methodologies of humanistic studies perfected
in the West, they are nonetheless the direct or indirect disciples
of Oriental and Asian scholars as regards the content of their
knowledge. They have thus, albeit unconsciously, inherited an

overall conception of humanistic studies (at a time when such a conception was giving way in Europe to fragmentary specialities) - a fruitful conception which very rapidly ensured the exceptional development of their work.

For their part, the scholars of the Orient and Asia very soon took over the methodologies put forward by the West, and which, incidentally, they had helped to perfect, while retaining that overall conception of humanistic studies which constituted an integral part of their traditions. In addition, they learnt Western languages, thus enabling themselves to communicate with the scientific world of the West (while at the same time the West was attaching much more importance than in the past to the use of one or more Oriental languages).

Thus there is now an increasing symbiosis of methods, interdisciplinary conception and communications between the scientific worlds of East and West in the field of humanistic studies covered by what it has been generally agreed to term henceforth: "Oriental and Asian Studies".

East-West scientific dialogue

However, it was necessary to await the era of decolonization before this progressive symbiosis could result in a completely open dialogue on a footing of equality and without mental reservations.

Its advent profoundly transformed the relations between Eastern and Western scholars, who became used to talking on an equal footing, in an atmosphere of trust and mutual respect, thus forming a truly universal scientific community.

This beneficial change immediately made its positive effects felt in the field of humanistic studies of the Orient and Asia, where it was an essential condition for progress and thoroughness. Whereas formerly information mainly circulated in one direction (with the literate Oriental acting as informer to the Western Orientalist), it now became increasingly reciprocal, owing to exchanges of documents and publications, scientific correspondence, mutual collaboration in reviews, the mutual practice of constructive criticism, joint participation in learned societies and undertakings, and the holding of conferences on a wide international basis, in which representatives of the cultures studied enjoy all the authority conferred on them by their intimate knowledge of the questions discussed.

Exchanges of persons between East and West are regularly increasing, for teaching and research in the field under consideration. These affect both young researchers (harbingers of the future) and experienced specialists.

This quantitative increase in exchanges is accompanied by an even more important improvement in quality, which ensures that henceforth there is an authentic inter-cultural dialogue. Since there is no longer any question of superiority or inferiority in connection with intercultural exchanges, which are carried out with a view to increasing knowledge and understanding of facts, the differences between cultures are ceasing to be a source of antagonism and are being appreciated positively and sympathetically as just so many factors contributing to the diversity of mankind in general, which prevent the "levelling into cultural

conformism and banality". (Cf. the text of Unesco Objective 1.2
mentioned at the beginning of the present Report).
    To be sure, much still remains to be done to ensure that the
cultural dialogue is' developed to the full; only a limited intellectual circle is fully engaged in such dialogues, expanding thoug
it is constantly (these studies are attracting an increasing
number of young people in nearly all regions). But it was undoubtedly essential to the success of this dialogue that it should
begin in a circle which was already well informed and prepared for
such an opening.
    The most pressing task of specialists in Oriental and Asian
studies is now to spread the results of this dialogue, upon which
the cultural future of mankind - and perhaps its harmonious survival - depends, among the international public by means of
popular treatises of an acceptable standard. Fortunately, they
are increasingly aware of this.(...)

ANALYSIS AND PROBLEMS OF CULTURAL IDENTITY

The contribution thus considered can only be specified after an
attempt has been made to define the cultural identity, including
the analysis of the features which compose it and the problems
which arise in connection with it.

Features of cultural identity
In the concept cultural identity, as understood internationally
today, the word identity is accepted in the sense of specific
character (made up of distinctive features) - but the collective
specific character of a human group rather than the oneness of
man. This at least is the way in which it is best to interpret
it here, since the cultural identity of the individual taken in
isolation is not a matter for international scientific activity.
    As for the term cultural it generally excludes somatic and
genetic features, at least as such. However, the psychological
impact of these features, felt collectively either by the group
which possesses them or by a different somatic group, can be
taken into account to a certain extent in the cultural identity
as an element of a collective ideology (e.g. contributing to or
detracting from solidarity or segregation, etc.). In that case,
it is not the somatic fact itself but the collective interpretatior
given to it, which constitutes a feature of cultural identity.
    In fact, by "cultural" we understand what is concerned with
the intellectual, psychological and spiritual aspects of a civilization.
    Obviously, language is one of the fundamental features of the
cultural identity. It is by means of it, and within its context,
that thought - or at least discursive thought, which is the only
sort that can be understood collectively - is expressed and transmitted. The diversity of languages and of their successive levels

and conditions, is one of the chief factors differentiating
human groups and imparting specific cultural features. Such differentiation, incidentally, varies in degree according to whether
the idioms compared are mutually incomprehensible or, as in the
case of dialects of the same language, make exchanges of information and linguistic communication possible, although some of
the meaning is lost.

As well as differentiating, language is a factor of union for
the group which jointly possesses it. By its language the group
recognizes itself and differs from those who do not speak it.

Community of language may be considered a necessary factor for
the collective cultural identity, but it is not a factor sufficient
on its own. (For example, there is a differɘnce of cultural identity between a Catholic and a Protestant of Belfast who both speak
English, or between a Hindu and a Muslim of New Delhi who both
speak Hindi).

The social organization of a human group confers on it various
cultural identity features, some of which are common to the entire
group while others are specific to the sub-groups which such organization may determine (differences in social class, age, sex -
which, too, are more or less marked in the language).

The religious status (understood in the widest sense) is a
factor contributing to the specific cultural character which varies
in importance according to the social environment. Except in
cases where inter-confessional antagonisms are exacerbated for
regional, social and historical reasons (as in the case of Northern
Ireland), there is a tendency for its force of distinction to
abate in highly industrialized countries where a lay tradition in
government has been developed. Here, it becomes a relatively
secondary factor in cultural identity.

Things are quite different in the majority of regions where
economic development is taking place, which are dominated by
traditional agricultural societies for which religion is not only
a body of deeply held beliefs but a well defined ethical system
and an essential regulator of social organization. Such a
situation exists in a large number of countries of Asia and Africa.

It should be noted that it is sometimes difficult to distinguish a religious fact from one which is not in the culture of a
society. Everywhere are to be found popular beliefs and practices,
which do not form part of the doctrine of the group's religion and
may even be partly in contradiction with it but which, in the collective consciousness, have characteristics of faith and obli-
gation quite comparable with religious characteristics.

These popular beliefs and practices on the fringe of or partly
unrelated to religion proper are complex but fundamental components
of the cultural identity. They often constitute the continuance
of secular internal traditions underlying religious acculturation.

Although more or less condemned by the intellectual classes
of the society or outside it in the name of orthodoxy or rationality, they are nevertheless an integral part of the real cultural
universe and should be considered as such in any analysis of it.

The beliefs in question are partly explicit (which sheds
direct light on the meaning of the practices bound up with them)

and partly implicit (in which case they can be deciphered by means of a practice). In certain cases, it occurs that a practice continues long after the belief which gave rise to it has disappeared (Cf. the Christmas tree in the Christian West). There then occurs a kind of sublimation, such as that which transformed what was formerly a magic ceremony into a festival (Cf. in France, the "Fires of Saint John").

Obviously, it is right to include festivals among the elements making up a human group's cultural identity.

Traditional techniques are also features of this identity. Some, such as those of the crafts, are essentially material (although elements of belief are often mixed up with them). Others, such as those of popular medicine, are midway between the rationality of material experience and speculation on the basis of beliefs (either the one or the other being preponderant according to cases). Lastly, there are others, such as those of magic or wizardry, which fall into the realm of beliefs.

Feeding habits, which are undeniably a characteristic factor of cultural identity, are related to material, environmental and economic conditions and to historical phenomena of acculturation or regulations of religious origin. In any case, they must be taken into account for the definition of the cultural identity and the respect of it, for the non-observation, through ignorance or contempt, of the rights of others to different feeding habits or, even worse, forcing them to violate their traditional or religious food laws are rightly resented as both physical and spiritual aggressions.

Textual traditions, obviously related to the language factor, play a considerable part in a people's cultural identity, whether of a sacred or profane character and whether written or oral. The written tradition has always been recognized as a primordial element in culture. It affects not only literate but also illiterate people by means of recitation (particularly in the case of sacred texts, such as the Koran). The oral tradition should be considered as equally and even more important in vast areas of Asia and Africa, where it is one of the richest and most lofty components of popular culture. It preceded written tradition and was the mother of it. It includes a great variety of genres just as the literatures do: mnemonic or operative, ceremonial or liturgical, proverbs, tales, epics, lyrical songs, didactical poems, etc. Its dignity and value are now fully recognized. It is the object of increasing interest. A knowledge of it is essential to those human groups who possess it.

Oral tradition is not merely a means of artistic expression. It also conveys knowledge, a view of the world, man and society. It plays a basic part in education, and its decline, even in a literate society, would be a tragic impoverishment, generating a serious cultural crisis and regression which, it is to be hoped, is still avoidable.

Artistic tradition forms a complex cultural entity, which is also highly pertinent for defining the identity of a society. A distinction can be made between plastic (drawing, painting and sculpture), architectural, musical and choreographical, theatrical traditions and others. It becomes manifest at different levels, according to whether it is the work of specialists or a common possession of the population.

All the elements of cultural identity I have listed (though the list does not claim to be exhaustive, and I am well aware that many other methods of classification are possible) are transmitted from one generation to another - and are modified - by education.

Any thorough study of cultural identity should include research into the methods and content of education in the human group under consideration. Education takes different forms, of which teaching is only one special aspect. It is comparatively easy to study educational systems of the scholastic type, concerning which abundant documentation can usually be collected. But less is usually known about the other means of education (by the family, the social environment, the natural surroundings, the means of communication) which are also specific to a society.

The latter are also worthy of the entire attention of the researcher in his inventory of culture, as also are ludic activities (games and sports), which play a by no means negligible part in the development of intellectual and physical faculties.

The specific features of sexuality in a given society, which we have a right to consider as forming part of the cultural identity, are very largely bound up with an overall and more or less systematized education in which the entire society participates.

In the content of any system of education, it will be as well to distinguish what is related to the acquisition of knowledge, skills, social behaviour, ethics and ideology (religious or otherwise).

This is a measure of the complexity of elements which must be taken into account in order to define and assess the cultural identity of a human group (a complexity which would be even greater if we were to consider that of individuals, which is not the case here).

To all the above considerations, which are synchronically applicable, must be added a diachronic factor which is essential for explaining and characterizing cultural facts - that of the historical dimension. The importance of this dimension, which specialists do not lose sight of, is felt deeply by the people themselves, whether literate or not, who attach the greatest value to their past and to a knowledge of it, whether resulting from the historiographer, the factual oral tradition, or the elaboration of symbolical myths (just as prevalent among the literate as the illiterate).

Cultural identity problems

By means of a scientific analysis followed by a synthesis of the factors I have just named, it is possible to attempt an objective approach to the cultural identity, but it would be foolish to pretend that such an approach is the exclusive reserve of a limited intellectual public rather than that of human collectivities.

As it happens, the latter adopt a subjective, all-round approach, favouring certain features and blurring or effacing

others, ignoring or failing to see clearly many others, and inter-
preting them in affective rather than in intellectual terms.

This method is often taken to extremes in the image which a
given group creates for itself of the specific cultural character
of another group. In such cases, hasty judgements, misunderstandings and phantasms are common.

But the image seen by the group of its own collective cultural
identity, while based on intimate experience, has considerable
difficulty in extricating itself from vague subjectivity. The
group is no more capable of analysing itself than is the individual
Its experience undoubtedly confers on it a profound awareness of
its identity, but it is a general, not a discursive, awareness
which it is difficult to explain in words and therefore to transmit.

On the other hand, the extraneous investigator, even if (as
is essential for any profound contact) he speaks the language of
the group, respects its customs and is in a situation of trust and
sympathy towards it, can only penetrate to an extent which varies
according to circumstances, into the consciousness of the group.

Such is the well-known paradox of cultural anthropology: only
the social group is fully conscious of itself, but cannot analyze
itself; the extraneous investigator, who is intellectually capable
of analyzing, has not the group consciousness and is aware only
of its reflections.

Does this mean that the researcher ought to be inside the
group? That, too, creates a problem, for the special training he
must undergo in order to carry out his research unconsciously
modifies his own cultural identity, according to which he evalu-
ates that of his group.

There is no perfect solution to this problem. In any case,
we must resign ourselves to the fact that we can never exhaust
the unfathomable wealth of the collective consciousness. But
an attempt should be made to get as near as possible to the essential facts and transmissible truths. It is possible to
achieve adequate approximations in various ways: either the
researcher is extraneous to the group (as most frequently occurs)
and succeeds in getting himself sufficiently accepted by the
group to be more or less integrated with them, or the researcher
forms part of the group and immerses himself in it again for a
sufficient period to regain to a large extent his awareness of
it, or again, a solution which may perhaps be the best, an extraneous, but adopted, researcher closely cooperates with a re-
integrated researcher who is part of the group.

The official Unesco Objective 1.2 text regarding cultural
identity states, under Principles of Action, at paragraph 1224(a):

> "The presentation of cultures in their authentic
> form must essentially come from within: cultural
> values must be interpreted and brought up to
> date by the people who are actually living them".

This is an excellent principle, providing that the text is not
distorted by shifting the meaning from "essentially" to "exclusively" and that the latter adverb is not mentally added to the
second proposition.

For any presentation of cultures made <u>exclusively</u> "from inside" would run a serious risk of failing in scientific object- ivity and, moreover, of not "getting over" to the outside world, unless its authors are exceptionally talented, since it is very difficult to free cultural introspection from an incommunicable subjectivity.

In the same way, any interpretation and actualization of cultural values carried out <u>exclusively</u> by those who possess them runs the risk of lacking both objectivity and credibility in the outside world. It could, no matter how wrongly, be considered as propaganda.

It is equally true that <u>any presentation of cultures which does not take the fullest possible account of the manifestations of the internal consciousness or the internal interpretations and actualizations of cultural values, would be completely dis- torted.</u> If it were a matter not of ignorance but of a deliberate refusal to allow those concerned to express themselves, it would even be dishonest.

In order to ensure that cultures are authentically and credibly presented, it is essential to take the expression of the internal point of view fully into account without any censorship, (for <u>men's view of their own culture is an integral part of their cultural identity</u>), to pursue the analysis of them in close cooperation with participants and non-participants, and to con- clude a statement of them by common agreement.

To isolate those concerned from the presentation, inter- pretation and actualization of the cultural values they possess would be contrary to an all scientific deontology and would completely distort the results. To exclude all external witnes- ses would be to detract from the credibility of the statement. To reject out of hand any cooperation with a specialist not pos- sessed of the culture in question would be to compromise both the objectivity and the effectiveness of the cultural message.

Incidentally, it should be noted that, if the presenta- tion (essentially in writing if it is to be disseminated) of any culture were exclusively reserved to its participants, the illiterate human groups, which still constitute the majority in vast regions of the world, would be unjustly deprived of any external expression of their cultural values, although the latter are worthy of a respect equal to that accorded to the values of the literate.

The great movement for promoting the appreciation and res- pect of cultural identity which is emerging under the auspices of Unesco must be developed into a vast and fruitful inter- national cooperation, without mental reservations or exclusivity. It should encourage a dialogue between cultures rather than a monologue by them.

This is affirmed in paragraph 1224(b) of the official text already quoted (<u>Objective 1.2</u>):

> "Intra-cultural authenticity must necessarily
> be supplemented by inter-cultural dialogue.
> For unless one is to run the risk of encouraging

national compartmentalization and sectarianism
in one or other form, it is important to ensure
that each culture is open to the influence of all
the others within a broad international framework.

HOW CAN AND MUST ORIENTAL AND ASIAN STUDIES HELP TO PROMOTE
APPRECIATION OF AND RESPECT FOR THE CULTURAL IDENTITY?

The reply to this question depends on an assessment of the impact
of this research on cultural identity and an appreciation of it,
and of the means that can be brought to bear. It also depends
on a deontology of this research into cultural identity.

Impact
There is no doubt that the results achieved by humanistic studies
have direct repercussions on the cultural identity of human groups.
    To be sure, it is the intellectual classes which first become
aware of them but a knowledge of them is rapidly spread to varying
extents and in different forms among all the population, even non-
literate groups.
    The fact is currently noticeable at national scale in all
regions of the world. In particular, the work of national or
foreign scholars who try to enlighten a people regarding their
past, their origins and history, or to bring out the values of
their culture, arts and traditions and their contribution to
science and technology have far-reaching repercussions on the
people's image of themselves. Obviously, the specialized scientific content of this work is not understood by all, but its
essential echoes (sometimes, it must be admitted, with distortions)
reach the least favoured and least educated strata of the population. (It may even occur that certain research remains materially inaccessible to the populations concerned, when the transient
researcher, having benefited from very useful cooperation in the
field, neglects to ensure that the universities and libraries
of the countries concerned have the benefit of it).
    There is nothing new about this phenomenon, and there are
plenty of examples of it in the major Western and Eastern societies with a historiographical tradition. But societies with an
oral tradition also collect to a varying extent items of information regarding writings about them, and react in their own
manner, sometimes integrating them into their folklore, particularly into their ethnic legends.
    The very remarkable acquisitions of archaeology over the
past two centuries have had repercussions on "national images",
which are among the most significant components of cultural
identity. Thus, no Egyptian fellah is unaware of the existence
of the monuments of ancient Egypt, and the entire population of
Arab and Islamic Egypt feels that it is profoundly part of the

thousands-year old culture of Pharaonic Egypt. In the same way, Iran as a whole has some knowledge of Darius and Persepolis, and integrates the grandeur of the Persian Empire into its national image.

Ethnologists know well enough to what extent the populations they study are interested in the results of their research and try to understand the essence of it, so as to acquire a clearer and more vivid consciousness of their own identity. It is common-place to see, in countries which, like Mexico for example, are made up of various ethnic groups, how members of such groups crowd into the ethnographical museums and are very curious re-garding what has become for them a subject for thought, and even of pride.

Generally speaking, it can be asserted that the scientific study of a culture helps to deepen an awareness, among those concerned, of their cultural identity and to improve the value of its components in their own eyes, providing, of course, that it is sufficiently well carried out for them to be able to re-cognize themselves in its results.

It also plays a by no means negligible part in the way in which other human collectivities look upon such identity.

This is a positive part to the extent that the research rec-tifies errors in judgement, invalidates preconceived ideas, puts forward the internal points of view of a society authentically, shows the logical train of thought of its cultural system and pro-vides the means of an understanding which is the essential con-dition for respect and sympathy.

For such means to be within the intellectual grasp not merely of a restricted circle of specialists but of the greatest possible number of human beings concerned by the question, the basic scien-tific statement (which may well be highly technical) should be extended by means of conclusions clearly expressed in ordinary language comprehensible to the public at large, which brings us to the problem of sound works for popular consumption, to which we shall refer again later.

Otherwise, there is a risk that erroneous interpretations will be proliferated, thus involving a host of misunderstandings the subsequent dispersal of which will be extremely difficult. Thus it occurs that the abstruseness of certain scientists may generate surprises which completely distort the meaning of their work.

Deontology

Since humanistic studies, in analyzing and presenting cultures, have a certain impact on the internal and external appreciation of cultural values - an appreciation which is one of the factors determining social behaviour and relations between human groups - they are invested with a very grave responsibility, which demands of them a deontology.

Among the elements of this deontology, there are some common to all science and which call for no comment on our part since they are universally accepted: scrupulous observation and checking of facts, strictly logical reasoning, critical and auto-critical discussion, objectivity of statements, etc.

But owing to the subject of his science - which is none other than his fellow men - the specialist in the science of man has special duties which I shall attempt to define.

The first of these duties is a respect for the human person not only in its individual form but also in its collective forms. The cultural values which are an integral part of the individual and collective personality must, therefore, be respected. They cannot be considered as just another object which can be damaged or broken for research purposes.

Investigation, in humanistic studies, must be undertaken with unceasing prudence, and research must never take the form of aggression - even though involuntary and limited to a more or less discreet pressure.

In particular, the researcher must avoid with the greatest care anything which may ruffle the national or religious suscepti- bilities of those being investigated, or anything which might be considered as a critical or normative intervention in the values of the society concerned.

The researcher must, in the same way, abstain from showing opposition to the society's habits and customs and take the greatest care not to violate its taboos (even those which are foreign to his own culture).

Here, incidentally, is a fundamental difficulty encountered by all field research in humanistic studies - the fact that, in order not to offend the susceptibilities of the group concerned it is necessary, while not necessarily having a thorough knowledge of it (which can only be the final result of the research), at least to have a general idea of it and, in a way, to have a presentiment of it.

For this purpose, preliminary precautions have to be taken. They may consist of a study, preceding the research proper, of all knowledge already available (and perhaps published) on the group concerned. In cases where the group has not yet been the subject of scientific study, one method of approach is to gather information in the first stage from neighbouring groups which are in contact with it and who have acquired some knowledge of its cultural particularities.

But the most recommendable and effective method is to secure the prior cooperation of a member of the group wherever possible - a respected member.

In any case humanistic studies research into a special group (whether from the point of view of language, organization, tradition, or any other feature of its cultural identity) can- not be validly undertaken except in cooperation on equal footing with members of the group, who should be informed quite clearly regarding the object of the research and the advantages deriving from appreciation and valorization of its identity, and should thus become active participants in it.

If research is undertaken by one or more foreign specialists in the country where it has to take place, it is highly desirable, if not essential, that it should be pursued in cooperation with scholars of that country.

In any case the majority of States have laid down regulations

on this point which every researcher should make it his duty to
respect scrupulously.

Respect for the cultures studied should not only be observed
towards the social groups and persons. It should also be observed
towards the material objects which are the expression of such
cultures.

Deontology in this field is particularly strict as regards
archaeological treasures. The plundering of national antiques
(by forceful appropriation of the produce of excavations, pure
and simple theft, or massive purchases of objects in unfair conditions) of which many economically underdeveloped countries were
victims during the nineteenth century and the beginning of the
twentieth is now unanimously condemned by the consensus of international opinion and by all scholars worthy of the name. But in
spite of the progress made, problems still remain in the field
of exports of archaeological treasures.

It is obvious that the solution to these problems can only
be found on the basis of agreements with governments, but the
scientific world should give an example of scrupulous vigilance
in this sphere.

The researcher's respect should also be extended to all
objects which represent or convey cultural values. Among the
most important are written texts, whether manuscripts or rare
books. Modern reproduction techniques are a great help in this
respect, since they enable scholars to have access to the contents
of such documents without the risk of damaging them.

Ethnographic subjects should themselves be treated with
respect, both in the way they are handled and the way they are
presented, by agreement with the societies which created them,
an aspect of whose culture they represent.

Particular respect should be paid to objects of a sacred or
symbolical nature.

All these rules of respect for cultures and the cultural
heritage (which could be dealt with even more fully and in greater
detail) are today, fortunately, accepted and practised by the
great majority of specialists. They are not related only to
international morality; they also concern, within one and the
same nation, the treatment of the cultural values of specific
human groups, particularly those known as "minorities" (ethnic,
linguistic, religious, etc.).

Scientific deontology where minorities are concerned is a
particularly delicate matter. For it sometimes occurs that, for
various historical reasons, tension occurs between such minorities
and the majorities who dominate the country. A scientist conscious of his responsibilities should do nothing to aggravate
such tensions. On the other hand, he has to devote the same
consideration to the cultural identity of a minority as to that
of the dominant group. He thus has to reconcile two duties -
that of intellectual honesty towards the minority and that of
loyalty to the State into which it is incorporated. This is
sometimes a difficult task.

In such an event, his line of conduct might be inspired
by the following principles adopted by the Unesco General Conference under Objective 1.2:

"For each nation, whether or not it is its own
master politically, whether or not it is a great
power, whether it has a full range of resources
and skills at its disposal or is still in the
stage of development, the assertion of cultural
identity is the basis for cultural pluralism.
Acceptance and respect for such pluralism, with
equal rights and on an equal footing, is today
manifestly a factor contributing towards peace
and understanding between nations." (1207).

Without in the least detracting from the above, I might add that
recognition and respect of cultural pluralism are also factors
for the peace and internal harmony of nations. This is the point
of view from which specialists in humanistic studies should consider the accomplishment of their mission, so as to contribute by
their work to that understanding, not only among nations but among
all human collectivities, which is indispensable to sympathy and
peace among men.

Contribution of Oriental and Asian studies : Reality and prospects
To the extent that they have already, after a long period of
evolution, adopted and applied the deontological principles which
have been listed above, Oriental and Asian studies have made what
appears to me to be an increasing contribution to the promotion
and appreciation, with a respect for pluralism, of the cultural
identity of various peoples of Asia and North Africa.

Even the more or less Europeocentric research of classical
Orientalism, once revised, completed and reinterpreted in a new
light, particularly by scholars of the countries concerned, have
made a decisive contribution to the definition of cultures and
the expression of their values.

Even the scarcely paradoxical opinion that the excesses of
Europeocentrism have caused cultural identity to be more vividly
and clearly acknowledged, as the result of a legitimate reaction,
is worthy of support.

Today it may be claimed that, apart from a few reactionaries
and nostalgics, scholars in this field are to a greater or lesser
but usually to a very high degree aware of their responsibilities towards the peoples whose cultures they study and consider
it a duty to present their values positively.

That being so, the vast potential represented by the increasingly large number of persons and institutions which throughout
the world devote themselves to Oriental and Asian studies, devoting the entire resources of humanistic studies to them, can be
systematically employed in the pursuit of the objectives laid
down by Unesco for the appreciation and respect of the cultural
identity, for these objectives henceforth enjoy the overwhelming
support of this important scientific body.

The essential cooperation in this field between scholars in
all regions of the world is increasing rapidly and has already
attained a sufficient level to start a veritable dialogue among
cultures. In this connection, Unesco's direct or indirect encouragement has been of undoubted effect.

Thus, apart from a few exceptions, scientific institutions
in this field are no longer operating in isolation but are opening
up increasingly, particularly as a result of personal exchanges,
to a fruitful international cooperation.

The moment has therefore come to organize the integration,
at international level, of the momentum of Oriental and Asian
studies into systematic activities with the aim of defining, safeguarding and appreciating, not only among specialists but also
and above all in the arena of world opinion, of the values which
characterize the cultural identity of the many peoples concerned
by these studies, in harmony with the point of view of those
peoples and of their representatives in the scientific community.

Popularization of the studies

This is an urgent task, but one which is more difficult than would
appear at first sight, for good popularization which does not distort the facts and transmits the essential information authentically has to conform to requirements which are partly contradictory.

It must present simple and easily perceptible truths in a
field which is extremely complex and, moreover, unknown to the
vast majority of the public. It must take account of the sensitivity of that public, while remaining faithful, in the presentation of external cultural values, to the feelings of those who
possess such values. Much tact and restraint are needed to
succeed.

In view of the fact that the aim of popularizing foreign
cultural matter is not the dissemination of dry, theoretical
knowledge but the creation of a climate of understanding and
sympathy, it is essential to give priority to the facts most
likely to be positively appreciated. The favourable tendency
thus created will make it possible at a later stage to tackle,
with all the necessary precautions and explanations, the facts
which would have started off a psychological process of rejection if forced on readers in the first place.

The consequence of this (which is unfortunately ignored by
certain international publications) is that the way of presenting
a culture outside specialist circles should not be uniform but
should be more or less adapted to the cultural environment where
it has to be disseminated.

Let me quote an example from real life: an international
Bible publishing company, moved by the laudable desire to popu-
larize the values of the Christian faith outside Christian circles and, in particular, to contact Islamic peoples, had chosen
to present in an edition for Turkish-speaking Muslims, the Gospel
story of the Cana wedding feast (St. John 2) when Jesus changed
the ablution water into wine. This miracle, which was particularly attractive in the eyes of the Scandinavian publishers,
could not fail to shock the people for whom it was intended who,
according to their beliefs, considered it a sacrilege to change
the sacred purification water into a drink forbidden by their
laws.

This anecdote illustrates the necessity of getting to know

the values appropriate to the public at the receiving end in order to make a positive presentation of foreign cultural values. In this connection, specialists in Oriental and Asian studies among others can provide sound advice.

But it is as well to awake them to the problems connected with popularizing their knowledge and make them more aware than they have been in the past of their very special responsibility in this field. Above all, they must feel it a duty to disseminate clearly, honestly and in a way adapted to their readers the essential results of their research concerning the cultural values of the various human collectivities.

The best context for such dissemination is that of international cooperation, and it is above all up to the international cultural institutions to encourage and assist them.

A method of approaching intercultural relations

Cheikh Anta Diop

A suitable way of clarifying the difficulties and setbacks in
intercultural relations would be to discuss the process by which
any two given cultures come into being, develop, enter into contact and succeed in influencing one another in space and time.

Let us take as an example, on the one hand, a European geographical area situated in a temperate climate with its specific
fauna and flora, its own history, its social and political structures and its manners and customs as they have emerged from the
milieu concerned, and on the other, its diametrical opposite -
a tropical geographical area.

To confine ourselves to objective facts which anyone can perceive, let us analyse the limitations imposed by historical and
geographical factors in the general field of linguistics as we go
from one area to the other.

Since most European languages (English, French, German, Portuguese, Russian, Spanish, etc.) have the same common origin, the
literary expressions and the poetical imagery created there are
woven from the same basic facts taken from the same environment:
thus words like oak, cypress, pine, primrose, snowdrop, ivy, rose,
wolf, bear, snow, etc., take part in the building of literary
images which usually have equivalents in all European languages,
but cannot be translated into the African languages of the tropical zone.

This example is an appropriate one for bringing to light the
specific nature of the problem of intercultural relations. Thus,
it appears that, in the field of linguistic expression, which is
the fundamental means of "total" communication, Europeans have
only minor difficulties in communicating with one another. A
literary work in any European language can be translated into
another with a minimum loss of meaning, since the fauna and flora,
and even the history are the same and ensure that strictly equivalent expressions are to be found in all the languages of the
geo-cultural area under consideration.

For this reason too the phenomena of acculturation and
cultural alienation are more attenuated among Europeans because
they occur within the same great civilization.

The situation is different when a translator tries to transpose the cultural message of a literary work, such as poetry,
from a European language into an African one or vice-versa. One
of three cases may occur:

1. The concepts and images, which convey the message are of the
specific type described above, and this makes a literary translation into a language not sharing the same culture impossible:
e.g. "white as snow", "bearing one's cross", etc.
2. The images and expressions are of the universal type (i.e.
sufficiently free from socio-geographical and climatic factors
for the words used in expressing them to be translatable into any
other language of any climatic zone without distortion);e.g. the
following English or French expressions: "la mer à boire",
"burning one's boats", "to be doubled up with laughter", "sentir
le cadavre", etc.
3. There is a third category of images which, though specific, can
nevertheless be rendered in the languages of different climatic
zones. Thus, the French expression "attendre sous l'orme" (waiting till the cows come home) can be rendered in Walaf, the
language of Senegal, by the expression: "neg ci ron dahaar gi"
- literally "waiting under the tamarind tree" - which conveys
practically the same meaning and flavour as the original French
phrase.

In passing, it can be shown that the systematic translation
into African languages of expressions of Types 2 and 3 would be a
way of enriching such languages without causing them to lose their
own essence. Incidentally, the reverse process is possible; that
is, expressions of Types 2 and 3 originating from African languages could be introduced into European (or other) languages.
Although a language, at each stage of its development, is a self-
sufficient system for expressing the entire universe perceived
by any of us, the integration of new, fresh images in this way
would undoubtedly enrich the language under consideration, whether
European or African, and would not constitute a duplication of the
existing stock of expressions. The result would be to facilitate
the translation of complete works on a world-wide scale, which
would be in line with Unesco policy.

The European - or other foreign - linguistic conscience would
find it much easier to accept such racy, but perfectly intelligi-
ble, expressions, if encountered in translations of books, than
neologisms which are nothing more than sounds absorbing the meaning of the sentence because, in the nature of things, they can
call up no exact image in the mind of the reader. This fact will
become more apparent in what follows.

It emerges from the above that an Italian or Romanian condemned to express himself in Spanish would be less alienated
and more at ease than an African in the same situation. Let us
suppose that the latter is a poet. Every time he conceives and
mentally elaborates a new image on the basis of cultural elements
from his homeland and tries to express it adequately in French,
English or Spanish, the poetical rhythm is broken by the "barbaric"
neologisms which clutter up the poetical field like a lot of
rubble;his own words are radically, desperately lacking - the
baobab is not the equivalent of the oak. The European (and
foreign, in general) linguistic and aesthetic consciousness has
not yet assimilated these words, which constitute nothing more
than sounds.

Unless the acculturation process has been completed, when the African poet nevertheless speaks of rosebuds (which he has never gathered), he becomes ridiculous and ineffective. He therefore does not render the feeling of exotic, wild nature in a truly original language of his own. Even Leconte de Lisle succeeded better than him in his "Poèmes barbares". This is the setback to which Jean-Paul Sartre referred in "Orphée noire" as an irony of fate. He wrote:

> "The black is perfectly at his ease in it (in French) when he thinks as technician, as a scholar or as a politician. It is necessary rather to speak of the slight, but constant un-hedging which separates that which he says when he speaks of himself, from that which he wishes to say. It seems to him that a boreal spirit steals his ideas from him, that it softly twists to signify more or less that which it wishes, that the white words drink up his thought as the sand drinks blood..." (J.P. Sartre, Situation III, Black Orpheus. Translated by S.W. Allen, p. 24).
> "It is impossible for him to express his negritu-de with words of precision which efficiently strike the mark at every blow. He can scarcely express negritude in prose. Yet it is common knowledge that this feeling of failure before the language when considered as a means of direct expression is at the source of all poetical ex-perience..." (op. cit. p. 24).

Sartre pursues his analysis even further:

> "The specific traits of a society correspond exactly to the untranslatable locutions of its language. Now what dangerously threatens to curb the effort of the Negro to throw off our tutelage is that the apostles of the new negri-tude are constrained to edit their gospel in French" (op. cit. p. 22)...
> "And since French lacks terms and concepts to define negritude, since negritude is silence, they use words always allusive, never direct reducing themselves to an equal silence" (op.cit. pp. 26-27).

Sartre, who of all Western intellectuals was one of the best-disposed towards Africa, was not speaking of the negro of average intelligence. The frustration he describes is that of the African poets - the very ones whose poems he analysed.

In any case, so far as he was concerned, the African poets expressed themselves in a French which was not that of Frenchmen. These authors, he said : "degallicize French before writing it"...:

> "It is only when they (the words) have disgorged
> their whiteness that he adopts them, making of
> this language in ruins a superlanguage solemn and
> sacred, in brief, Poetry" (op. cit. p. 26).

He adds that:

> "The drama of the negro is that he wants to rejec⁴
> our culture while using our language; even when
> we are absent, we are present in the most secret
> of assemblies: the colonist is the eternal
> mediator".

Naturally, Sartre shows that an allusive, poetical language, verg-
ing on silence, in a degallicized French is possible. This comes
to saying: the poetical images which you express in our language
are opaque to our French minds. We would need an exegesis to
understand them, but in that case all the poetical aura would have
evaporated.

It emerges from what has been stated that an African who
borrows a European vehicle of expression can only use scientific
or ideological literature, or poetry employing the universal
images of type 2 or the adaptable ones of type 3, immediately and
to the full.

Very fine verses, of an admirable beauty, written by African
negroes and belonging to this category (i.e. using universal
images (1)),could be quoted :

"Emotion is negro and reason Hellenic"(L.S. Senghor).
"Those who have explored neither sea nor sky" (Aime Cesaire).

These are the sorts of success which give the foreigner the
illusion that he too can penetrate into the cultural nucleus
specific to another people in order to exploit its wealth and
treasures.

But an exhaustive analysis author by author would reveal the
comparative poverty of the vocabulary making up the poetic images
of African writers in foreign, European, languages: a very short
list of adjectives, particularly the "moral" ones would indicate
the most frequently used: valorous, noble, passionate, languorous,
etc.

The use of picturesque terms describing shades of colour and
taste and olfactory - and even auditive and tactile - sensations
is circumscribed in African negro poetry to the extent that they
belong to the specific vocabulary bound up with geographical
factors.

This is how the limitations on the originality of African
literature written in a foreign language of the West should be
brought out, so long as the acculturation or alienation process
has not been completed.

This brief comparative study enables us ʹto make a clear distinction between three conceptual levels on the basis of the

---

(1) With reservations regarding the substance.

analysis of the specific character of the linguistic expression.
This is a general remark and could be applied to a comparative
study of any two foreign cultures providing they are sufficiently
different from one another.

To these three levels there correspond three types of conceptual systems which should be carefully defined, or at least
kept sight of in intercultural relations, if a more profound
analysis is to be made of them, while dealing with the difficulties methodically one by one.

In fact, for the pursuit of our analysis we shall confine
ourselves to the two main levels - the specific cultural fact
(the incommunicable) and the universal cultural fact:
specific concepts; universal concepts.

THE ARTS

Having examined the specific character of linguistic expression
and the limitations it imposes on intercultural relations, let
us see if the other means of expression - the artistic ones such
as sculpture, painting, music and dancing - are privileged in
this respect. At first sight, these arts appear to be universal
because their mission is to create plastic shapes and rhythms
which our senses can grasp directly, without having to depend on
the spoken word. We therefore have the impression that, in the
case of the plastic arts, there is no irreducible and impenetrable
nucleus in the field of cultural relations, where all the specific
elements of a given culture are concentrated.

Let us take negro sculpture, which has undoubtedly had a
strong influence on Western art in the twentieth century. In
studying this phenomenon we notice that the Western artist has
borrowed from his anonymous African colleague not so much a canon
of beauty as the right to free himself from the classical canons
of the golden section and anatomic strictness - factors which, in
various forms, governed European art from Phidias to Rodin. Liberty in the creation of plastic shapes and rhythm constitute the
great lesson which modern art has derived from negro art. Obviously, it is difficult to separate this feeling of liberty from the
plastic creations which it engenders, and nearly all modern
artists create forms related to those of negro art; the relationship and influence are obvious - even among artists who would
prefer to deny them.

The fact remains that, quite apart from snobbery, the average
westerner lacking in artistic experience and training is usually
ill-prepared to appreciate the aesthetic value of a negro artistic
product. And Malraux, who was a great connoisseur of Western art,
even went as far as to deny purely and simply the existence of
negro art, in spite of its obvious influence on the art of the
West, which he adored.

In this connection, Japanese and Chinese painting is not universally appreciated in the West, although this is a universal language the meaning of which is clear at first sight.

Owing to this very fact, the details and the whole of the painting or sculpture (negro art) finish by revealing a universe in which incomprehensible details outweigh the universal features common to all mankind, and the human message conveyed by the work of art does not get through for lack of education.

Thus, in the present world state of artistic education, even in the sphere of the visual arts, cultural habits tend to favour: the existence of cultural nuclei the (cultural) substance of which can only be grasped and appreciated from the inside.

Turning to African music and dancing, we come to similar conclusions, even if, in our imagination, we strip the dancing of its ethnographic and brutally erotic hallmark. A western musicologist, inspired with the best intentions, admitted, after making a considerable effort to adapt himself, that he could discern nothing but a cacophony in listening to Mourid religious songs and music in Senegal. Other Westerners say the same thing regarding the songs of the *griots,* which are among the finest epics of the pre-colonial period.

I heard a great Western intellectual describe a Hindu musical party where all the Hindu audience were in ecstasy, whereas he sat, completely cold and indifferent, quite incapable of appreciating the music.

It might therefore be said that, in any culture, there are two spheres. First, there is a specific level to which, in fact, corresponds a specific conceptual system. This is the most concentrated level at which are elaborated the basic elements of the culture, which maintain it like a hearth radiating its effects. This nucleus can explode or perish like a cell, in which case there is no further cultural radiation. And yet, by virtue of everything stated above, it is impossible to express all the phenomena which take place by means of universal concepts. If anyone who is a stranger to this culture tries to penetrate it, he comes up against a psychological barrier - one might almost say a barrier of potential.

There is a second level of culture which corresponds to universal concepts. If I might use an atomic metaphor to illustrate my meaning, it is as if cultures interfere with one another mainly at the level of their radiation outside their specific nucleus, and as if this sphere were that of universal relations.

But such an atomistic conception could very soon lead to dangerous and erroneous mechanistic views.

It is also necessary to study the factors which might be referred to as cultural constants - i.e. elements which even radical revolutionary cultural transformations leave unchanged, such as profound aesthetic feeling - the graceful gesture in dancing, art and sport, for example.

Lastly, it may be observed that, no matter in what way the problems are considered, the conclusions of this statement remain the same. But the latter is merely an introduction to the debates which are being organized.

Thoughts on an intercultural relations research policy[1]

Alphonse Dupront

It would appear that any considerations on cultural exchanges should, in accordance with Unesco's necessarily world-wide activities, be inspired by two basic facts: 1. the full autonomy inherent in any culture, and therefore the recognition of the extreme diversity of cultures, each in its own autochthony; 2. the necessary development of exchanges and links, transcending occlusions and tensions, for the gradual realization of universal values, which are essential to the development of a world inter-communication culture.

The present introductory memorandum takes these principles into account and seeks, in an essentially interrogative form, to propose for joint consideration three analytical approaches for tackling the vast problem which we are required to confront. The first, as appears natural, would consist of attempting to determine, even if only approximately, the most fundamental collective notions for the mutual understanding of the phenomenon and thus to provide ourselves with instruments for our communication, which are as well adjusted as possible. The second, which is as simple as it is obvious, would be to constitute our own analytical material by bringing to light some of the most characteristic aspects in which inter-cultural exchanges take place in a manifest diversity of forms. It appears that such an operation of reconnaissance and collective realization should result in a third reflective process - that of considering the future development of such exchanges within the context of a world inter-cultural policy.

I. ESTABLISHMENT OF INSTRUMENTS OF KNOWLEDGE AND COMMUNICATION

In providing ourselves mutually with a vocabulary to ensure the authenticity of our own discussions, we also make clear the ne-

---

(1) Since this text was drafted as a potential introduction to the Working Group's discussions, it could not be given any-thing but an interrogative form in its analytical approach.

cessity of establishing more generally, from our own consideration
a corpus of basic notions which are both essential to grasping
the inter-cultural phenomenon and sufficiently clear in their respective contents to ensure complete mutual understanding in the
use of this vocabulary.

From this point of view, three kinds of notions, particularly
rich in values, would appear to require clarification in the interest of common lucidity.

In the first place, such key notions from our Western vocabulary as civilization (with the sometimes different overtones of
the plural civilizations) and culture (idem for cultures).

To what extent have these notions acquired general application throughout the diversity of cultures? And to what extent
have their contents been changed by passing from one culture to
another?

Would it not be as well to make an inventory of words and
expressions, the contents of which are roughly equivalent, in
cultures where these notions are not current?

For a "culture" to be qualified as such, it must occupy a
minimum of space and time. Hence the question: are there reason-
able measurements both of geographical extent and temporal depth
for culture really to exist? What content values should be imputed to the recently launched notions of counter-culture and
sub-culture?

Can a culture which has been artificially rediscovered from
its distant roots be recognized as a culture?

Secondly there are the problems related to the universal. An
exploration of the present vitality of the diversity of cultures
would appear to be essential from the basic Unesco point of view.
Different lines of research are conceivable, all converging on a
measurement in situ of the efficacity or presence of these values
in the life of the contemporary world. For example:
1. A western history of notion such as man, humanity, mankind,
humanism envisaged in themselves and in their historical connotations.
2. A differential study, among pilot cultures, selected as di-
versely as possible, of the values considered as being those of
all men or considered, in such cultures, as being liable to universalization or even generalization. Would there not be exemplary research regarding the powers, expectations or needs of
the universal in contemporary humanity, through the multiplicity
of its creative approaches?
3. An inventory of the archetypes of the universal on the basis
of autochtonous cultures generally.
4. A selective enumeration, in a number of pilot cultures, firstly
of universally current and applied disciplines of knowledge
(exact sciences, natural sciences, social and human sciences and
various technologies) and secondly, of those shown to be not subject to universalization.

The third major category of notions, essential to any analysis of the intercultural, brings us back to the diachronic approach
with the fundamental problems of traditions and modernization.

It is possible to draw up concise definitions but the reality
is infinitely more complex. In creating instruments for analysis

and real knowledge, does it not seem to be essential to have a
material fully covering the diversity of cultures?
   Three aspects at least should enable us to constitute it:
1. The inventory of a collective awareness of traditions or of
what is traditional in the mental systems of autochthonous cultures.
2. The study, still in the diversity of cultures, of the various
mental systems contributing to the notion of modernization, its
constraints, its force, as well as any rejections of it. Here
one should not neglect the essential fact of processes of desacralization, which is bound up with the problem of modernization.
3. The temporal fact (temporal dimensions; collective awareness
of time; multiplicity of times, etc.) in a few major pilot
cultures.

II. INVENTORY AND ANALYSIS OF FACTUAL DATA

At the same time that the instrument of knowledge, interpretation
and transmission are being prepared, it is obviously necessary
to conduct a very wide-ranging reconnaissance of the present
state of development of inter-cultural relations on a world-wide
scale. It is only possible to philosophize about the intercultural, to decide on lines of action and to situate them in an
instant consciousness of planetary unity if the study of the
existing situation has provided the material for incarnate thought.
A Herculean labour to be sure, but one which it should be possible
to tackle by means of a number of approaches which are as varied
as they are convergent. Some of these are suggested below:
1. Cultural destruction.
2. Acculturation.
   The latter can be studied according to two methods. The
first is historical, and the obviously typical example is the
analysis of forms and processes of acculturation of the conqueror
by the conquered. The other is rooted in the present and consists
of an inventory and analysis of examples of acculturation in the
contemporary world, either in a given geographical zone or through
the study of specific cases of cultures which have a typically
acculturating effect on autochthonous backgrounds such as, in
contrasting circumstances, the Mozarabian culture and its survivals or the elaboration of Japanese culture.
   In any study of acculturation, it would appear essential to
record, alongside the positive facts (reception), the negative
facts (rejection).
3. Contrastive analysis of closed or self-sufficient cultures
and those of the "melting pot" type.
4. Inter-cultural reception of "universal" forms with very careful study of the negative repercussions in autochtonous cultures
and a scrupulous inventory of any subsequent equilibria.

Among these forms, most of which have been given currency by the West, theologies may be selected from the religious point of view, the classification of western sciences and their conceptual vocabulary from the systems of knowledge point of view, and the vocabulary and, transcending the language and mental forms of technical implementation, the underlying vision of the world and of a homogeneous universe from the technological point of view.

In respect of this last, would not measuring the impact of a homogeneous mental angle on the economy, equilibria and mental cohesions of autochtonous cultures be extremely important for a lucid view of a world cultural relations policy, respectful of the diversity?

The problem is so important that, in order to tackle it both objectively and in depth, it appears that it would be as well to proceed by case studies.

In tackling problems of this kind, such examples as the establishment - so widespread today - of "turnkey" factories in numerous so-called underdeveloped countries, or one of the sensitive forms of homogeneous technicity including concrete architecture or, lastly, the situations of conflict, reciprocal attrition, resigned or lucid co-existence and possible complementarities between western medicine and pharmacopoeias and traditional ones. This latter example makes it possible to illustrate a remarkable case of a "return journey" with, inter alia, the increasing introduction of Chinese acupuncture into western countries.

In these means of communication through widespread cultural areas, a study of the part played by vernacular languages would appear to be necessary, together with their possible repercussions on the autochtonous cultures concerned and any value they may have for the transmission of the authentic experience of the cultures using them. In this connection, might it not be suitable to suggest sample surveys conducted concurrently in English-speaking, French-speaking, Spanish-speaking and Portuguese-speaking areas to achieve the important advance of transition from the imposed instrument to the tool lucidly and pertinently used, for the better service of the user?

Is it not also important to bring to light the cultural consequences of trade and human exchanges in the form of increasing tourism, from the point of view of "universal" relations?

5. Differential or thematic studies.

Here the choice may be considerable and determined according to a wide variety of criteria.

By way of example only, suggestions regarding subjects to study in a number of cultures: the imago urbis or the specific forms of contemporary urbanization or relations between town and country, consciousness of the body, the basic colours, consciousness of history and division into periods, intact forms of relation to the cosmic, original myths (myth and temporality), consciousness and practice of the sacred.

6. The stereotypes.

Under this supremely important intercultural relations heading
in which agonic forms of the profound psychism of the collective
mental attitude free themselves until they attain crystallizations degrading for all, two types of research would appear to
be necessary.

The first would enumerate the vocabulary of adversity towards
- and labelling or non-recognition of the "other" in the relations
between - certain groups of culture. For example, the foreigner,
the Barbarian, the more or less hereditary enemy, or, at a different level, the savage or the primitive.

The second would make an inventory, again between given
cultural groups, of the collective, quasi-natural stereotypes,
so as to discover their historic origins, and the processes by
which they develop and finally become set; we would thus achieve
a liberating collective psychoanalysis, if one may be allowed
the expression.

III. PROSPECTIVE RESEARCH ON THE DEVELOPMENT OF INTERCULTURAL
     EXCHANGES

It seemed essential to submit to the consideration of the Group
this third and last approach to the problem as a whole. All of
us consider that this is necessary, if we look upon ourselves
not just as analysts - lucid ones to be sure - of the present,
but also as discreet but effective guides for the future.

From this point of view, it would appear that two levels
of research on the future can be defined very concisely and
almost immediately:
1. That of fundamental research which would use the results and
lessons derived from former research - a research which would,
therefore, within the programme of a coherent project, take
place either subsequently to the analysis of the various data
or concurrently with it.

It should be possible for this to result in the gradual
establishment of a methodology for the study of inter-cultural
relations - a methodology at present either very fragmentary
or non-existent - and in the constitution of a system of intercultural pedagogics - which is certainly indispensable for
speeding up the healthy and free development of intercultural
relations.
2. That of an experimental research, conducted strictly in vivo,
to prevent its becoming an excessively facile abstract, and thus
ineffective, construction.

Here again, the resources are infinite and the material for
teaching and mutual enrichment that it could provide practically
unexploited.

The following are also worth consideration:

a)   a survey, carried out in a number of universities which receive large contingents of foreign students, of the conditions
under which such students are integrated into the different
cultural milieux of the countries concerned;
b)   an inventory and analysis, either in these universities or
in other cultural environments as widely different as possible,
of the methods of teaching used in presenting the autochthonous
culture and of any results due to the cultural origin of the
students;
c)   an observation, interpretation and assessment of the "trade"
phenomenon (1) generally, covering both commercial and cultural
exchanges, between two given cultural sectors;
d)   a detailed study of the intercultural exchange, following
on a preliminary study of the psycho-social forces inspiring it,
of mass tourism, so as to avoid a situation where it gives
results contrary to what might be expected - the hardening of
mutual lack of appreciation and the proliferation of new stereotypes.

As has already been stated, the sole purpose of the above
suggestions is to make a preliminary contribution to our joint
deliberations, which should take form rather innately than in
accordance with rigid extraneous guidelines, at the meeting
point of efforts which are as rewarding as they are various.

The present text is therefore only a possible starting
point. Let it remain so.

---

(1)   Original French: phénomène "commerce".

Extending cultural studies to cover intercultural studies

Vadime Elisseeff

This brief document, coming in addition to those already existing, does not pretend to characterize the chief types of cultural or intercultural studies on which the working group will have to make a decision, but merely to list some of them. Nor does it aim at defining the conditions of establishment, the nature, the composition and the procedure of an international organization for coordinating, promoting and assessing such studies. On the basis of experience acquired in the programme of cultural studies, it seeks rather to determine some of the practical problems which can arise and the requirements which emerged from former projects, bearing in mind the final report of the meeting held in Belgrade in October 1976 to "study the preliminary aspects of the intercultural studies project", and the work carried out by the Secretariat in collaboration with the Geneva "Institut d'études du développement". (Cf. the Belgrade Final Report - October 1976 - and the working document drawn up with a view to this meeting by the Institute).

I. THE FIRST RESEARCH WORK ON THE MUTUAL APPRECIATION
   OF CULTURES (1956-1966)

In the Approved Programme and Budget for 1977-1978 in accordance with the decisions of the Nairobi General Conference (19 C/5 approved, 4005), it is pointed out that cultural or intercultural regional studies will be carried out "in order to spread knowledge and foster international understanding through the mutual appreciation of cultures...". This is the basic aim of a task patiently pursued since the founding of the Organization, but one which was first formulated only ten years after its foundation. It was at New Delhi in 1956 during the IXth General Conference that the representatives of Member States proclaimed that the understanding necessary for peaceful cooperation among peoples could only be based on a thorough knowledge and appreciation by each people of the civilizations of other peoples. It was in order to contribute to such understanding that an exceptional ten-year programme was decided upon, in the form of a Major

Project related to the mutual appreciation of the cultural values
of the East and West (1957-1966).

Thus, the final objective was reinforced by emphasizing
appreciation instead of knowledge and appreciation jointly. At
the same time, the two terms "civilizations of peoples" used in
the Resolution were replaced by "cultural values" and "East and
West" respectively in the Project as formulated, since it was
considered that this defined the purpose of the study and situated
it more clearly in a geographical context.

The choice of that context was made in accordance with the
urgencies of the time. For most of the Member States fell within
this geographical area - those with a western tradition both in
Europe and America on the one hand, and those of the Arab and
Indian world, the Far East and South-East Asia, on the other.
While recognizing the specific nature of the terms "civilization"
in the widest spatial and temporal sense, and "culture" in its
most restricted territorial sense and in a more compact duration,
the Major Project, in order to avoid dispersion which might have
caused confusion, was also obliged to limit its activities to
cultural values, it being understood that it was not yet a
matter of universal points of view but of individual ones.

This policy and the philosophy of the Major Project were
elaborated and pursued over a period of ten years by a
coordinating unit of the Secretariat assisted by an international
consultative committee which met six times. This committee consisted of a dozen specialists from all over the world, a proportion of whom were replaced every session, so as to widen the
basis of consultation while ensuring continuity.

The Major Project was to be applied to three distinct spheres
of activity: research; education so far as school curricula and
text books were concerned; information (dissemination, exhibitions
and translations). Associated institutions and miscellaneous
centres were set up in Tokyo (1961), New Delhi (1962), Beirut
Damascus and Tehran (1964), designed to promote "the formation
of networks of regional centres for the study and presentation
of cultures...". To this was added: "thus, the major Project will
have laid the basis for a campaign designed to continue autonomously" (para. 7).

An account of this campaign was periodically distributed by
means of a two-monthly bulletin which summed up the activities of
each Member State, and particularly those of the East-West
national committees and of the Secretariat. This is not the place
to cast the final balance of this decade, but it is as well to
mention the many activities in connection with translation, the
collection of audio-visual material and the organization of
travelling exhibitions, many research projects undertaken through
the intermediary of "associated institutions", bibliographical
and sociological activities, comparative studies and reports by
various national commissions, covering a wide range of text books
on a number of little-known or badly presented cultures.

At the end of its term of office, the Consultative Committee
made a report in which it estimated that the chief objectives had
been attained. As from 1964, an assessment of the Project was
published in a number of instalments in the "Orient-Occident"

Bulletin: translations of literary works, personal exchanges, cooperation among associated institutions for the study and presentation of cultures, education, information on social sciences, international talks, out-of-school education and the activities of non-governmental international organizations.

In fact, nearly all the divisions of the Secretariat have done their best to ensure that all aspects of their work could contribute to a better appreciation of cultural values; the spirit of the entire activity of Unesco and of all Member States was imbued with it, especially as, during its last meeting, the international Consultative Committee, pointing out that, since 1960, it had participated in extending certain items of its programme to include countries of Africa and Latin America, was able to conclude by expressing the hope that its activities would be extended to all geographical sectors. Thus, at the thirteenth session of the General Conference at Paris in 1964, Chapter 3 A of the draft programme for 1965-1966 (13 C/5) included African studies (3.44) and the History of the scientific and cultural development of mankind (3.45). In the introduction to Chapter 3 A there was a recommendation to concentrate resources on achievements the effects of which could be extended beyond the time limit laid down for the major Project, which was 1966. There was also an appeal for help from researchers and specialists to the effect that the impulse imparted by the major Project would be extended by the autonomous and permanent activities of the Universities.

II. THE DEVELOPMENT OF CULTURAL STUDIES (1967-1976)

For the decade following on 1967 the programme of cultural studies became the subject of the activities of a new organic department. Research was chiefly devoted to a study of cultures themselves, rather than the more limited study of cultural values. There were many points of application, and the methods used were varied, since it was necessary to be able to benefit from current work on the occasion of each study, give it breadth and depth and ensure that not only the different areas but also the different disciplines benefited harmoniously from it.

It is interesting to take stock of the subject matter of the first cultural studies as described in the Director General's Report on the activities of the Organization in 1968. At the fourteenth General Conference, under the heading of Resolution 3.i323, we have: I. The contribution of Japan to contemporary arts; II. The study of the civilizations of peoples of Central Asia; V. Guide to sources of the history of Asia. Sub-headings III, IV and VI deal with the development of oriental studies and assistance to Member States for the same purposes. Under the heading of Resolution 3.324: I. General History of Africa; II. Studies of African linguistics; III. African cultural contributions to Latin America; IV. Guide to sources of African history. Under the heading of Resolution 3.325: Study of the cultures of Latin America

(especially investigations of literatures). Under the heading
of Resolution 3.326: Studies of European cultures (works on
history, philosophy and sources).

This programme was greeted with a certain amount of criticism concerning its lack of cohesion and the sporadic nature of
the Organization's action. A considerable effort was then made by
the Secretariat. This was evident from the time of the XVth and
still more of the sixteenth General Conference, when the challenge
of imparting more coherence to the programme while extending it
to other cultural areas was taken up. Thenceforward, in addition
to the cultures mentioned above, special projects covering the
study of Malaysian, Oceanian, Scandinavian and Slav cultures were
included. Increased attention was given to oral traditions and
the contemporary aspect of the cultures concerned.

The 1977-1978 programme lists cultural studies at Chapter 4,
Section 4.11, sub-sections 4.111.1 to 4.111.7, making seven
different study projects, some of which are further divided into
a number of sub-projects. Five projects consist of studies concerned with all continental areas, including certain privileged
geographical areas such as Central Asia and the Caribbean. Care
has been taken to fill in certain obvious gaps and to impart a
trend in line with present-day concerns - collections of summaries
histories of central Asian civilizations, general History of
Africa - in each of these areas. Here the classic problems inherent
to work of this kind arise, as well as a number of special problems according to which the researchers should orientate their
contributions.

At local study level, special interest is devoted to certain
notions: that of creativity has been inserted into the studies
dealing with artistic expression and that of cultural identity
serves to detect the roots and antecedents of traditional cultures.
New factors assert themselves: the increasing importance attributed
to oral traditions, hitherto under-estimated in favour of written
sources, and particularly that emphasized by Project 4.111.6:
"the impact of technologically advanced societies on culture".

The programme approved for 1977-1978 (Nairobi, nineteenth
Session, 1976), where the subjects and the areas meet one another,
displays a considerable number of cultural studies and shows
what progress has been achieved over this last decade. Experts
and specialists, often consulted for their opinion, are not
always aware of the progress patiently and laboriously accomplished by the Organization in this field. The new role of the specific natures of cultures which has brought us from a respect
for the plurality of culture to a respect for cultural identity
is the most striking result of the cultural studies undertaken.
A new stage begins with the present decade, and the Nairobi
General Conference adopted a working plan in section 4.11 -
Studies and Circulation - by stating that "the activities described under this Section are designed primarily to promote
cultural identity as a factor of national independence and as a
force for social coherence" (para. 4004); it is pointed out with
equal firmness that emphasis will be placed "on intercultural
aspects and on a multidisciplinary approach so that historical

links and contemporary solidarity among different cultures will
be revealed." (Para. 4005).

The need for carrying out intercultural studies arises from
two causes. As from the start of the first cultural studies programme, the considerable risk of dispersion was universally
apparent, and it was not the least of the merits both of the Secretariat and the responsible authorities of Member States that
care was taken concerning the articulation and priority of
research. This delicate equilibrium had to take the state of research, the human and material potential and the delays and shortcomings affecting certain areas and certain disciplines into
account. Since the last General Conference but one, there has
been an openly expressed concern for coordination, and at Nairobi
the wish was formally expressed that a committee for the coordination of intercultural studies, harmonizing the studies of
different cultures and balancing the needs of each objectively,
should be set up.

At the same time, research into the various processes
characterizing the birth, evolution and development of cultures
and their role both in the present and the future have given rise
to intercultural studies designed to clarify problems of cultural
interpenetration and interference. This was the problem which the
Major Project was supposed to tackle between 1957 and 1966,
though prematurely without doubt, for in the bibliography published
in the working document drawn up by the Geneva Institute for the
Study of Development on the occasion of the Belgrade meeting, we
find only a dozen works anterior to 1960, apart from classical
ones such as those of A. Comte, Durkheim, Marx and Toynbee, and
nearly fifty since that date.

III. A COORDINATION GROUP FOR INTERCULTURAL STUDIES

Intercultural coordination and intercultural research are two
complementary activities of intercultural studies. They are
clearly announced in the Programme and Budget approved for 1977-
1978 (19 C/5 approved, February 1977, para. 4041): "In accordance
with the orientation given by the General Conference stressing
the intercultural dimension and the need to establish a body for
international coordination to that effect, a study of the scope
and nature of this coordination will be carried out and a working
group of representative scholars from all the main regions will
be convened in cooperation with ICPHS, for the purpose of establishing a plan aimed at promoting, systematizing and evaluating
the activities undertaken in the field of intercultural studies".
The aim of the first activity might include making an inventory
of knowledge in the field of culture and in that of intercultural
studies and assessing the results achieved in the field of cultural
studies. The second could include an attempt to distinguish the
evolutive processes and, by comparing diachronic studies, to outline possible patterns. This consultative body would therefore
have two distinct but complementary functions, with the results

of one being used as grounds of reflection for the other, and
the research of the latter inspiring the finality of the former.

A. Nature of work
In order to be able to carry out its task to the full, any committee responsible for these two functions should be in possession
of a record of past and current research. A list and a graph
would make it possible to detect shortcomings and compensate
for them on the basis of their extent and the resources required.
The basic documents for establishing this record would be supplied
under the responsibility of the existing international consultative committee or similar bodies in respect of each subject.

   To be sure, it is difficult to impose a choice of work on
those participating in research but it seems to us to be essential
to keep them informed regarding the progress of all organizations
contributing to the attainment of the general objectives in this
field. In any case it would be as well to convey the results
obtained by means of cultural maps and atlases, when suitable.
These were warmly recommended as working instruments on a number
of occasions, and the Belgrade meeting wisely raised the matter
of the way of preparing and using them.

   In this connection, it should be remembered that, of the
four research areas proposed at Belgrade (Cf. Final Report, paras.
10 to 14), two already lend themselves to representation on maps;
these are: (a) the results obtained from studies depending on a
territorial approach and revealing the existence of such and such
cultural phenomena; (b) thematic studies dealing with a tangible
or intangible transcultural subject.

   Cultural atlases, maps giving the results of research or
working maps made according to the principles of modern cartography constitute, as is stated in the Final Report, a working
method. As such, it is related to theoretical studies pursued in
the third area of research, which is devoted to patterns, methodology and the epistemology in general.

   The fourth area of research proposed, which is basically
merely a special aspect of the thematic studies, deals with the
phenomenon of the industrial society versus the traditional society. Although more difficult to pursue than the two first
mentioned, it can also, like the previous one, give rise to the
preparation of graphs showing the strength and weaknesses of
the theories and the bonds uniting the various aspects of the
problem.

   It thus appears that an inventory of research undertaken
under various headings by the different projects is inconcei-
vable without the establishment of graphs and maps, or in short
of cultural atlases, which are essential working instruments and
not mere illustrations of documents.

   Concurrently with the drawing up of such records, it would
be essential to have available a table summarizing the chief
trends in intercultural research. This already appears from the
remarkable Geneva working document submitted at Belgrade, where
the participants accepted the idea of intercultural studies in
the widest sense of the term "including all fields of human competence such as technology, art, thought, social organization

and the economy". This table is recommended in the Belgrade
Final Report, particularly for the purpose of "improving the
methodological context by assembling analyses entrusted to researchers of various origins and horizons concerning the theoretical and conceptual approaches in use".

One of the essential points of this recommendation seems to
have been the term "researchers of various origins and horizons".
Without overdoing the search for a balanced approach, it may
appear legitimate to distribute comparable subjects to authors
not only of different backgrounds but also of opposing ideologies.
The open method of publishing opposing theories was largely
followed during the preparation of the History of the Scientific
and Cultural Development of Mankind. Lengthy articles in the
Journals of World History, as well as chapters of the History,
give marginal notes expressing opinions diverging from those of
the author. This procedure caused a certain stir at the time,
but at the scale of an international organization such as Unesco,
it appears to me to be an essential guarantee that justice will
be done to each cultural group and that any excessive ethnocentrism
will be avoided.

B. Ethical basis
In addition to the objective inventory and the critical analyses,
consideration should be given to the ethical dimension of any
international undertaking of this sort. The aim of improved mutual
appreciation could still be given priority without affecting the
inestimable virtues of intellectual research. This problem had
already arisen during the establishment of the East-West Major
Project and gave rise to lengthy discussions as a result of which
a joint declaration was unanimously adopted.

This joint declaration played the part of a deontological
charter in all Project activities. It made a considerable contribution to defusing all the sources of conflict which arise on the
occasion of different judgements. It might be worth while at least
to benefit from that experience - while not perhaps copying it
literally - in order to ensure that the work proceeds as smoothly
as possible.

Every researcher in intercultural studies has to be fully
conscious of the psychological and political obstacles impeding
improved mutual appreciation and of the appearance of new
situations which call for a revision of viewpoints and a consciousness of the equality of nations in the world order. Any
cultural or intercultural study is based on judgements of values
and affective reactions which are liable to affect adversely the
objectivity and calmness of research, since the latter depends on
the former.

It is therefore accepted that in any case the notions which
might involve an affective reaction - such as borrowings and influences, dominations and isolations - should be commented on and
explained by the light of historic facts reconstituted in their
total verity. But at the same time considerable emphasis was
placed on the fact that it was as well to avoid any expression
liable to have a psychological or political effect on human dignity
or mutual respect. Furthermore, in order to facilitate appreciation,

the facts should be transposed into wide chronological perspectives so as to bring to light their relative duration and the
place they occupy in historical evolution generally into geographical ones so as to situate the regional action of the cultural
factors within the context of inter-regional relations and socio-
economic ones so as to explain cultural facts in terms of the
various levels and ways of life. We discover these three points
of view in the three variables which the cartographers of the
second (Atlas) Belgrade committee wanted to have more precisely
defined in respect of each study: (1) in space; (2) in time; and
(3) in terms of social levels.

It is possible to define each of these variables by following
the time table laid down for each phenomenon and defining its
space within a political or geographical whole, but the important
thing is that the facts should not appear isolated or out of context. The term perspective is perhaps more appropriate, for while
respecting the notion of variable, it helps to prevent excessive
focusing from involving distortions of judgement. The chronological perspective should be wide enough to dominate the event
and transcend momentary contradictions. It alone can thus contribute to establishing contemporary facts or recalling forgotten
facts which broaden the cultural identity of a people. The geographical perspective brings out not only the context, not only
the phenomena of synchronism, but also the correlation and inter-
relation appropriate to intercultural studies in areas whose
political frontiers may hide what is at stake. The socio-economic
perspectives may attenuate the harsh character of certain glorious
or wretched episodes by situating them in diachronic phases which
reduce the brilliance of the spotlights. For every culture has
its high and low points, and it is not very scientific to
generalize from them.

By adhering constantly to these three perspectives and
occasionally correcting the synchronic by means of the diachronic,
many present-day contrasts which are the source of mitigated
appreciations would disappear. People today are always talking
of "Japanese politeness"; they are amazed at the number of
salutations involved in the slightest meeting, at the calculation
of distances for introductions and the gestures involved in
crossing thresholds; but an analysis of these movements and
steps shows that they are very similar to those related to court
protocol as it existed and still does exist here and there in the
palaces and barracks of Europe. The remarkable fact is not its
existence as a cultural product but its social proliferation and
present-day survival; in other words, it enables everyone to
appreciate it unreservedly, since it is liable to be reversible
for some and has the chance of being imitable for others. This is
the sense in which "every culture is endowed with a universal dimension", not only because it can be understood and respected by
all peoples, not only because it can express human excellence in
an original way, but also because it often remains comparable and
equal in value according to time and space.

C. Choice of tasks

In view of the experience acquired, of the directives of the
Nairobi General Conference and of the recommendations of the
various preparatory meetings, what appear to be the most urgent
tasks? It would be useless, or at least not very realistic, to
hope that the inventories, balance sheets and analyses can be
completed by the end of the next biennial period. But it would
be possible to select from each area proposed in Belgrade the
most advanced project which also has the most intercultural
aspects.

We must therefore choose a geographical area in which different cultures are interwoven, each of which has been sufficiently
studied for their confrontation to enable us to grasp the texture
and process by which they are interrelated. While a number of
these crossroads of history have already been suggested and even
designated - the Belgrade Report quotes "the Caribbean, the Sahel
region, the Balkans, South-East Asia, the confines of East Africa
/Madagascar/Indian Ocean, etc." - it has to be recognized that
their systematic study has hardly begun. Without wishing to be
peremptory about it, I would suggest that the Central Asian
Studies Project combines the best characteristics to act as the
point of application both of an assessment and of a problem. A
second subject could be based on studies already at an advanced
stage, the results of which could be used as the methodological
basis for others. For example, the comparative study of the part
played by neighbourship in the development of the civilizations
of the Mediterranean and the Indian Ocean, and possibly its application to South-East Asia or the Caribbean.

Thematic studies covering a tangible or intangible transcultural subject have given rise to much research both of the
technical aspects (navigation, sailing, compass, roads, vehicles,
methods of traction, textiles, wood, glassware, tools, weapons,
flora and fauna, etc.) and the intellectual and cultural aspects
(religious iconography, literary subjects, traditions, ethnographical subjects, gestures, etc.). These should be given every
encouragement, for they constitute the concrete substratum of
the flow of exchanges. Myths and scientific interpretations of
the universe have sometimes been dealt with abundantly, even
though their number is still insufficient. Here again is a road
to follow, but it would perhaps be as well to take a thoroughly
studied notion and submit it to a new methodological examination.
The example of the cultural atlas of the Socialist Republic of
Serbia might be used as a starting point.

Theoretical studies can also be based on diachronic studies,
with which partial progress has been achieved in various sectors,
such as that of relations between the State and the family in the
field of civic training and family education. The extent of the
epistemological contribution of intercultural studies could be
based on an analytical and critical inventory of the contributions
of Marxist and non-Marxist historiographers to the study of feu-
dality and feudalism.

Studies on the subject of "industrial societies and traditional cultures", which participants in the Belgrade Meeting
centred on the impact of modernity, could be related to the

subject suggested dealing with the urbanization of four villages
in four continents. But it appears to me to be desirable to consider a study likely to deal more widely with the concerns of
the communications sub-sector, such as the real or unreal worlds
created by the mass media: dualism of social life and the life
of the individual, of "what people have been told" and "what they
have experienced".

D. Priorities of subject
Many other subjects, vying with each other in interest, could be
included. The choice will be difficult, but it will be as well to
give priority to those on which work has already reached an advanced stage, for the main consideration, as was emphasized in
Belgrade, is the selection of a methodology. In the absence of
concrete cases there is no methodology in this field, and the
risk of superficiality is such that it should be guarded against
straightaway.

     Many writers of reports, too often not very well informed,
construct seductive theories in quite good faith, but sometimes
overhastily. Hence the necessity for attaching supreme importance
to the collection of information, to the patient task of
accumulating facts, before constructing explanations or theories
out of thin air. To the well-known remark according to which
truth may be stronger than fiction, it may be added that facts
are always more rich than theories. Erudition, which is often
criticized, is the only guarantee of the legitimacy of a
historical or sociological, anthropological or ethnological,
interpretation. All the specialists know this, but everybody
else must wake up to the fact and act accordingly, prepared to
await the results of one research project before undertaking
another, no matter what the attraction or apparent urgency of
the latter.

E. Methods of setting up a coordination group
Faced by this enormous, multifarious task with its strict intellectual and moral demands, which should be articulated, pruned
down, encouraged, promoted, systematized and evaluated, as
stated in Para. 4041 of the 1977-1978 Programme (19 C/5 Approved),
we have seen what could be the task of a consultative group
chiefly that of ensuring that a study is practicable, that it
fits into a project within the meaning of the final objective,
and that it is undertaken with all scientific guarantees in a
spirit of generous impartiality.

     Since the enthusiasm which can be engendered by an idea or
project ought to be tempered by the research capacity implied in
any intellectual activity, it is important that the committee
should be able to benefit from the fullest possible information
on the institutions and their resources. Here, a representative
of the ICPHS is in a position to reply in the shortest possible
time and to guarantee the soundness of an undertaking.

     If we could appoint one man to each function and one to each
culture, we might perhaps have an ideal committee, but its size
would be more that of a congress than a consultative meeting.
Experience along similar lines gives grounds for supposing that

a score of members constitute a viable committee, not including observers, and that a dozen constitute an efficient group.

A dozen to fifteen seats could be distributed on a geographical and disciplinary basis. It would be possible for a first session to appoint officials from consultative committees (or their equivalent), corresponding to the research which is most advanced as things are at present. If the disciplinary dominants of these officials are explicit enough, they can help to cover the field of certain disciplines. Among them, priority should be given to those disciplines which can be applied in the approved programme of cultural studies, while a few general theorists can be added.

The principle which seems to be the wisest and most appropriate for producing results in the immediate future is the adoption of a simple working method, with well defined thematic and geographical limits. It would be possible, for example, to use the study on the cultural values of Asia in contemporary societies (18 C/5 Para. 4.012) drawn up at the Tokyo meeting (10-16 March 1976) and emphasize the methodological aspects of the part of the Final Report of that meeting devoted to "research into cultural interaction trends in Asia". Whatever the solution, each Member State should consider the method selected not as a reward for the interest of its research work but as a priority methodological example, initiating, through its potentialities for securing results rapidly, the establishment of subsequent projects to which everyone can henceforth contribute by adapting his own programme.

3. *Report of the proceedings of the consultative meeting*[1]

Followed by an analytical list of research subjects

The Ad Hoc Working Group set up jointly by Unesco and the
International Council for Philosophy and Humanistic Studies to
draw up a programme of intercultural studies met at Unesco on
21 and 22 March 1978.

The Group, consisting of 23 members[2] opened its proceedings with an address by Mr. Makaminan Makagiansar, Assistant
Director-General for Culture and Communication

At the end of the last meeting, Mr. Emmanuel Pouchpa Dass,
Director of the Division of Cultural Studies, submitted a summary
of the requirements, suggestions and subjects which had come to
light during the meeting which, it should be pointed out, was
carried out in an atmosphere compounded of an acute sense of the
problems involved, a common determination to achieve a true
consciousness of communication among cultures and an equal eager-
ness to contribute not only to bringing about a programme of
studies but also to developing a policy of the "intercultural"
as one of the loftiest tasks confronting Unesco and contemporary
mankind. Mr. Conil Lacoste of the Division of Cultural Studies
commented briefly on the information paper submitted by Unesco
and directed the attention of the Group to the essential continuity of the project in relation to its previous history and to
its gradual maturing, while suggesting prospects of broadening it
so as to impart to what had hitherto been research and expectation
the decisive breadth of an indispensable service.

The present report will take into account both the multitude
of suggestions put forward during the exchanges and the pro-
positions contained in the preliminary reports.

The material provided by the four sessions of the Working
Group and by the preliminary studies would appear to fall under
three headings - the guiding lines of a policy of the "intercultural", the formation of the instruments of such a policy, and
possible applications to ensure increased and improved intercultural communication. In the following pages the material will
be discussed under these three headings.

---

(1) This report was prepared by Professor A. Dupront, Honorary
    President of the Université de Paris-Sorbonne.
(2) Cf. List of participants at the end of this volume.

I. MAIN FEATURES OF A POLICY OF INTERCULTURAL STUDIES

1. It was necessary to define the aims pursued in intercultural
studies. These may be set forth as follows: continuous effort
to make progress in the reciprocal knowledge of cultures, accepted
as collective indigenous identities;analysis of the dynamism in
various forms of intercultural relations in the past and in the
present; bringing to light the organizational "values" of cultural identities; developing studies, experiments and research
contributing to an intercultural policy, with a strict respect
for the autochthonism of cultures, while ensuring constant coordination between fundamental and applied research and at the
same time showing a better understanding between cultures and
possible common values.

2. The aims defined above proceed from an underlying philosophy
regarding the contemporary consciousness of the roads leading
to world unity. This philosophy consists of two essential, and
finally converging, lines of thought.
    One, at the "existential" level, recognizes the diversity
of cultures and their reciprocal "foreignness". From a recognition
of the specific character of cultures and of the fact that sometimes they are not transmissible, accepted as a discipline of
knowledge and communication, there should arise both an awareness
of the necessary unity and a practical increase in authentic communication. Here, the consciousness of oneness proceeds from the
full acceptance of the diversity.
    The other, required by metaphysics, discovers in the organi-
cism and deep-rootedness of indigenous cultures, considered in
their present aggregate, the fundamental elements of a community
of mankind. This, as was forcefully stated, is the transition from
the historical, with all its humanistic aspects, to the cosmological and the ontological. Attaining the ontological, in an
approach appropriate to each of the cultures, is to manifest
common origins. Thus, there was talk of ontological research
in the development of intercultural relations - a research in
which the various approaches of philosophy should play an
essential part as regards the interpretation of values, their
circulation and their embodiment in the various cultural
entities. Thus, study of the intercultural results in a "new
awareness" of the world. Its progress, and any programme related
to it, will proceed from a both ethical and spiritual discipline
and dynamism.

3. The above reflections provide the guiding lines of a methodology for the organization of research along four essential
directions:
a) Historical and analytical study of universal values and forms
of a world in which indigenous cultural identities have not been
previously recognized as fundamental realities of the world
organization (including an assessment of the part played by
languages of communication and technological vocabularies).

b) The study, from the point of view of intercultural relations, of cases and situations according to an essentially differential method, i.e. entirely devoted to the manifestation of specific characters and of the irreducible in culture. This will be organized in a multiform combination of three approaches - synchronic, diachronic and prospective - and even, for historic cases proper, an associative induction approach.

Particular importance will be attached to the study of acculturation phenomena, studied in vivo - in their dynamism.

In the same way, the analysis of reciprocal knowledge between two major cultural areas can establish two forms of recognition in the development of intercultural relations - that of a knowledge of oneself by the other and that of reciprocal opacities, or even crystallizations of refusal or of "un-knowledge". In this connection, for example, it was suggested that a reciprocal confrontation between India and Africa could be evolved. Exchange of knowledge between Europe and the Islamic World might also be considered. And it would be of outstanding cathartic value to reverse the usual order of things and to have Western cultures studied by personalities from other cultures.

c) The search for fundamental values, through the diversity of cultures, and possible expressions or bases of unity. This would be a cultural ontology to be created from nothing, which might become one of the loftiest tasks of Unesco.

d) In addition to these mental approaches, the basic discipline of any cultural study makes it necessary to consider such culture as the total creation of the human group concerned, its specific expression or its identity. That being so, all exterior signs of that culture - productions, forms, and material and spiritual or mythical instruments - should be taken into account.

In other words, the global approach is the governing principle of all studies of intercultural relations, and the only valid global approach - as was most aptly pointed out - is to be found in the development of strictly inter-disciplinary research (1).

In the discipline of this approach the most certain method appeared to be to impart the widest possible field to intercultural studies so as to grasp, in this vast mass of material, the special problems thus "situated" in broad organic contexts (2).

4. The pursuit of the guidelines suggested above will require the testing and fertilizing effect of time. The policy of the intercultural outlined, if considered necessary, will only assume meaning and usefulness in the context of a fully assured continuity. The Group, therefore, before dispersing, insisted on assuming its responsibilities regarding the future development of intercultural studies by adopting, as the most reliable conclusion to its proceedings, the following motion:

> "The Working Group convened in accordance with the decisions of the Nairobi General Conference to establish the guidelines for a programme of intercultural studies unanimously agreed to set up a body responsible for coordinating, harmonizing and assessing these studies.

(1) For annotations (1 to 13), please refer to the end of the text.

"It trusts Unesco, jointly with the
International Council for Philosophy and
Humanistic Studies, to determine the most
suitable form to impart to this organ."

This organ, according to the Working Group, should be of a flexible
nature but surrounded by a group of people chosen for their
scholarship or interest regarding intercultural communication
and responsible for informing the group on a given cultural area.

II. CONSTITUTION OF THE INSTRUMENTS OF AN INTERCULTURAL STUDY PROGRAMME

Obviously, the basis of a policy for the development of intercultural communication depends on the quality of the instruments
available for the pursuit of research and studies of the intercultural. But as things stand at present, no clear awareness of the
essential resources, no overall research discipline, no coordination or even information regarding experiments, tests or
studies carried out in this direction appear to have been achieved.
    In view of this urgent situation, it would appear to be
essential:

1. To draw up an inventory by major cultural sector of research
projects thus far carried out.
The dispersion of research in watertight compartments and excessive reciprocal ignorance make essential, through the application
of intercultural knowledge and in order to ensure improved economy of resources, an inventory of all published or current works
regarding relations between cultures.
    It would be as well if this inventory, which could be com-
pleted by stages in order to ensure the reliability of information,
could be compiled simultaneously with the constitution of the group
of correspondents designed to implement the overall policy, as
proposed above.
    Like any other methodically pursued inventory, this should
increase in value as it evolves and thus bring out the lines of
force which at present contribute to analysing or activating the
most important features of the relations between men and cultures.
It should not only collect materials, but also act as a guide to
the subsequent development of the studies.
    Hence, the need to collect in the most exhaustive possible
way, diachronic as well as synchronic studies, thus clearly
designating the areas still unexplored.
    Since moreover it forms part of a continuous process, this
list should constitute an account of past experiments, particularly
Unesco's pioneering experiments in the study of exchanges between
East and West. This account should also be an assessment and
therefore a development of the positive results of previous
attempts as well as a source of methodological indications (3).

2. The constitution of a working language of intercultural communication.

The fundamental finality of the operation: providing, for the establishment of research on a world-wide scale, the essential elements enabling everyone to understand what the other means on the basis of his world of original values.

This implies a two-fold task: drawing up a vocabulary which can validly be used by all as an instrument of research, and the study of fundamental notions at the heart of the major human problems in the world situation as it is today.

A list of key-words, with an analysis of the content of each, should make possible a greater certainty of meaning for research generally, and even joint projects, than is attained today, with too many essential notions that are either used with different meanings or are ambiguous in ordinary conversation.

Thus, during the meeting, the following key-words, notions, concepts and forms were mentioned: culture with its two meanings; civilization and its reciprocal relations with culture; related to culture, class culture, "sub-cultures", "cultural levels", mass culture, popular culture, traditional cultures, counter-culture; cultural identity; universal and universality; creativity; modernity and modernization; humanism; values; peace, tolerance; ethnic group; nation; State, etc. (4).

Without a vocabulary with well established connections in the study of intercultural relations, no interdisciplinary and international research is possible, with the result that there is no reliable communication in a joint search for knowledge.

The constitution of an instrument of this sort, if it is to be the basis of communications on a world-wide scale, must far transcend traditional methods of lexicography and content analysis, which were established in relation to linguistic families fully recognized and set, particularly in Western cultures. Certain key-notions, such as "culture","civilization" and "universal", brought into circulation by science and by Western domination, have been either imported, or approximately adopted, or ignored, or translated by mental processes differing widely from those used in the West, in a number of non-Western cultures. Hence the necessity for the prior listing of the key-notions which are in use, their content as adopted by the various cultures, and, in cultures where they are not in use, the words or expressions with more or less equivalent contents.

Method òf inventory to be cross-checked, in the general respect of cultural authenticities, by an analytical approach leading from the thing to the word. Thus, in the sample-cultures, selected on as wide a basis as possible, the genetic study of values considered, in the internal dynamism of these cultures, as of all men or as being amenable to universalization or generalization.

Incidentally, this research vocabulary constitutes an essential instrument for the study of the two outstanding problems related to a worthwhile knowledge of the intercultural: that of determining the fields of intercultural relations and their respective dimensions; and that of the extent to which the languages of communication are valid for the authentic transmission of

cultural identities. We therefore have both a measurement of the
value of the language for constituting cultural identity and
analysis of the phenomenon of transition through the languages,
with all the adjustments necessary for more reliable communication
brought to light.

3. Formulating a deontology for intercultural studies.

Two aspects of intercultural knowledge can be used as a starting
point for this deontology, which is considered indispensable.
A. The problem of collecting oral traditions. In view of the increasing evidence of an immense heritage of oral traditions to be
conserved for that common fund which the diversity of cultures
represents, the intercultural methods of collection should be very
carefully studied - not in order to establish rigid, standardized
rules but to determine the essential attitudes for attaining a
truer, and more respectful knowledge in encounters with the other.
For intercultural knowledge is made up of imponderables,
particularly where oral evidence is concerned. Advice and urgent
recommendations, presented in the form of research worker's or
collector's manuals or guides, should be made available, so that
intercultural research can achieve its proper objective which is,
in cultural encounters, the delivery and reception of that profound
message which can only be transmitted in the greatest mutual frankness and reverence.
B. Determining the best conditions for authentic knowledge:
a) Mental attitudes: discipline of open-mindedness and real
willingness to know the "other" - not the "foreigner".
b) Knowledge of the autochthonous language and direct experience
of the cultural milieu studied.
c) Mutual appreciation of the respective value of studies of a
given culture carried out by scientists "belonging" to it or by
"foreign" scientists. It would appear to be necessary, on the
basis of evidence, experiences and published contrasting studies,
to consider and appreciate the quality of the knowledge and the
extent to which work carried out on one and the same culture by
"native" and "foreign" scientists is transmissible, in order possibly to achieve cooperation in research which, at a particularly significant level, would be a channel of reciprocal knowledge
and communication in depth, and therefore of authentic intercultural exchanges.

4. Constitution of material for the study of an overall dynamism of the intercultural.

The material must be collected by the most widely differing methods
for an analysis *in vivo* of the various aspects of the dynamism of
intercultural relations. Let us not hesitate to acknowledge it:
this is a truly immense task, regarding which the Working Group made
a large number of suggestions which can, however, be classified
into a few essential options each covering a specific series of
case studies.
    Confronted by the contrasting wealth of the numerous sugges-
tions, the Working Group very rightly pointed out, with the
wisdom of a wide experience of research, that any conceptualizing
or educational consideration regarding intercultural relations

and their development had to be based on case studies selected
in essential areas where a relation dynamics might reveal itself,
in both a diachronic and synchronic dimension,both being equally
balanced (5).

There appear to be a number of important areas which can give
rise to case studies:

A. Analysis of basic data

a) Establishment of a polyvalent material for the analysis of
intercultural relations:

The linguistic content analyses suggested above regarding
conventional terms or their equivalents cannot suffice as the
equipment for general research undertaken by inter-disciplinary
research workers from different indigenous cultural environments.

It is therefore essential:

(i) to carry out a phenomenological analysis of culture
as such, both in its global form and also as the consciousness
experienced and even mythologized of the cultural identity,
enumerating the chief factors fashioning each from both points of
view. In particular, determining the cultural non-variants and
their respective hierarchies or, to use a semiological approach,
the constitution of emic units (culturems or behaviourems),which
are organic to the cultural phenomenon taken as a whole (this
last suggestion comes from the Arutiunov Report).

Two differential methods can be used complementarily to confirm an analysis the conclusions of which remain fundamental.

One, relating to language and to communication generally,
can determine, within each indigenous cultural complex, the untranslatable and the intransmissible (words, collective representations, habitual mental schemas, ways of life, customs, etc.).
A similar method provides an introduction to a psychology of the
profundity of cultural oneness (oneness at the heart of the
identity)(6).

The other, by a detailed study of cases, assesses the transmis-
sibility value of the common language for communicating the cultural identity - a liberating verification which also attains a
cultural specificity.

When analysing the organic elements of culture, a fundamental
distinction will be made between cultures with written traditions
and those with oral traditions.(7) In the same way, while it certainly appears that almost every culture is intercultural in its
phenomenological being,the development of this internal, and sometimes constituent, interculturality, should make it possible to
impart full polyvalence to the operational concept of culture -
which is the objective sought.

Particular attention should be paid to the part played by
language as an element in culture, not only on account of its
importance as a major element of the cultural identity but also,
in polycultural States or those with considerable differences
among the social strata, as a means of social advancement - i.e.,
in many cases forced acculturation (8).

(ii) to study the major organic cultural groups formed around
unifying principles, though without laying claim to a general
typology, which would be premature at this stage. Thus, the
culture of sea-folk, cultures emanating from the same source of

food, such as rice; cultures bound up with the various forms of animal economy (horse, cattle, sheep, etc.) (9).

Similar methods could be applied to the study of the ethnic reality, to the development of "ethnic processes", with their own constancies or differences, to the constitution of what Soviet ethnology calls the "ethnic consciousness"- in view of the research pursued in the U.S.S.R. along these lines (Arutiunov Report).

In the same way, an analysis of the constitutive mechanisms of cultural groups and the classification of the elements or forms, media or expressions of this dynamism, particularly a study of the processes of building "national" cultures or of the channels through which a culture organizes itself as self-sufficient or totalitarianizing (10).

b) Prospecting the fundamental requirements in cultural diversity, particularly representations and symbolisms. Or, as was suggested, the study of mythologies.(11) All these methods result in the constitution of anthropological material established, contrary to traditional methods, from the point of view of both the existential differential and of a possible universal.

c) Measurement and consequent definition of the fields of intercultural relations (the extent of the cultures under consideration, whether macro- or micro-culture and the social quantitative as well as the qualitative will play a decisive part in this); studies of areas of encounter (particularly Central Asia or similar areas to be determined in other parts of the world); repertory of forms of cultural coexistence.

d) Revealing and analysing intercultural relations bound up with various forms of migration (episodic; seasonal; temporary or permanent settlements, etc.).

B. Relational systems

a) Study of relations between cultures and socio-economic structures - a capital relational problem for which, in order to avoid any misunderstanding it is important that the existential contents of the notion of culture should be determined beforehand.

b) Phenomenological analysis of the birth, life, and death or exhaustion of cultural identities. Particularly, bringing to light processes of establishing peaceful or tolerant relations between cultures, or relations giving rise to organic conflicts affecting their balance or possible coexistence.

Hence the importance of the part played by proximity in the development of the civilizations of the Mediterranean or of the Indian Ocean, with possible application, by differential or comparative methods, to the world of South East Asia or of the Caribbean (Elisseeff Report).

Particular attention will be paid to clinical cases of cultural destruction, both past and present.

c) Dynamism of accultural relations: a vast chapter in the study of intercultural relations, in which the following lines of research can be granted prima facie a privileged place:

- forced acculturations: relations between the dominant and the dominated cultures within the same society and between different societies (colonizer and colonized); national culture and foreign minority). Under the general heading of this line of research the

following urgent problems were mentioned: the phenomenon of the
rejection of "sub-cultures" in a given unifying society; the
forced encounter of traditional peasant cultures with urbanized
culture of the Western type (Aroutiunov Report); the insertion of
immigrant workers into industrialized countries; the study of
the phenomenon which was given the name "culturism" by the
meeting itself - i.e. coercive imposition of a culture, with all
the psychic and mental complexes involved, both for the oppressed
and the oppressor (12).
- Cultures with a typically acculturating effect on an indigenous
background such as, in different ways, Mozarabic culture and its
remains or the assimilation of Japanese or Romanian culture
(Dupront Report).
- Closed or self-sufficient cultures (same Report).
    These acculturation studies should bring to light both the
positive facts (reception) and the negative facts (rejection),
as well as the inter-reactions, which are often more extensive
than would appear, between the dominated and the dominating
culture, at both national and international level (13).
d) Consciousness of the "other" : inventory, in each system of
intercultural relations, of what is mutually recognized as being
unusual, strange, foreign, or even untranslatable.
    Study of facts, forms and problems connected with tolerance
between cultures.
    C. Thematic and transcultural studies
The following subjects relating to transcultural research were
particularly noted during discussions and in suggestions
embodied in reports:
- analysis of cultural complexes (myths, legends, traditions,
collective behaviours, etc.) regarding the reality of the sea;
- attitudes, principles and behavioural patterns of cultures
regarding consciousness of the family, its organicism and human
field, its measurement of time, its life of traditions, etc.;
- study of hydraulic techniques in a number of cultures, with all
their implications of successful technology, mastery of the
element and mental reactions towards water as an element;
- a differential analysis, through well defined cultural
ensembles, of the structures and collective consciousness of
relations between social life and individual life (Elisseeff
Report). An enlightening approach would be the comparative and
differential study of individualistic structures (Western) as
opposed to community structures (Africa, Asia and Latin America);
- intercultural study of the mental states resulting from becoming
aware of both what is "communicated" and what is "experienced"
(Elisseeff Report);
- the forms of consciousness of man's destiny in indigenous
cultures (e.g., in the West, the problem of the hereafter);
- inventory of the various mental schemas which, in indigenous
cultures, contribute to the notion of modernization and define
its restraints and dynamism, as well as any rejections of it;
- the analysis of the mechanisms of the collective consciousness
of modernity could be carried out in parallel with that of the
mental complex of "traditions" and of the consequent processes
of desacralization (Dupront Report).

- the fact of time (temporal dimensions; collective consciousness of time; multiplicity of times; time and eternity, etc.)
and its physical, psychical and spiritual expressions in certain
major cultures (Dupront Report).

The perfecting of an exploratory methodology on the basis
of a few examples might lead to overall research, necessary both
for the development of intercultural communication and for the
discovery of values of archetypes - the possible foundations of
a consciousness of the universal or at least of common reference
systems.

Such an array of themes, no matter what the order in which
they are dealt with, must produce transcultural evidence. This can
also be achieved by two other convergent approaches:
- the first consists in organizing parallel and coordinated
studies in relation to some major specialized discipline. Thus,
the organization of international cooperation in the fields of
anthroponymy and toponymy (Arutiunov Report) ; to which might be
added, for certain cultural areas, hagiotoponymy.
- The second consists of the multi-disciplinary study of common
problems, such as bilingualism in the world of today and the
reciprocal acculturations resulting from it (Aroutiunov Report).

Or again, a subject which is fundamental to the exploration
of the present age and is a growing threat to indigenous cultures -
the repercussions of technological transfers, the circulation of
technological languages and their intercultural communication
value, and more generally, a study of the "electronic civilization"
and of its effects on cultural identities and popular cultures.

III. APPLICATIONS OF RESEARCH

1. The first stage is the development in each cultural environment of knowledge about other cultures. There are too many worlds
which are sufficient unto themselves on the surface of the globe.

Emphasis was thus placed on the importance of training young
people in a knowledge of the major present-day cultures; particularly at the primary and secondary education level, broadening
and deepening intercultural information in Western societies -
thus compensating for the former, European type, universalization.
Programmes of information through the media could be arranged,
and the distribution of works of quality among the public at large
envisaged.

2. This gives rise to the essential problem of the teaching of
foreign cultures. To be operative, such teaching can only be
elaborated empirically.

Two approaches were suggested along these lines:
a) The educational exploitation of the relations between the
intercultural and the interdisciplinary. Owing to the fundamental
demands of the global approach, any valid interdisciplinary
research is an apprenticeship for the intercultural; in the same
way, any intercultural study, whether relational, thematic or

transcultural, should be defined as interdisciplinary (Bazin Report).
b) Increasing movement of students through various cultural environments provides considerable material, which is extraordinarily vivid and has thus far been insufficiently exploited for preparing a cultural pedagogy, which is still rudimentary and biased.

In this connection, the following could be envisaged:
- either a study, in a number of Universities receiving large contingents of foreign students, of the conditions of integration of such students into the various cultural milieux of the countries concerned;
- or an inventory and analysis, in Universities belonging to cultural areas as widely differing as possible, of the pedagogical methods worked out for the analysis and transmission of the indigenous culture and the evaluation of the results achieved according to the cultural background of the students (Dupront Report).

Incidentally, the case studies, as outlined above, will of necessity provide - if the analysis of the materially and mentally organic elements of the cultural whole and their motivating components of consciousness, dynamism and even rejection is sufficiently pursued - a mass of information likely to throw light on the elaboration of an intercultural relations pedagogy.

3. Action in the field of major collective experiments providing material both for analysis (fundamental research) and for concrete orientations (applied research).

The following were suggested:
a) observation, interpretation and possible assessment of the phenomenon of "trade" generally (material, human and cultural exchanges) between given areas (in French: phenomène "commerce");
b) a thorough study of the exchange of knowledge which takes place as a result of surprise meetings arising from developments of mass tourism, in order to deduce lessons which will prevent this temporary mobility (so extensive in present-day societies and appearing to result from a deep-seated need) from having results opposite to what might be expected from them, by reinforcing reciprocal misunderstandings and recharging old stereotypes or producing an increasing number of new ones (Dupront Report).

Such are the main concepts which came to light during the debates, to which Mr. Jean d'Ormesson, Secretary-General of the International Council for Philosophy and Humanistic Studies brought an essential personal contribution.

The present Report is an attempt to consolidate, in a consciousness of the finalities appropriate to the Working Group, the contributions of all. It was also the best way to help Unesco set down some of the fundamental principles for the definition of a policy awaited for by everyone.

ANNEX

List of Research Subjects

The following systematic list of research subjects was drawn up with two aims in view - first, making an inventory of a maximum number of the suggestions regarding intercultural studies submitted during the meeting (speeches and preliminary reports) and the previous meetings; second, in order to impart unity to the whole, making a classification of this great wealth of material along the lines of the major divisions of the general report.

I. CONSTITUTION OF THE INSTRUMENTS OF AN INTERCULTURAL STUDY PROGRAMME

A. Inventory of intercultural studies and research (published studies, current research) thus far carried out.

B. Constitution of a working language of intercultural communication:
- Drawing up an intercultural glossary of the key-notions of the various cultures (to be done in successive stages either according to basic concepts or by major cultural areas).
- Inventory and constitution of the "corpus" of an intercultural vocabulary. Particularly the vocabulary of opposition and non-recognition of the "other" (the "foreign", the "barbarous", the "hereditary enemy", the "savage", the "primitive")
- Inventory of established elements for the preparation of an intercultural atlas and evolving a policy for preparing culturo-historical and ethnographico-historical atlases; attempts to standardize methods of collecting material, its graphical representation and the classification of subjects.

C. Deontology for intercultural studies:
- The "foreign" look in the theoretical and descriptive approach to cultures.

- Consciousness of "otherness" (alterity); case studies, suggested methods and attitudes.

D. Constitution of material for the study of the overall dynamism of the intercultural:
1. Analysis of basic data:
a) Studies of the various processes of knowledge;
- Inventory of "operational" concepts for a methodology of the intercultural.
- The incommunicable in the intercultural: inventory and analysis of intercultural incommunicables. (Limits of communicability of poetic expression).
- Dictionary of "untranslatables".
b) Culture and ontology: fundamental values and attitudes; ontological approach in various cultures.
- Culture and myths.
- The plurality of cultures as a safeguard of universal culture.
- The "media", creators of another cultural "reality".
c) Cultural identity and universalism.
- Intercultural and "universal".
Convergent research could be conducted in the following directions: Studies in various sample cultures of values of universal application; inventory of the archetypes of the universal; enumeration, in various sample cultures, of the disciplines of knowledge and technologies universally applicable and of those, particularly the disciplines, which are not.
- Research into the repercussions of time and space on cultural specificity, particularly the relativity of "cultural difference" in terms of history.
- The "trade" phenomenon (material and cultural exchanges) between two given cultural sectors.
d) Immigration and cultural mixture.
- Mass tourism in relation to mutual understanding or misunderstanding and the production of stereotypes.
2. Relational systems:
a) Socio-economic structures and culture.
b) Comparative study of the part played by vicinity in the evolution of the civilizations of the Mediterranean, Indian Ocean or the Caribbean.
- "Nation building" and the survival of autonomous cultures.
- Cultural destruction.
- Cultural aggression: culture imposed and culture subjected.
c) Study of the acculturation process in history and in the world of today: positive effects (receptivities); negative effects (rejections).

- The dynamics of cultural rejection.
- Cultural imperialism, responsible for both the destruction and the safeguarding of cultures in the colonized countries;
- The trend towards the "homogeneous" and its impact industrial establishments (the "turnkey" factory, standardization through concrete, etc.).
- Comparative studies of cultural "change" under the effect of the media and of Western technology.
- Sample studies of the evolution of peasant-society institutions among certain indigenous populations (South-West United States, Mexico, Andean plateau, coastal plantation areas of West Africa and the Philippines, East Africa, Southern Siberia, etc.) in contact with European cultures.
- Closed and self-sufficient cultures.
- Ethnocentrism and its effects on intercultural relations.
- The "melting pot".
- Bilingualism and the process of bi-cultural development.

d) Consciousness of alterity ("otherness"): case study; proposed methods and attitudes (already mentioned).

II. THEMATIC AND TRANSCULTURAL STUDIES

- Study of migrations and transcultural accultura- tion of symbols, myths, rituals, ceremonial and artistic elements, etc.
- The family in the various cultures.
- Studies of systems of family relationships and changes in them in different societies.
- Research into the essential dualisms in the various cultures: social and individual life; what is communicated and what is experienced.
- Collective consciousness of time and the multi- plicity of times in the various cultures.
- Studies of the collective consciousness of history and forms of periodization in various sample cultures.
- Inventory of mental schemas of tradition and modernization in various sample cultures.
- Consciousness and practice of the sacred; modernization and desacralization.
- Study of the toponymic model and of microtoponymy in the various societies.
- The imago urbis and the specific forms of urbanization; town-country relations.
- Comparative study of urbanization phenomena in four villages in different cultural areas

(Finland, Western Europe, North Africa and
another continent).
- Consciousness of the body in the various cultural
  systems.
- The fundamental colours of the cultural universe.
- Inventory of collective stereotypes by major
  cultural areas.
- Western medicine and pharmacopoeia and traditional
  medicine and pharmacopoeia.
- Comparative studies of harmonies and antagonisms
  regarding artistic culture in the various societies: personalized artistic culture and anonymous
  traditional culture; production by craftsmen and
  imported culture of the urban-industrial type;
  impact on local artistic industries of commercial
  demand and mass-production, with inverse processes.
- The theme of the "foreign" in the theatre.

III. RESEARCH APPLICATIONS

- Drawing up educational programmes covering the presentation
of other cultures. The same action should be taken as regards the
content of the media.
- Study, in a number of universities and in the milieux of
the host countries, of the degree of integration possible among
foreign students.
- Inventory, in a few sample universities, of the methods
of presenting indigenous cultures to foreign students, and
assessment of results.
- Publication of the results of intercultural and interdisciplinary research conducted in Finnish peasant environment
under the direction of Rector Kirkinen.

FOOTNOTES

(1) It was stressed that the global approach has become that
normally adopted by Western orientalists. The latter, in
fact, have been "acculturated" by the methods employed
in Oriental science, which does not acknowledge any
separation between the different branches of knowledge.

(2) Unless the area which intercultural relations should cover
is first identified, broadening the scope of the exercise may
prove to be as dangerous as it is ambitious. By contrast, a
very wide-ranging investigation of the material in all its
complex and multiple real-life forms should enable "fields"
and "themes" to be clearly pin-pointed and should give rise
to the implementation of a programme of specific studies
that would be both pursued with exactitude and situated in
an existential context (case studies).

(3) Not forgetting, in connection with Unesco's past experience,
the outcome of the various Conferences on Cultural Policies.

(4) One of the concepts on which views varied most widely in the
course of the discussions was that of "cultural identity",
and the actual validity of the term was queried on a number
of occasions. This plainly entails analysing its content,
drawing up a list of instances where it is "accepted" or re-
fused, determining cases where its relevance or inadequacy is
acknowledged, and ascertaining the type of medium to which it
can be applied.

(5) Reference was quite rightly made to the danger involved in
developing an intercultural research methodology established
at the level of theoretical discourse without starting out
from the study of precise facts, or at least without its
evolving in parallel with such a study.

(6) In other words, untranslatable "cores" existing in any culture.
That common and incontrovertible feature highlights a point
that is fundamental to a methodology of intercultural studies
and, as far as communication in depth is concerned, dictates
that ways and means be sought of conveying the untranslatable
or of making it heard. Poetic translation, which can be
regarded as reaching into the heart of the incommunicable,
could be said to offer a particularly choice field for such
research (cf. the analyses contained in Cheikh Anta Diop's
paper).

(7) The group's attention was drawn to recent research on ancient
Chinese. Contrary to the generally widespread pattern, oral
tradition was by no means a forerunner to the development of
the written language. In the case in point, the source common
to both was a system of gestures. The existence of this
fundamental preliminary accordingly introduces a possible third
distinction into the original character of cultures.

(8) Examples of language as a class sign or criterion were cited in the cases of Belgium, Spain, France (Brittany) and Canada.

(9) The plant environment or, from another standpoint, the system of tools used, can also be viewed as principles of differentiation and as keys to the coherence of certain cultural units.

(10) There was a variety of reactions to the "nation-building" concept. Either the construction of a so-called "national" culture is an accomplished fact that has now been superseded, in which case homogeneization in the context of the nation is, on analysis, revealed as being a form of violence, or else, in the case of on-going nation-building, "cultural racism" could be denounced, as it was in a particular example. Nation-building is therefore an equivocal concept and a source of misunderstanding as far as intercultural studies are concerned, and we should not be inveigled into assimilating nations with States. Any exercise in thinking or research into the intercultural issue must use either concept advisedly.

(11) Stress was laid on religious systems as being among the most powerful factors in cultural identity.

(12) Current instances of rejection or revival were cited in respect of Spain, France and the United Kingdom (Scotland and Wales) and, in the case of Scandinavia, of the reaction of the Lapps to the dominant culture. Since, over the course of time, any form of rejection generates a dynamic of its own, the diachronic dimension is essential if a valid analysis is to be made. More broadly speaking, studies of acculturation are meaningless unless light is shed on diachronic developments, and this accordingly becomes essential in every case.

(13) Among antagonistic relationships, it would be essential to make a study of the two major complexes represented by racism and xenophobia through an approach that should be lucid and, while not necessarily objective, should be free from the passions which naturally go to form their make-up.

III. Promotional aspects

Education for the mutual understanding of cultures
(Unesco, Paris, May 1979)*

---

* "Committee of Experts on the Education for the Mutual Understanding of Cultures"
(Unesco Headquarters, Paris 28-31 May 1979).

1. *Guidelines note*

Elements of information and conceptual landmarks

This meeting of experts deals with a partial - but fundamental and particularly concrete - aspect of the "intercultural" research programme drawn up by a working party set up jointly by Unesco and the International Council for Philosophy and Humanistic Studies (ICPHS), in which some experts among those assembled here today participated. (1)

ANTECEDENTS AND LINKS WITH THE UNESCO PROGRAMME

Meanwhile, the Unesco General Conference, during its twentieth session held in Paris in October/November 1978, confirmed that Member States are keenly interested in intercultural studies, and particularly intercultural communication from the point of view of understanding and peace.

    This appears clearly in the Resolution concerning the programme of activities in connection with the "promotion of appreciation and respect for the cultural identity of individuals, groups, nations or regions" (Objective 1.2 of the Medium-Term Plan 1977-1982) approved for 1979-1980. By means of this Resolution, the General Conference authorized the Director General to organize activities relating in particular to the two following themes: "Contribution to the mutual appreciation of cultures and to international cultural understanding" (Theme 4/1.2/04) and "Recognition of cultural pluralism and respect for the identity of people belonging to minorities" (Theme 4/1.2/06), particularly activities contributing to "understanding between peoples based upon the recognition and mutual appreciation of the values and the dignity of each culture, thus establishing international cooperation on the basis of equality and mutual respect" (cf. Approved Programme and Budget for 1979-1980, Programme Resolution No. 4/1.2/1).

    The importance of the notion of cultural identity in the view of Unesco, as well as in that of the United Nations specialized agencies and other organizations and institutions covering other

---

(1) See the list of participants at the end of this volume.

spheres which at first sight appear to be but distantly related
to cultural matters, is due to the major role now attributed to
the cultural dimension of development by the international community. The expert and the technician can no longer ignore the
fact that technology is not culturally innocent in the most
ordinary conditions of its transfer process; the economist now
knows that expansion can no longer be expressed in absolute
terms and that growth and development have ceased to be synony-
mous. Without insisting on this problem of the social and cultural aspects of development, we would merely point to the double
procedure implied by the relationship of the individual or group
to the cultural identity. (1)

In purely economic terms, the <u>consciousness</u> of cultural
identity constitutes the indispensable - though indirect - stimulant for endogenous, integrated development, freed from "ready-
made" patterns. As a motivation of a community or the leaven
of a national growth, in view of the sanction of facts and results, it can no longer be ignored by the planner. But even
supposing that the equitable distribution of resources on a world-
wide scale has been achieved,that would not necessarily imply
the harmonious cohabitation of cultures.

This brings us to the second aspect: on the ethical and psyco
logical level, <u>appreciation and respect</u> of the cultural identity
are the key to a development based on human dignity and individual
and social evolution. In short, it might be said that quantitative
development depends on consciousness of the cultural identity,
and international understanding on a respect for it. Obviously,
it is the second aspect with which the theme "Education for the
mutual understanding of cultures" is concerned, even if it is
asserted that appreciation of the culture of "others" presupposes
that our own roots are authentic.

It was in order to take this double attitude into account
that, in the biennial programme and the medium-term plan adopted
by the General Conference, cultural studies are essentially grouped
under two distinct (though complementary) headings: "promotion
of cultural studies at regional, sub-regional and national level",
which is in line with the studies by geo-cultural area pursued
within the Cultural Studies Division for a long time, and "contribution to the mutual appreciation of culture and to international cultural understanding" which, over the past two or three years
has added to cultural studies based on a traditional geographical
distribution the diagonal dimension which they were lacking and
which gives rise to the subject of the present meeting.

Incidentally, in the "list of research subjects", which
follows on the report of the consultative meeting of March 1978,
will be found a number of suggestions which are closely related
to the subject under discussion today. These include:

---

(1) Cf. Unesco: <u>Medium-Term plan,</u> 1977-1982 (Document 19 C/4
     approved) and the abridged version intended for the general
     public entitled: "<u>Thinking Ahead. Unesco and Challenges of
     Today and Tomorrow</u>" , op. cit.

- drawing up an intercultural glossary of the
  key-notions of the various cultures;
- dictionary of "untranslatables";
- the foreign look in the theoretical and
  descriptive approach to cultures;
- consciousness of "otherness" (alterity);
  case studies; suggested methods and attitudes;
- limits of communicability of poetic expression;
- the "trade" phenomenon of material and
  cultural exchanges;
- dynamism of cultural rejection;
- the "mentality of the homogeneous";
- ethnocentrism and its effects on intercultural (and international) relations;
- inventory of collective stereotypes;
- the theme of the "foreign" in the theatre.

In more direct relation with the educational and pedagogical aspect of the theme suggested today, there is to be found under the heading "Research applications":

- drawing up educational programmes covering
  the presentation of other cultures;
- study, in a number of universities of the
  degree of integration possible among
  foreign students, etc.

A vast programme, to be sure, certain items of which - as the rapporteurs were aware - have already been the subject of extensive studies (including some by members of this new committee of experts), which were however devoted rather to outlining an area of research than to laying down a strict programme. In suggesting that the experts here present should consider the theoretical implications and practical methods of intercultural education, the Secretariat's intention was both to adopt the priorities laid down by the General Conference and to initiate a discussion likely to facilitate the approach to a number of subjects selected by the previous meeting (from which the committee of experts might be called upon to make a further selection in accordance with the priorities for the continuation of the project).

The theme of this meeting fits into the programme of intercultural studies, the guidelines of which were laid down by the two previous meetings (1). As its title indicates, it also covers other fields than culture, education explicitly and the social sciences by implication. Within the Sector responsible for these, the Philosophy Division is planning a meeting to "clarify, through basic reflections of a philosophical and epis-

---

(1) Cf. supra the final report of the March 1978 meeting already quoted and that of the Belgrade meeting.

temological nature, the conditions and methods for the study of cultures and to examine the problems relating to communication between cultural groupings". But the theme is directly related to problems of communication and dependent on its technology, since intercultural communication may be considered as a special case of relations with others, to some extent "complicated" by the cultural alterity factor (1). Mention should also be made of the programme pursued in the Social Science Sector regarding the transfer of technology and its secondary cultural effects.

A problem of culture and a problem of communication: the subject for debate hinges round this integration of culture with communication which seems to have such difficulty in getting past the stage of juxtaposition, although it has everything to recommend it and everyone is in favour of it at both national and international level. At its twentieth session, the General Conference was very insistent on this point and recommended that the Director General "continue, during the 1979-1980 biennium, the action to ensure the unity of conception of the programme concerning culture and communication and to accentuate the convergence of activities designed to attain the objectives of that programme" (General Resolution 4/01). Seen from this point of view, the theme submitted to the committee of experts almost appears to be part of a pilot scheme.

THE FACTORS AT WORK

This is only a partial theme, since, as it tackles intercultural reality from the limited angle of education and from an active point of view, it does not exhaust the vast field open to cognitive and elucidating research. Regarding the wealth and complexity of intercultural relations and acculturation phenomena there has been talk of a "metasystem of interactions involving almost unlimited possibilities of exchange" (2). It is, however, a fundamental theme, for the generalized decompartmentalization of human society, together with the headlong development of communications (mobility of persons, invasion by the media) makes

---

(1)　Prof. E.P. Lovejoye (University of California, Santa Barbara, USA) who participated in the committee of experts as an alternate for Prof. Klineberg, pointed out that, for the psychologist, the dialogue between two individuals of the same culture is at the start quite a complex one, since it implies the interaction of no less than six voices: the two speakers, each with his individual consciousness, plus the perception that each has of the other and the perception of himself that he thinks the other has of him.

(2)　Cf. supra the working document prepared by I.U.E.D. for the Belgrade meeting, 1976.

"the education of difference" and the apprenticeship of alterity a priority aim not only from the ethical but also from the practical point of view. The time when the intercultural factor was chiefly manifested in comparative studies and was measured by the tact of diplomatic speeches or the exotic thrill of the traveller is past. The number of intercultural training courses organized for those - whether diplomats, businessmen or experts - whose work brings them into contact with mentalities and practices foreign to their own cultural context, to which no dictionary can provide the key, is sufficient proof of the existence of the problem.

First of all we must agree on a few definitions. The word culture itself is usually understood in two senses: (a) culture in the restricted sense of intellectual and artistic production, and (b) culture as "the related aggregate of ways of thinking, feeling and acting" conferring a distinctive character on a collectivity; we are here dealing with the second of these (1). In the present discussion we are not concerned with comparative literature or aesthetics, but with education and the pedagogics of the intercultural in the wider sense; with seeing by what educational and pedagogical means - particularly at schools and universities but also in everyday life - it is possible to contribute to the dismantling of prejudices, misunderstandings and stereotypes, to the dispersion of the psychological opacities that form a screen between the different cultures at both group and individual levels, and to broadening the minds and understanding of those who happen to be living abroad and find themselves adopting the "foreign" approach. Reciprocally, this is also applicable to those who receive them in the host country.

Culture in the restricted sense is not, therefore, at the heart of the matter, although this does not in the least detract from the interest of such studies of a more academic character (e.g. on the communicability of the image and the coincidences of semantic fields in the literary expression of different cultures, or more generally on problems connected with translation and transposition), and should not prevent anybody from wondering about the psychology of the feeling of strangeness in approaching "foreign" painting, literature or music.

Discussion should also take into account two other features, related to each other incidentally, which further contribute to characterizing the notion of culture - its homogeneity and its area of expansion. For the question arises what are the limits and criteria of representativity and cohesion on the grounds of which a "number of ways of thinking, feeling and acting" may be considered worthy of the name "culture". This is the problem cultural homogeneity (with, at the extreme, the double-edged sword of the "Reinkultur" concept), i.e. the maintenance of the same characteristics of civilisation at a certain degree of density and stability within a given territory, and the problem of dividing

---

(1) Ibid.

the world up into geo-cultural units, a matter which has given
rise to much speculation. A document already quoted gives the
following details: "The geocultural units considered as fundamental for a future world order vary from five (Mazrui, 1975) to
ten (Club de Rome, 1974) and even twenty-four (Kothari, 1974).
The more the number increases, the nearer do we get to a system
based on the nation-State" (1).

These considerations should be related to the distinctions
which, in order to facilitate intercultural analysis, should, it
has been suggested, be introduced between cultures according to
the size or extent of cohesion of the human groups to which they
correspond. We thus arrive at the following typological scale:
micro-cultures (micro-society and particular group); national
culture; regional culture; macro-culture (understood as the
dominant culture of a system of societies - such as capitalism -
or practically as a synonym of "civilization", depending on
whether the emphasis is placed on the synchronic or the diachronic) (2).

PROBLEMATICS AND DEVIATIONS OF INTERCULTURAL RELATIONSHIP

A reminder is scarcely needed that the problem of meeting between
cultures is so vast and difficult to grasp, revolves round such
a complex phenomenon (consciousness of the other) and brings so
many disciplines into play (from cultural anthropology and social
psychology to linguistics and including sociology, history, economics, communications sciences, and introspective and behavioural
psychology of the individual and the collectivity), that a discussion of it can be approached in many ways. Only a few reference
points and suggestions for analysis, some of which take the interrogative form, will therefore be proposed here.

We start with a paradox: how can cultural communication be
promoted when the specific nature of a culture is that it is untranslatable and incommunicable? The "psychology of the profundity of cultural oneness" is rooted in the intransmissible (Final
Report of the Meeting of March 1978).

Discussion could be undertaken regarding the situation to be
changed: shortcomings, deviations and pathology of the intercultural relation.
Lack of communication. Non-communication and its psychological
motivation: many concrete examples illustrate at all ages and in
the most widely varying situations and environments the stalemate
which may result from certain "mental" incompatibilities.

---

(1)   Ibid.
(2)   Cf. Roy Preiswerk: Le Savoir et le Faire (Relations inter-
      culturelles et développement) , No. 2 of Cahiers de
      l'I.U.E.D., Geneva, 1975).

Pathology of the intercultural: The mirror-deforming stereotype
(Otto Klineberg's research); prejudices and misunderstandings;
negative vocabulary of otherness - "foreigner", "savage", "native",
"tribe", etc. (in French: "l'étranger", "le sauvage", "l'indigène",
"la peuplade"...).

Question: is the stereotype avoidable? Does it not constitute an essential, structural step in the process of perceiving
the "other", and one which should be corrected rather than eli-
minated?

The pitfalls of ethnocentrism: The examples quoted are legion.
The problem of distorting facts and the ideologies underlying them
in school textbooks is one of the best known (Columbus discovered
the New World: new for whom?). There could be discussion on
whether ethnocentrism is mainly of a deliberate or an unconscious
nature: is there such a thing as well-intentioned ethnocentrism?
There is an abundance of reports from travellers, missionaries
and experts· in the field which bring out, with varying degrees of
subtlety, the involuntary unsoundness of certain attitudes.

So far as behaviour is concerned - and even more important what
might be called "micro-behaviour" - the careful observation of
what are apparently the most harmless mannerisms and attitudes
may provide revealing indications regarding the devious trans-
vestisms of ethnocentrism, which are often quite unsuspected.

An analysis of ethnocentrism must obviously vary according
to the place and environment of the meeting (migrant workers,
school, university, tourists, research workers, international
relations agents, etc.).

But here again, purely and simply disclaiming a state of
things leads nowhere. The question has been raised whether for
a long time there has not been a tendency to assimilate ethnocentrism with racism. The point was reached of wondering whether
it was not "inextricably bound up with the very existence of
cultural diversity". Thence again, the idea of a sort of "comparative ethnocentrology": "To what extent (for example) does
non-western ethnocentrism manifest itself through those same
mental categories which have been found in Western ethnocentrism?" (1).

Without referring outright to the most spectacular deviations, the psycho-sociological analysis of the mechanism of communication and the inventory of the phenomena of interaction and
behaviour brought into play in the intercultural dialogue proposed by certain specialists are revealing enough.

In a document analysing, for operational purposes, the relations between certain social forms of behaviour and the intercultural adaptation of technical advisers working in developing

---

(1) R. Preiswerk and D. Perrot, Ethnocentrisme et histoire:
     l'Afrique, l'Amérique indienne et l'Asie dans les manuels
     occidentaux, Paris, 1975.

countries (1), B.D. Rubin lists seven criteria, four of which we
consider especially relevant here:

- Display of respect;
- orientation to knowledge;
- empathy (or putting oneself in the place
  of the "other");
- interaction management.

Less clearly defined in the same report, the "interaction pos-
ture" refers in particular to the ability to react to the "other"
in neutral and purely descriptive terms, and the opposite tendency of communicating only by assessing and arguing.

The fact is that these are interactions inherent to communication in general. But it would be easy to show, in relation
to each of these criteria, the complication introduced by the
cultural dimension: how, for example, do you judge marks of respect, if the manifestation of them varies from one latitude to
another?

It is only in consideration of all these factors that the
promotion of this "new consciousness of the world" mentioned in
the report on the March 1978 meeting can be envisaged and the
educational practices worked out.

EDUCATIONAL ASPECTS: MATERIALS FOR AN APPRENTICESHIP IN ALTERITY

Even if the problem is chiefly concerned with culture in the
widest sense of the term, the works of art and of the intellect
condense the soul of the civilization which gave birth to them.
This gives some idea of the importance attached to the diffusion
of such works. Unesco is contributing to this by means of its
collection of translations of representative works, its collection of records and its travelling exhibitions (which today are
much more than mere displays of visual art and make an attempt
to emphasize their cultural context) - an activity which should
be pursued, broadened and intensified. The Organization's activities in the field of scholarships, travelling fellowships,
courses and exchanges take the same direction.

In more direct relation with the educational and pedagogical aspects, what equipment is available?

----

(1) Brent D. Ruben and Daniel J. Kealey: Behavioural Assessment
     and the Prediction of Cross-Cultural Shock, Adjustment and
     Effectiveness (Preliminary report to the third annual con-
     ference of the Society of Intercultural Education, Training
     and Research, Chicago, Illinois, February 1977).

Stereotype studies, the analysis of conflicts and tensions related to racism or merely intercultural misunderstanding, are
extremely useful; but it is difficult for younger people (children, adolescents, students abroad) to gain access to them,
although it is they who will be responsible for preparing the
world of tomorrow.
Of more immediate effect may be collections of anecdotes and
true stories bringing out the unsoundness of ethnocentrism, i.e.
the propensity to judge "others" in terms of our own criteria (1),
the attitude of an individual or group "that places itself in a
centre around which the world revolves" (2).
Investigations have been undertaken in certain universities in
order to see how the culture and customs of foreign students are
regarded by the "receiving culture", and vice versa. The results
could make a useful contribution to defining solutions and suggesting methods.
The training of diplomats, businessmen and foreign-aid experts
is increasingly giving rise to concrete pedagogical techniques
such as "training exercises", the simulation of inter-cultural
dialogues bringing out the implications, etc. (3).
A few recent works (particularly J. Condon and F. Yousef:
Introduction to Intercultural Communication; Edward T. Hall:
La dimension cachée) are beginning to constitute the library
which is needed to provide an introduction to the intercultural
problem for the general public.
Two studies prepared on the occasion of the present meeting by
Mme M. Abdallah-Pretceille and Professor Lê Thành Khôi consider
the problem of education for intercultural understanding at the
level of the child, the adolescent and the school, and at that
of the adult, the university and the general public respectively.

In practice
Participants at this meeting may be invited to advise Unesco:

> - by making suggestions regarding the struc-
>   ture and programmes which they consider
>   might contribute to the promotion of edu-
>   cation for the mutual understanding of
>   cultures, at the various educational
>   levels;

---

(1) Cf. for example, V. Guerry: La vie quotidienne dans un
     village baoulé (Abidjan, INADES, 1970) and certain worth-
     while re-interpretations of historical events in the
     March 1979 number of the Unesco Courier (articles by
     Hugo O. Ortega and Beryle Banfield).
(2) Cf. J. Cueva-Jaramillo: "Ethnocentrism and Cultural Conflicts:
     The Anthropology of Acculturation", Cultures, Vol. V, No. 3
     (Unesco, 1978).
(3) Cf., in particular, the works and publications of the
     S.I.E.T.A.R. (Intercultural Transactions through Education,
     Training and Research), Georgetown University (USA).

- by considering means of awakening the
  interest of the youngest, who are still free
  of prejudices, to intercultural matters,
  particularly during this International
  Children's Year;
- by contributing their own personal experience
  and the results of research work in which
  they may have been associated;
- by recommending priorities among the list of
  themes for study contained in the final
  report of the proceedings of the consultative
  meeting held in March 1978 and those more
  directly related to the educational aspect;
- by contributing either during this meeting
  or after it, to drawing up a bibliography
  in line with the theme.

In view of this programme and these responsibilities, an awareness
of the composite nature of not only any culture, but also of any
individual, may act as a stimulant. In the last resort, are we
dealing with anything else but achieving outside ourselves that
cultural integration which is accomplished in each individual by
the fact of being born and inheriting acculturation? And if
this appears to you to be excessively optimistic, perhaps we
ought to let Pierre Bungener remind us that "en certaines cir-
constances, l'Utopie seule est raison" (1), so as not to let
ourselves be intimidated by the immensity of the task.

---

(1) Cf. Pierre Bungener, Le développement in-sensé (Lausanne:
     L'âge d'homme; 1978).

2. *Preparatory documents*

The intercultural in schools[1]

Martine Abdallah-Pretceille

The child and the school ought to constitute the two main targets of such a programme, and yet we are obliged to tackle the subject of the intercultural in schools by noting deficiencies. Although a number of attempts to take action along these lines have been made - particularly under the pressure of the presence of foreign children in classes, the noble intentions of a school to promote the understanding of the Other and to prohibit racism have not often gone beyond the stage of verbal statements which are occasionally introduced into lessons on ethics and civics. Apart from national anti-racism days - which, in reality, are merely an opportunity for washing away guilt, an easy way of providing oneself with a clear conscience - no serious permanent activity based on a clearly defined attitude, clearly defined objectives and a perfected methodology, has ever been undertaken. The presence of foreign children is often considered as a handicap - as a difficulty to be solved. It is high time that, on the contrary, it should be considered as a source of richness - as an opportunity which the school has a duty to seize.

On the basis of a critical analysis of the few attempts already made, I shall attempt to define the objectives and suggest a few guidelines for an intercultural methodology.

SCARCITY OF EXPERIMENTS

Intercultural activities at the elementary school, even where they exist, have not gone beyond the experimental stage and the context of teaching the children of immigrant workers. These two limits are a sufficient indication of the utter ambiguity inherent in such educational schemes. I shall base my analysis on a few

---

(1) Although this study is strictly confined to the national context - which prevents the facts and analyses it contains from finding more widespread application - it offers, from the starting point of the situation obtaining in one country, a series of practical pointers on which the committee of experts found it useful to base its discussions when it came to tackle the more tangible aspects of its agenda.

characteristic experiments supported by the French Ministry of
Education and carried out with the help of research and training
centres such as the CREDIF. (Centre de Recherche et d'étude
pour la diffusion du Français), the IRFED. (Education et Deve-
loppement : Institut international de recherche et formation),
and the CEFISEM. (1) or under the impulse of personal
initiative.

The pilot experiment conducted by IRFED was carried out in
a Franco-Portuguese context, at the request of the European Social Fund, at the Henri Wallon School in Fontenay-sous-Bois. It
was begun in 1971-1972 and completed in 1975-1976, and covered
not merely one class but the entire school. Apart from the intercultural education undertaken among the children, IRFED also took
an interest in the specific training of the teachers called upon
to work in such situations and studied intercultural training
problems in other fields - that of adult immigrants, social
workers, families, etc. (2).

In 1975, the European Economic Community drew up a project,
supervised by CREDIF, related to teaching immigrant children their
original language and culture. This project remains in the experimental stage and is only concerned with a few languages - Italian,
Spanish, Portuguese and Serbo-Croat. The scheme provides, in
addition to three hours' teaching of the language of origin per
week, for an hour of intercultural activities common to foreign
and French children and an hour devoted to meetings with parents.
This incidentally, is what constitutes the original feature of the
project as compared with the hours of teaching of the language of
origin within the context of the leisure and cultural activities
provided for by Circular No. 75 148 of 9 September 1975. This
experiment affects only about 250 children (3).

In 1975-1976, R. Gloton started an intercultural project
covering the entire school at the rue Vitruve in the 20th
arrondissement of Paris instead of merely a few classes.

Apart from the fact that an intercultural project was
justified by the high percentage of children of Arab origin, it
was facilitated in this particular school by the fact that the
school is experimental in status and therefore has a flexible

---

(1) CREDIF : 11, avenue Pozzo di Borgo, 92210 - Saint-Cloud, France
    IRFED : 40, rue de la Glacière, 75013 Paris, France.
    CEFISEM : Centre d'études, de formation et d'information sur la
    scolarisation des enfants de migrants (Centre for research,
    training and information on the schooling of immigrant
    children).
(2) Outline of an intercultural methodology for the training of
    teachers and social workers dealing with immigrant workers,
    Analysis and conclusions of a pilot-study and experiment.
    December 1975.
(3) See the various reports published by CREDIF. (B. Blot,
    S. Boulot and J. Clévy) on the teaching of the language and
    culture of origin of foreign children attending elementary
    schools (Studies of surveys carried out successively among
    masters, children and teachers with a view to ascertaining
    their ideas on the subject).

pedagogical structure. The work of all children attending the
school is concentrated on class projects - "classe verte",
circus performance, theatrical performances, etc. The
"fundamental" learning is based on the requirements created by
the projects. Thus, mixed groups (French and foreign) and Arabic-
speaking groups (three hours' language teaching and three hours
of project per week) are organized (1).

In addition, certain CEFISEMs, such as the CEFISEM-CEFREM
of Marseilles, organize occasional activities with a view to
awakening people to intercultural problems and providing training
in them.

The above information will suffice to indicate the
institutional context within which these experiments took place.
But no matter what the context, all these different experiments
are based on similar postulates.

The very fact that they all fit into the framework of
education for the children of immigrant workers and into this
framework alone proves that the basic objective of intercultural
activities does not here lie in an understanding of cultures but
in improving the adaptation of foreign children to the French
school system:"Ensuring that foreign children retain a knowledge
of their language and culture of origin may even constitute a contribution to the adaptation of such children to the school" (2).
The fact that notice was taken of cultures of origin was caused
by the extent of the difficulties, and even scholastic failures,
of such children. Moreover, the prospect of a possible return to
the country of origin has also been taken into account by the
educational authorities, which hoped by these means not to cut
off the child from its culture of origin. The cultural dialogue
is only considered as a means of remedying a defective educational
situation. Intercultural education, considered from the point of
view of the all-round education of the child, is therefore a
secondary element in this context.

The intercultural project at the rue Vitruve school was
carried out with the object of "providing Arab children with a
national culture for which they felt the need" (3). The Marseilles
CEFISEM-CEFREM define the aim of cultural activities as "enabling
children and adolescents from an under-privileged social environment to assume their own cultural identity and getting the school
to recognize their right to be different - or in other words making
a positive discrimination"(4). For IRFED, the words "therapeutical
means" are directly associated with intercultural pedagogics,
which are based on the orientation of a curative system of teaching
designed to reduce the traumatism from which immigrant children
suffer. Intercultural activities are considered by certain teachers
as mere media for logical and linguistic operations, as factors
facilitating the relaxation of affective and linguistic inhibitions.

---

(1) Cf. Langue et culture arabes à l'école de la rue Vitruve
    (1975-1976), Association française des arabisants.
(2) Circular No. 78 148 of 9th April 1975, Bulletin officiel de
    l'Education nationale, No. 5, 17th April 1975.
(3) Document of 5-6th December 1978.
(4) Ibid.

While such a dimension can be taken into consideration, it is regrettable, from an educational point of view, if it is the only one.

These formulations of objectives which remain superficial - and even caricatural - are worthy of being subjected to a critical analysis in an attempt to extirpate from them their paternalistic and ethnocentric implications, in spite of a declared willingness to achieve better understanding of the Other. It must be admitted that the Western cognitive model is so pregnant that it weighs heavily on attempts to approach and opportunities of opening up. "Teaching", "restoring a culture of origin", "under-privileged socio-cultural environment" - are not these very terms tainted with paternalism? Would we use the same ones if we were speaking of French culture? Our way of tackling the problem of the Other's culture is, subconsciously or not, still impregnated with ethnocentrism. Here we coincide with the theories expressed by Roy Preiswerk, who asked whether "the scientific approach applied by the West does not constitute an obstacle to a knowledge of other cultures" (1). It is necessary for the researchers, teachers, educators, and so on, who take an interest in the problem of understanding among cultures and in intercultural activities, to ask themselves about the ideological and theoretical background conveyed by the collective thought which directs their cognitive behaviour.

The above remarks demonstrate the necessity for a detailed analysis of the various types of statements made on a subject of this sort.

So far as content is concerned, intercultural activities are often restricted either to the linguistic field or to history, geography, folklore, festivities or arts and crafts. This assimilation of culture to the most easily perceptible manifestations, and its reduction to a historical or geographical dimension is all the more significant in that it implies methodological orientations which, in reality, correspond neither to the new educational objectives as laid down in the various instructions and circulars published since 1969 nor to the concept of culture as such.

From this point of view, culture is presented on the basis of isolated elements, as a sum   of atomized items of knowledge. The internal dynamism inherent to any culture is absent from all these different methods of approach. But what is important is not so much to find out about a few cooking recipes or types of craft as to try and find out how these elements are incorporated into cultural life generally. Knowing how to make mint tea does not imply an understanding of the important part played by it in social exchanges between those belonging to the culture concerned.

Intercultural meetings are very often considered as a coming and going between events of two countries at the same period. A

---

(1) R. Preiswerk: "Intercultural relations and development", Le Savoir et le Faire, in Cahiers de l'Institut d'études du développement, PUF, Paris 1975.

system of comparative pedagogics is established, with all the dangers and errors potentially inherent to it. IRFED has based intercultural training on a "contrastive approach to cultures", to employ (and extend) a term used by linguists: "It makes it possible to analyse differences and understand the gap between the reactions of different socio-cultural systems to one and the same problem. Adaptation to different situations can then be effected within the subject and the group, rather than by virtue of an extraneous constraint". The complete transposition of a method appropriate to the linguistic sphere into another sphere in itself constitutes an intellectual feat the scientific value of which may be challenged. Moreover, the validity of contrastive linguistics as a means of learning a foreign language is strongly disputed. IRFED's determination to "consider data regarding the culture of the country of origin and the culture of the host country for the purpose of education not as haphazardly interacting parallel systems but as a system of differences, the interaction between which must be analysed in order to facilitate its control and make it into a source of enrichment" was in strict conformity with the aim of intercultural education as it has been laid down, viz: "to help the child to construct a new mode of regulation on the basis of the sources of cultural influence to which he is subjected" (1). It appears, therefore, that the methodology should be reviewed, in spite of its coherence with the objective laid down.

Moreover, we are obliged to admit that intercultural activities are always undertaken from a dual point of view. Arab culture as compared with French culture, Spanish culture as compared with, etc. No plurilateral analysis of several cultures is ever considered. We should also note that such activities are always more concerned with presenting the foreign culture (foreign so far as France is concerned), whereas not only is French culture never presented or studied, but also the notions of exchange and cultural dialogue are practically absent.

The supervision of French teachers by educators (in the case of IRFED, CREDIF and the rue Vitruve school) or by pupils' families appears at first sight to conform to a concern for authenticity. However, such a practice will not stand up to a detailed examination. In addition, it has the major disadvantage of complicating the educational structure. The fact of "asking families to inform children and teachers about their specific cultural features" (1), while conforming to the admirable intention of opening the school to the environment, in fact provides no valid guarantee ragarding intercultural activities. Cooperation of this sort can only be justified if it corresponds to real team work uniting international researchers engaged on intercultural studies.

Another postulate common to these various experiments involves the setting up of a system of intercultural pedagogics, requiring the formulation of specific structures, the participation

---

(1) Marseilles CEFISEM-CEFREM

of staff who have undergone a specific training, etc. But by imparting a sophisticated character to this type of teaching, there is a risk of confining intercultural studies to a ghetto - which would be the very opposite of the openness hoped for. The intercultural is, and must be, an integral part of an overall educational process. It is not a matter of considering the problem of understanding between cultures in terms of an additional subject but in terms of awakening to the intercultural dimension of all teaching and all education.

The empiricism which marks intercultural activities should be replaced, so to speak, by a scientific and methodical approach to the problem of the need to define in the first place the field and instruments of work, the need for multi-disciplinary consideration of the problems of understanding cultures and cultural dialogue. An authentic approach to the Other can only be made if it is based on the prior objective consideration of all the psychological and sociological implications of the activity, and of educational activities in particular. It is odd to note that, when the West plans a programme as generous as the approach to another culture, it almost invariably omits to submit its intellectual approach to a critical examination. Declarations of intent, as numerous as they are noble, would appear to be intended to make up for this methodological shortcoming.

And yet, more than in any other field of research, intercultural activities ought to be subjected to a strict examination, for to speak of culture is not to work on a pure concept or an inert group but to try and understand the Other through what identifies him and what affects him deeply. Respecting the Other is above all being exacting in regard to oneself and to the cognitive bases of one's activities.

MULTI-LEVEL DEFINITIONS OF INTERCULTURAL

It seems that intercultural activities have been proceeding without teachers having taken the trouble to define the very conception of culture in advance. Without necessarily adventuring into the maze of multifarious definitions, the teacher cannot dispense with a conceptual analysis, for intercultural activities assume a different direction according to the priority given to the various aspects of culture.

Every culture has its roots in the collective subconscious. Men are, in any case, generally unconscious of the cultural meaning of their thoughts and acts. Thus it is that no approach to another culture, and no attempt to explain one's own culture can be completely transparent and fully objective. The dialectical link between culture and personality forces us to admit that no culture can be fully understood, that we can only strive towards an understanding which, no matter how subtle it may be, is always incomplete. It is therefore indispensable for the teacher to subject his lessons on culture to permanent revision.

It would be futile to make a choice among the many accepta-

tions of the word "culture". The task of the teacher is not to make
such and such a definition his own but to know something of the
different shades of meaning applied to the word. The education-
alist cannot take a single science as his basis; he must, as far
as possible, integrate the contributions of the various disciplines if he is to give a credible foundation to his method of
teaching. It is from this point of view that we shall now consider
certain aspects of the concept of culture.

Along the lines of a structuralist approach, pedagogical
guidance should be based on the study of correlations, for "the
cultural features of a society are not merely adjacent, they are
bound together; they form a system, a configuration, they have a
meaning, and once we have grasped this meaning, it will define
the spirit of the culture of that society "(1). In order not to
give an excessively mechanistic definition of culture by
emphasizing a collection of objects, practices, rites and
superstitions which are submitted as ethnographical documents,
the educational task in the teaching of the intercultural should
be pursued on the basis, not of an isolated cultural element
but of the structuration of elements. The child should learn to
discover characteristic systems of meaning. To draw up a list of
cultural features and remain at the nomenclature stage is to
fossilize culture; it means not going beyond the documentary
stage and proposing an anti-scientific approach.

A culture does not exist without a human group; it is a
social experience and as such cannot be taken to pieces; it
must be seen as a whole. A culture cannot be learnt or taught;
it has to be experienced. Intercultural contact, particularly
where children are concerned, is essential for better mutual
understanding. Subsequent activities must, therefore, be inserted
into a movement between a general perception of the culture and
an analysis of the facts, particularly as the cultural features
are not all significant and pertinent to the same extent. A
culture, therefore, cannot be approached without at the same time
apprehending the context of its historical and social development.

One form of culture has always held a privileged position
in the Western educational system; this is "Culture with a capital
C". While works of art, monuments and architectural and literary
achievements should be taken into account, they should not form
a screen to hide the cultural values conveyed by the individual.
Nevertheless, these sublimated manifestations of culture may constitute excellent tools for understanding between cultures, for
"it is easy to communicate from one culture to another by means
of the arts and literature, which quite rightly, transcend the
codes and determinisms of each group by assuming them. Each work
of art creates its own order of internal necessity which, as
Malraux said, places it outside the context of history" (2).

To define the cultural identity of a people is a matter of
an intellectual challenge, particularly as the notion of culture

(1) J. Stoetzel: La Psychologie Sociale, Paris, Flammarion, 1963.
(2) L. Chambard, Les Amis de Sèvres, No. 3, September 1976,
    quarterly review.

is in reality a plural notion. Firstly, culture is in perpetual
movement; defined as the whole of a group's possible reactions
to the stresses of the environment, it is liable to permanent
adaptation, for "cultures grow and change. They eliminate certain
elements and acquire others during their history" (1).Dealing
with a culture demands integration with this dynamism. In an
intercultural approach it is therefore more important to try to
perceive this movement than to attempt to establish an exhaustive
picture of a culture, which can never be anything but partial
and haphazard. Secondly, "any society divides its members into a
number of categories and assigns various sectors of the entire
culture to each category" (2). The result is that "no individual
is familiar with the entire culture to which he belongs, far less
does he express all aspects of it in his own behaviour" (3). The
reservations already expressed regarding the guaranteeing of
intercultural activities by favouring the participation of those
belonging to the culture concerned were expressed by the light of
these considerations. For to what extent can an individual claim
fully to represent his culture? When teachers say that they want
to obtain information on cultures of origin from foreign children,
we can only tremble at the thought. From what point will training
be determined not in terms of its content but of initiation into
a method of research?

"Owing to this difference in cultural participation, it is
wrong to consider a culture as the common denominator of the
activities, ideas and attitudes of the members forming a society.
Such common denominators may be established for individuals who
have a particular common status"(4). The very notion of culture
should be considered in relation to the existence of the sub-
groups which secrete sub-cultures within an overall society.

Intercultural activities are very often confined to an
isolated representation of the "other" culture. Although numerous
inter-connections exist or have existed, they are not considered.
And yet they could very easily act as a starting point and provide
the basis of questions. For no culture is automatically free from
all past or present influences. No matter what the discipline
may be (mathematics, history, architecture, etc.), it should not
be possible to fail to make a reference to the intercultural at
some point. Let us quote as an example the influence of Arab art
on Roman art, the foreign origin of certain names of towns, the
roots of words, and scientific discoveries. It is remarkable to
what an extent our teaching has been, and often still is, marked
by a prodigious blindness. Calling a halt to ethnocentrism - and
particularly Eurocentrism - means agreeing to consider our knowledge relatively and place it in an intercultural context.

---

(1) R. Linton: Le fondement culturel de la personnalité (p. 37)
    Paris, Dunod, 1967.
(2) R. Linton: The Study of Man, quoted by J.C. Filloux in the
    preface to the book by R. Linton (op. cit.).
(3) Ibid.
(4) Ibid.

I do not claim to have covered the entire problem with these few observations; my only aim is to demonstrate the necessity for situating our educational activities in a wider context than the purely pedagogical one. In the intercultural field, taking a stand on the conceptual plan has repercussions on the choice of teaching methods. No educational strategy is completely disinterested; the conscious or subconscious choice of a philosophy underlies every action.

PSYCHOLOGICAL PREREQUISITES AND SOCIAL DIMENSION

By the same token as any other discipline (French, mathematics, the disciplines known as "éveil"(1) such as history or natural science), intercultural activities should be based on the psychology of the child and take account of the characteristics of child mentality (egocentrism, syncretism, animism, realism and artificialism). It is desirable that studies should be undertaken with the aim of working out, not so much a programme as useful concepts, whether specific to the intercultural field or not. Thus, notions like the structuration of time and space - notions which are more particularly constructed in the context of the "activités d'éveil" - also constitute the basis of intercultural studies.

Another direction of research can be followed on the basis of the parallelism between the importance of the "me-and-the-other" couple in the development of emotional life (cf. H. Wallon) and the part played by the Other in the development of the cultural identity.

A perfect mastery of the scientific mechanisms governing interethnic and intercultural relations in the child and the adolescent would make it possible to devise a practical system of pedagogics conforming to the child's development and adequate to the values, codes and successive systems of reference which condition its socialization. Studies conducted hitherto are scattered, partial and have been carried out by teams of researchers all belonging to the same culture. The validity of intercultural studies will only be ensured from the time when they are pursued by multi-disciplinary and multi-cultural teams.

One of the functions of intercultural activities is to prevent racism and promote a better understanding of cultures. Now the very fact that an aversion for the dissimilar does not exist in young children and that the acquired nature of this phenomenon has been demonstrated is a proof of the urgent necessity for undertaking basic research to enable the teacher to suggest activities respecting the child's evolution and modes of relations.

---

(1) "Activités d'éveil" - literally "awakening activities", i.e. those related to awakening the child's interest in the world around him.

By way of an example only, and without claiming to be exhaustive, we give below some of the conclusions of various
research projects which, incidentally, should be exactly
inventoried. The following constitutes a simple list (1).

- The ethnic identification of oneself precedes
  the ethnic recognition of other groups.
- Children of minority groups develop an ethnic
  consciousness much sooner than others.
- From the age of 4 or 5, consciousness of self
  as a racially different person emerges.
- With children who do not belong to a minority
  group, identification takes the form of member-
  ship of a national group.
- It is only at the age of about 10 that the
  stereotypes regarding other peoples appear.
- The ability to identify oneself and identify
  others in terms of race or nationality develops
  in the child well before he is in possession of
  the appropriate abstract categories.
- Lambert and Klineberg noted that there is a
  general tendency for children of 6 to see other
  peoples in terms of difference, whereas at the
  age of 10 the tendency to see other peoples in
  terms of resemblance is at a maximum.
- Stereotyped thought is not due to a resurgence
  of egocentrism but to the influences to which
  the child is subjected during his socialization

The psychological basis of education for the mutual understanding
of cultures should be characterized and determined if intercultura
teaching is to be strict and therefore effective.

In addition to the psychological dimension there is the socio-
historical one, for can the problem of understanding cultures be
solved without reference to their economic, social and historical
contexts? For example, can it be denied that relations between
French children and immigrant children are often of the unequal
type, for many reasons: numerical size of populations, the fact
that the latter belong to socially under-privileged classes, and
that they come from former colonies or protectorates?

Any discourse about the Other, the culture of the Other and
intercultural relations must, therefore, revolve round political,
economic, social and intellectual movements of the epoch. Does the
revival of interest in intercultural activities in schools really
conform to a purely intellectual concern? Being aware of the
environment within which an intellectual movement takes place
does not in the least destroy the value of that movement: on the

---

(1) All the following are extracted from the study by M.C. Munoz.
    Le développement des stéréotypes ethniques chez l'enfant.
    Approche psycho-sociologique. Doctorate thesis, Paris EPHE
    1973. 265 pp. (The author has attempted to give a glimpse of
    the state of research, pp. 77 et seq.).

contrary, it gives it its true dimension and prevents it from
being deviated from the purposes originally fixed for it. This
viewing of one's reflection from a distance appears to be
essential in order to avoid a situation where the noblest and
most generous intention at the start is overtaken or even distorted and detoured from its proper path. In order to convince
ourselves that such risks of "ideological deviation" are not
purely hypothetical, it will suffice to refer to a few ideas.

Does not the claim to have a right to differ and the pro-
clamation of a teaching of the difference, quite apart from the
ambiguity inherent in the term itself (difference meaning something less, something more or something foreign?), run the risk
of confirming relations on a basis of inequality? For example,
C. Camilleri has clearly shown (1) that "providing the dominating
group takes its distance (particularly when dominance becomes
domination), it selects differences in the dominated group at the
expense of resemblances, for in this type of relation perception
is guided from the beginning since anything which makes it
possible to be assimilated to those from whom it is wished to
separate is ignored". Selecting the differences may involve the
individual in the dilemma either of perpetrating a social system
based on inequality or of deteriorating the identity of the Other
by enclosing it in a rigid, conformist and fossilized culture.

"OTHERNESS" AND RECIPROCITY

Existing intercultural activities are defined, inter alia, by
their determination to give the culture of origin of foreign
children its rightful value. Quite apart from the paternalistic
connotations of the phrase, this vague expression in fact
corresponds to activities which are still excessively marked by
a certain intellectual wolliness and lack of precision in expressing objectives and in pedagogical strategy. F. Fanon had
noticed the complexity of such an attitude: "Encapsulated culture,
which has vegetated since foreign domination, has been restored
to value, it is claimed. And this sudden restoration to value,
which is verbal and without structure, from the start glosses
over paradoxical attitudes" (2). Intercultural activities are
nearly always organized round the culture of the Other, who thus
becomes a subject of curiosity. The possibility of mutual understanding and reciprocal exchanges is never considered. Although
carried out with a declared intention of creating frankness and
understanding, we might perhaps ask ourselves how our activities
are seen by the Other. Is there not a risk that the talk of
rehabilitating the culture of origin will be resented by the

---

(1) C. Camilleri: "L'image dans la cohabitation de groupes étran-
    gers en relation inégalitaire", Cahiers Internationaux de
    Sociologie, Vol. LIX 1975, pp. 230 to 354.
(2) F. Fanon: Pour une révolution africaine, p. 43.

child, the adolescent and the immigrant as a way of reminding
him of his situation as an exile? Any intercultural approach
should be made in a dialectical movement between ourselves and
the Other. Collaboration with researchers belonging to different ·
cultures would make it possible to objectify the ideological
and theoretical background underlying every activity and explain
it.

Moreover, the way in which intercultural activities take
place raises another problem in cases where it is we who try to
revive in the Other a culture which we consider he has lost. By
inserting ourselves as mediators, are we not making a transfer?
For, as A. Gokalp points out: "The fiction that the original
culture is a paradise lost makes us forget that nearly everybody
is experiencing, at present, cultures which have been profoundly
changed by the aggressiveness of the industrial society. It is
as if we in France preferred to appear to be unaware of the fact
that the unifying ideology of the primary school, industrialization and urbanization have profoundly transformed, and even
destroyed, traditional cultures, with the result that we try to
relive the fantasm of our own original culture, which we have
forgotten, through the immigrants" (1).

For intercultural activities to result in a real dialogue
- and not just a caricature of a dialogue - their theoretical
basis must follow multi-disciplinary paths. In the same way, they
can only ensure true understanding of cultures if they can free
themselves of the affective and moralizing sphere to which they
are so often confined and are based on scientific discoveries
and principles. Education must take over the rational element
which exists in the intercultural. Intercultural exchanges should
no longer be left to the spontaneous efforts and good will of
participants, but should be organized on a sound basis. There is
ample proof of this in the sample survey conducted by Cl. Tapia
(2) among the pupils of a primary school for girls chosen, firstly
on account of its heterogeneous public, and secondly, because of
its location in the most culturally homogeneous area of the district - a zone of influence of the Jewish community hailing from
North Africa". The author protests against "one of the most
generally accepted ideas regarding the improvement of relations
between groups" that "contact is always a good thing. It is said
that people should try to get to know one another and that, once
this aim has been achieved, all their preconceived ideas will
disappear and they will become good neighbours". Cl. Tapia shows
that "physical interpenetration by culturally heterogeneous popula
tions in a restricted geographical area cannot result in mutually
favourable attitudes and opinions among such populations unless
there are regulating institutions and organizations in this milieu
Will the school be prepared to act as the regulator?

----

(1) A. Gokalp: "Le paradis perdu de la culture originelle", in the
    review Autrement, No. 11 (Nov. 1977).
(2) Cl. Tapia: "Contacts interculturels dans un quartier de Paris"
    in Cahiers internationaux de Sociologie, Vol. LIV, 1973,
    pp. 127 to 158.

This conceptual, psychological and sociological approach to the problem of mutual understanding of cultures at school makes it easier to discern the objectives of, and define the pedagogical approach to, intercultural education. The intercultural consists both of an end and a way of learning. As such, it cannot be based on teaching of the methodical type. It is not in the least defined on the basis of pin-point knowledge. It is not a matter, then, either of trying to establish a programme or of drawing up an extra chapter for a scholastic subject. Better mutual understanding of cultures cannot be effected on the basis of improved knowledge and know-how. Intercultural pedagogy must be incorporated into all disciplines, since it is essentially defined as an intellectual approach, an attitude of mind, a behaviour. The role of the school is to enable children to develop and master the art of approaching the Other.

Every phenomenon or subject of study must be perceived in an intercultural context. The intercultural approach must be inserted into education in the same way as the psychological, sociological, historical or mathematical approach. Thus intercultural activities will lose their artificial character. Education is intended for the individual as a whole and not as a sum of behaviours which are sometimes contradictory. In the same way, the aim of the intercultural is the overall training of the child.

The intercultural approach, owing to the learning situations and the investigative method it proposes, provides the child with the opportunity of devising and mastering its own conceptual tools in the image of other subjects. Intercultural activities ensure the development of the spirit of observation, providing that the word observation is understood in its scientific meaning, where observing is not confined to sensitive and qualitative perception but consists of understanding the subject of study (a cultural feature in this case) and inserting it into a system of meanings. The methods of analysis and systems of interpretation which a child learns to construct in order to take into account the structuration of a culture should only be considered as working hypotheses which, as such, can be either confirmed or invalidated. The connection with the training of the scientific mind is obvious in this connection. Moreover, to the extent that approaching culture, whether one's own or otherwise, means being able to decipher this code, the development of the symbolical function of intelligence is favoured. While to be cultivated is to be capable of "establishing relations, analogies and differences, and of structuring and synthesizing the knowledge acquired" (1), any attempt to approach a culture emanates directly from general, basic education.

The importance of an education for the mutual understanding of cultures at moral level is self-evident. The eradication of prejudice, stereotypes, racism and ethnocentrism will be effective only when the intercultural has been rationally taken over by the educational system. Respect for the Other is the result of a systematic apprenticeship like any other form of learning. Knowing

---

(1) J. Stoetzel: La psychologie sociale, op. cit., p. 67.

how to find one's place in a culture, and being capable of understanding the relative values of cultures are aptitudes which,
like other intellectual aptitudes, cannot be based on intuition
alone.
     Intercultural teaching, being a form of intellectual and
moral training, enable the child to get to know itself as a person
and individual. For there is a dialectical movement between self-
perception and perception of the Other. "People are not necessarily
conscious of the relations between their thoughts, their language, their habits and cultural elements" (1). Awakening to these
relations may occur when the individual is in contact with a
foreign culture. But whereas on the one hand the culture of the
Other can act as a mirror for my own culture, I on the other
hand can only perceive the Other if I know myself. Mutual understanding of cultures is therefore the result of a reciprocating
movement: "Recognition of the Other is derived from a look at
oneself" (2) and conversely, "one cannot know one's own culture
if one does not know others"(3).

THE PART PLAYED BY "AWAKENING ACTIVITIES"

On the basis of these facts it is now possible to devise and
suggest a teaching method. The objectives of intercultural pedagogics are not only incorporated into present-day educational
plans but are the pre-condition for their success. The elementary
school in particular provides an exceptional context for such
education. The use of the leisure and cultural activities period,
and the practice of "activités d'éveil" and the inter-disciplinari
which they imply, provide intercultural activities with an adequate, flexible pedagogical structure. Objectives complete and
interpenetrate one another; the working methods are identical.
The school ought to enable the child to bring out the socio-
cultural dimension of the environment. By basing their learning
strategy on the environment, "activités d'éveil" cannot fail to
take into account the cultural field. At the same time, making
other forms of culture accessible to children can only be done
in terms of "éveil". In terms of overriding psychological, sociological and pedagogical considerations, it would appear that
intercultural activities should be based on certain principles,
which we submit for discussion (incidentally, the list is not
exhaustive):

                    - Any approach to another culture should conform
                      to an interest or need of the child. Apprehend-
                      ing a foreign culture means making a movement
                      towards the Other.

----

(1) J. Stoetzel, op. cit., p. 67.
(2) L. Chambard, op. cit.
(3) R. Linton, op. cit., p. 11.

- Perceiving a foreign culture goes hand in hand
  with perceiving one's own culture.
- A culture cannot be understood from oral dis-
  courses delivered by masters. Knowledge of the
  intellectual type is useless, and may even be
  dangerous. At this stage, knowledge can only
  be a supplementary tool which must be integrated into "an approach towards..."
- At elementary school level, children must
  be able to experience intercultural exchanges.
  The organization of an international inter-
  school correspondence network - by Unesco for
  example - would enable teachers to widen
  children's cultural environment especially if
  there are no children belonging to other
  cultures in the class.
- Intercultural activities should be reflexive
  rather than descriptive (importance of active
  methods).
- The aim is not so much to teach a culture as
  to teach children to read cultures - their
  own and those of others.
- Intercultural activities can follow the procedure of "activités d'éveil" - questioning,
  general grasp of the problem, analysis and
  synthesis.
- Intercultural activities should enable pupils
  to construct their own method of approach to
  intercultural problems.
- As far as possible, they ought to be extended
  into their family life, outside school hours.

Since intercultural activities should, in the same way as "activités d'éveil", be based on questions put by the children, the role
of society in general and the school in particular is to put
forward an environment likely to give rise to questions and arouse
interest. Owing to the fact that the activities cannot be considered on the same footing as a single voluntary act, that they
are rooted in a relation with the world and are a response by the
individual to the constraints of the environment, it is essential
that the teacher attaches particular importance to the part
played by impregnation in his teaching - impregnation being understood in the sense, not of conditioning but as a natural means
of stimulating and fostering the awakening of the child. For how
can we hope to encourage intercultural research and make the child
aware of other cultures in an unrelentingly monocultural environment? The classroom and the school can easily integrate cultural
elements (books, disks, everyday objects, works of art, etc.)
belonging to other cultures into their daily surroundings.
Libraries should include works written in foreign languages (translations are not enough). Foreign pupils who write in their own
language should have the production of their culture recognized.
This would be facilitated by a centralized translation service.
    F. Debyser proposes that semiological analysis, as a means

of approaching and penetrating a culture, whether one's own or that of others, should be introduced into education. The analysis of pictures and symbols makes it possible to understand a culture: "It has been said (A. Grosser) that comparing civilizations often leads one to conclude that what seemed to be different was identical and what seemed to be the same was different. The aim of comparative semiology would be to compare cultural signs and connotations. Equivalent signs may have identical significations. Contrastive or differential semiology will ensure an interpretation avoiding the difficulties likely to be caused by cultural analogies and mistranslations. Semiological analysis, being in fact an interpretation applied to the facts of civilization and modern myths, provides us with a methodology of cultural understanding". (1)

While the essential feature of intercultural teaching is a spirit transcending all disciplines, there are fields where the cultural dimension is essential. I have already mentioned "activités d'éveil"; learning a language - whether the mother tongue or a foreign one - also favours this approach, for language and culture are closely interwoven. Whereas the word is a means of clothing my own thought, of recreating and reconsidering the world surrounding me according to my own personality, language "encloses us in a system of speech and of the thought appropriate to it" (2). Each language has its own way of recounting human experience. "They (languages) do not cut out non-linguistic reality in the same way; languages are not the same unvarying blueprint of an unvarying reality, nor are they universal nomenclatures". Thus, a language cannot and never ought to be removed from its cultural background. Speech is defined not only as a structured social behaviour but as a behaviour adapted to the cultural environment. But it appears that the learning of languages often takes place without any explanation or awareness of this cultural dimension. Only when, as a result of progressive education the individual has become aware of the specific nature of the mental organization and of the cutting out of the reality of the world induced in his speech will he be able to understand the Other. Decentralizing faculties should be developed by all possible means. Only the mastery of an oral and written linguistic code is taken into consideration at present, while the communication function is often neglected and the cultural code ignored. Why? And for how long?

It is only by breaking out of the narrow context of education for immigrant children, passing from the experimental stage to generalization and ridding ourselves of empiricism and affectivity that intercultural activities will discover their true dimensions and be integrated into education for the mutual understanding of cultures. This is all the more urgent because the opening of frontiers, the exchanges facilitated by the increase in tourism may, paradoxically enough, become a source of obscurantism if people have not been educated to look, see and put questions instead of speaking in terms of values.

---

(1) F. Debyser: Les amis de Sèvres, op. cit.
(2) J. Guénot: Clefs pour les langues vivantes, Paris, 1964.

BIBLIOGRAPHY

Allalt, Buffard ,Marie: la Fonction miroir, Aix-en-Provence, Laboratoire d'économie et de sociologie du travail, 1974, 211 p.

Banton, N.: Sociologie des relations raciales, Paris, Cujas, 1970, 437 p.

Bastide, R.: Le prochain et le lointain, Paris, Cujas, 1970, 296 p.

De Varine, H.: La culture des Autres, Paris, Seuil, 1976.

Fanon, F.: Pour une révolution africaine, Paris.

Gauquelin, M.: Connaître les Autres, Paris, Denoël, 1970, 256 p.

Guillaumin, C.: L'idéologie raciste - Genèse et langage actuel, Paris, La Haye, Mouton, 1972, 248 p.

Klineberg, O.: Etats de tension et compréhension internationale, Paris, Médicis, 1951.

M'Bareck: L'influence de la civilisation sur la compréhension des images chez les Marocains et les Français. St. Cloud annual course, 1975-76.

Michaud, G.: Identités collectives et relations interculturelles, 1978, 256 p.

Munoz, M.C.: Le développement des stéréotypes ethniques chez l'enfant. Approche psycho-sociologique. Doctorate Thesis, Paris, EPHE, 1973, 265 p.

Nouailhac, A.M.: La peur de l'autre, Paris, Fleurus, 1972, 328 p.

Laing, R.D.: Soi et les autres, Paris, Gallimard, 1971, 241 p.

Sarano: Connaissance de soi, connaissance d'autrui, Ed. du Centurion, 1967, 207 p.

Le Savoir et le Faire.Relations interculturelles et développement. Cahiers de l'Institut universitaire d'études du développement (Geneva) Ed. PUF, 1975.

Reviews

Autrement, No. 11, Nov. 1977. Special number:"Culture immigrée."

Nicole Geunier: "Conte et diversités des cultures", Bref, No. 14, May 1978, p. 5 to 24.

Bulletin international des Sciences Sociales, Vol. III No. 3, 1951.

Y. Bernard: "Espace habité et modèles culturels", Ethnologie française, Vol. 8 No. 1, 1978.

C. Camilleri, "L'image dans la cohabitation de groupes étrangers en relation inégalitaire", Cahiers internationaux de sociologie, Vol. LIX, 1975.

Maucorps et Bassoul, "Conscience de la conscience d'autrui et empathie des relations interpersonnelles, Psychologie française, 1958 (3-4), p. 286-306.

Pedagogie, No. 4, April 1971, p. 295-372, "Affronter la différence".

Pluriel, a review which emphasizes inter-ethnic, racial and cultural relations.

Cl. Tapia: "Contacts inter-culturels dans un quartier de Paris", Cahiers internationaux de sociologie, Vol. LIV, 1973.

Forms and sources of misunderstanding: pedagogical prospects and proposed activities

Lê Thàn Khôi

It can be taken as an established fact that education ought to contribute to international understanding - a principle expressed in the Universal Declaration of Human Rights, Article 26 of which states: "Education (...) shall promote understanding, tolerance and friendship among all nations, racial or religious groups".

A recommendation passed unanimously by the International Conference on Public Education in Geneva in 1968 lays down that

"Education should contribute to making the world and its inhabitants better known to young people and to engendering in their attitudes towards other cultures, other races and other ways of living a spirit of appreciation and mutual respect. Education should bring to light the relations between the environment and the ways and levels of life. While displaying objectively the differences between political, economic and social systems, it should lay emphasis on the values, aspirations and needs common to the life and consciousness of the various peoples.

Education should show that the advance of human knowledge is the result of the contributions from different peoples of the world and that all national cultures have been enriched by contributions from other cultures and continue to be so".

Here, as elsewhere, there is considerable discrepancy between the internationally accepted standard and the facts. In reality, what dominates relations between nations and between individuals belonging to different nations is misunderstanding, indifference or contempt, particularly where different cultures are concerned, and even more so when the colour of the skin is different.

Let us look at some of the different forms of cultural misunderstanding and the reasons for them, before formulating a few proposals.

FORMS OF MISUNDERSTANDING

Throughout the world there are a number of different cultural
areas each characterized by certain common features (language,
religion, cultural tradition, etc.) which both reconcile and di-
vide them: the West, Latin America, Africa south of the Sahara,
the Arab-Muslim world, the Hindu area, the area of Theravada Bud-
dhism (Sri Lanka, Burma, Thailand, The Lao People's Democratic Republic, Democratic Kampuchea) , and the Chinese area (China, Korea,
Japan and Socialist Republic of Viet Nam). To be sure, these areas
are not absolutely homogeneous, and numerous countries combine
various influences, among which political influences are by no
means the least important; but what concerns us here is that,
within each of these areas, there is more mutual understanding
than there is between one area and another, particularly when cultures which are unequally developed from the material point of
view are concerned.

The extreme form of misunderstanding is racism, and the press
of industrialized countries provides daily examples of the attitude of nationals toward immigrant workers and even toward "colour-
ed" students. Even when there is no racism, such countries show
an implicit tendency to esteem their own culture at the expense
of other cultures, to which they are indifferent.

Here are some of the replies given by students of the Third
World to a survey carried out by the intercultural psychological
laboratory (University of Paris V) on their "perception of cultural
identity":

"Here people know nothing about our country, and relations are
much more indifferent (than in my country)... Foreign students are
fairly cut off and there is no opportunity for meeting French
students, although it is only through such contacts that you get
to know the way other people live..."   (Mauritius)
"The French are a little hypocritical and chauvinistic, but nice
all the same".   (Haiti)
"It takes time to make friends with the French".   (Venezuela)
"On the French radio and television there is scarcely ever any talk
of the West Indies - except when a Minister goes there. Nothing is
known about the culture of the West Indies except perhaps its folklore. Real West Indian culture - the arts and literature (we have
a West Indian theatre) never appears in France.   (Martinique)
On the other hand, it is often through contact with others that
cultural identity is perceived:

"Here, you know a Brazilian when you see one, not in Brazil, because there we are all very mixed up and very different. This
awareness takes place here, we feel ourselves foreigners". (Brazil)
"You become aware of your cultural identity when you go abroad
and begin to note the differences. It is by leaving your country
and going elsewhere that you begin to make comparisons and thus
gradually define your identity".   (Venezuela)

A survey carried out by Claude Tapia in a district of Paris
(Belleville) shows that the fact of several populations living side
by side (French nationals, Jews from North Africa, other immigrant
workers) results in very few real contacts between them. While
"the children of the country know little of the culture of a
people with whom they are in contact every day (the Jewish
population), the immigrant children are even less capable of distinguishing the cultural features of another group" (Tapia, 1973).
However, another survey carried out by M. Mauviel on a population
of French parents whose children attend schools where there are
many immigrant children shows that a large proportion of them
(74 per cent) declare themselves to be in favour of joint intercultural activities for French and foreign pupils; only 14 per cent
were hostile to the idea. Contrary to widespread opinion, prejudices and stereotypes co-exist among the same individuals with the
desire to get to know and understand more of the difficulties which
foreigners encounter. It is interesting to note that the parents
most in favour of intercultural activities are themselves of
rural or semi-rural origin. Is this not an indication that, in
spite of differences in nationality or in religion, they share
with the immigrants certain common cultural features, particularly
the experience of communal life and attachment to the wider
family? (Mauviel, 1979).

It is in education that an ignorance of the cultural differences is particularly harmful, since it results in a negation
of the other, even where it is not a question of pure and simple
racism.

In the United States it has been noticed that teachers become
irritated when their Puerto Rican pupils do not look them straight
in the eyes. In fact, the latter are merely showing a sign of respect - it is impolite to look anyone straight in the eyes. This
cultural feature, incidentally, is not specific to Puerto Ricans.
It is also to be found in Asia and Africa, and the same is true
of European teachers who have to deal with pupils coming from
these continents. In the same way, the linguistic behaviour of a
teacher may cause communication to be jammed when he addresses a
"slow" group and an "advanced" group in a different way as may be
the case with blacks and whites; for blacks who have come from the
ghettos, the style used reminds them of the approach adopted by
welfare workers in conducting their investigations, and the
pupils automatically react by refusing to co-operate (Unesco, 1973).

Although childhood is the most impressionable age, the ideas
and pictures contained in school books are a serious infringement
of truth and of respect for human rights when they convey racist
or ethnocentric ideology. A recent issue of the Ûnesco Courier
(March 1979) gave a few examples of this. "The colonial and sla-
very experiences," wrote the American Beryle Banfield, "are presented as beneficial to Third World peoples providing them with
discipline and skills previously unknown to them".
As regards the Maoris of New Zealand, "the destruction of
Maori culture is dismissed, and the use of force to impose an
alien culture is justified as necessary to keep the peace". In
North America, the culture of the Indians of the Eastern forests
is portrayed as inferior to that of the Europeans, although "the

society they developed was in many ways more politically sophisticated than that of the Europeans in terms of the participation
of women in the political decision-making process and the general
level of citizen involvement. The political organization of the
six nations of the Iroquois Confederacy served as the model for
the colonies when they moved to set up a new nation".

Ethnocentrism and racism are not confined to the West. They
are also found in the Third World, or at least certain parts of
it. In the same issue of the Unesco Courier , Hugo Ortega examines
the way in which the history of America is portrayed in certain
works recently published in Argentina. Everything is presented
from the "white" and "Western" point of view. America is "discovered", which means "that the continent, its people and its
wealth only acquired value because they were discovered and recognized by the centre of the world, in other words Europe. It
is hardly surprising, then, that civilization (clothes, big ships,
white men and the faculty for naming places and people) should be
equated with Europe and that barbarism (the Indians and the "new"
world) should be equated with America". The former inhabitants
of the American continent are described in pejorative terms -
half-naked, savage, with a headdress of feathers, irrational
and inferior to the white European. All that constitutes a negation and a sort of cultural genocide.

SOURCES OF MISUNDERSTANDING

What factors explain the lack of understanding of different
cultures, particularly on the part of cultures which consider
themselves as "superior"? There are many of them, and they are
at work from childhood, at the most impressionable age, in the
family, at school, through the mass media and the environment
generally. They are known as ethnocentrism, ideology, nationalism
and racism.

In this context, ideology is taken to mean the system of
ideas and judgements predominating in a society at a given time.
It is generally the product of a class or a group (political,
religious, etc.) which has been imposed on the society as a whole.

Ethnocentrism is the attitude of a group or culture which
tends to grant itself a central position in relation to other
groups and other cultures. It is distinguished from racism, which
presupposes a hierarchy based on skin colour or biological here-
dity.

Nationalism is a special form of ideology which, like ethnocentrism, tends to transcend social classes and groups and integrate them into a nation - i.e. a political and economic community
characterized by the consciousness of its unity and a defined
territory.

Of all these factors, ethnocentrism is the oldest and most
universal. The Chinese considered themselves to be the centre of
the world, as witness the name they gave to their country:
Zhōng Gùo (the Central State). They called all foreigners

"barbarians", as did later the Greeks and the Romans. Mediaeval
Christianity for a long time discussed the question of whether
Africans and Amerindians had souls, and looked on Marco Polo's
Book of Wonders as a fable. In the contemporary period, colonial
conquests and the fact that Western civilization has been imposed
on the entire world have nourished the ethnocentrism of the West
(and also its racism, which was unknown among previous peoples).

In this connection, it is important to draw attention to the
responsibility of the university. Although it was supposed to be
the seat of impartial research and of the dissemination of objective knowledge, it occurs all too frequently that many research
workers do not respect the rules of scientific method. Ideology
and ethnocentrism manifest themselves not only in the interpretation of phenomena, but from the beginning of research in the
formulation of hypotheses and the collection of data. Here are a
few examples.

Generally speaking, all research is governed by the guiding
principle of hypothesis - i.e., in the true sense of the word, a
presumed relation between two or more facts. But if a hypothesis
is to be worthy of its name, it should not be a false hypothesis
- i.e. a proposition which is adopted initially as an explanatory
principle and which the methodological apparatus is used to
verify, with the result that we find ourselves at the end with
what we had at the beginning.

Thus it is that psychologists have claimed to demonstrate
the "underdevelopment" of certain peoples by means of tests intended to estimate their capacity for abstract thought, chosen
on the basis of a hazardous initial postulate and devised in an
insufficiently diversified way, in order finally to arrive at
perfectly arbitrary conclusions.

Facts are never "raw" facts. They are built up. Their perception by the individual depends on social and cultural factors.
There is no reality or object of knowledge independent of the
subject and even of the technique used. Thus, the optical
illusions of the blacks in relation to the whites are due to differences in visual environment, i.e. ecology. Simple geometrical
shapes such as the square do not exist in certain environments
where familiar objects are cylindrical, conic or hemispherical
(huts, roofs, calabashes, pots, etc.). The majority of Ivory Coast
languages only distinguish between and use three colours - black,
white and red - which may explain the greater success with
Bonnardel's cubes (which only use these three colours) than with
Kohs' cubes. Hudson showed his South African children a picture
in which a man was aiming with his lance at an antelope with an
elephant between them in the background (and therefore smaller
than the antelope). Most of them said that the man was aiming at
the elephant which is nearer to him on the picture and Hudson
concluded that they had no perception of depth. Omari and
MacGinitie consider that this interpretation is distorted by the
graphic material used: in the first place, these were animals
with which the children were relatively unfamiliar; next, the
motivations which they imagined (since the elephant is dangerous
for man) led them to deduce that it was the target. The two
writers therefore devised a revised version of the test in which

the elephant is replaced by a cow and the man is not attempting
to kill. The results confirmed their hypothesis, since significant
differences appeared between the performances of two groups chosen
at random who had been shown the two series of pictures. In addition, in contradistinction to the information provided by Hudson,
results improved considerably with age (Omari, 1976).

An interpretation of a phenomenon should not isolate it
from its context, but put it into relation with society as a whole.
In this way, ethnocentrism will be avoided. We must try to understand a society on the basis of its own standards of reference
rather than pass inconsidered judgements on the basis of the
standards of the observer.

Let us take a well-known example of intercultural psychology:
among African children more rapid psychomotor development has
been noted than among European children until the age of about 18
to 20 months, followed by a sudden slowing down at the time of
weaning. How should these differences in development be interpreted? They are not due to racial but to cultural factors. The
mother benefits throughout her pregnancy from food which is
richer in protids and lipids, she feeds her baby herself at any
moment day and night when the child needs it, and when it is
frightened, it lives continually with her, carried in her arms,
astride her back or stretched out on the same mat; thus, not only
does the child not perceive any feeling of refusal but its tensions are reduced. Weaning, which is often sudden, interrupts
this harmonious universe. For an ethnocentric writer this phenomenon would constitute "the first stage in the direction of submission and fatalist resignation to all forms of constraint imposed by clan life" (Knapen). In African eyes, on the other hand,
it is a matter of a central function of socialization: frustration
makes the child aware of its dependence and obligations not to a
person (its mother, as in the case of the European child), but to
what she represents, i.e. the safety-making world of the group,
which causes it to interiorize its educational standards.

In all these examples we can see two manifestations - ethnocentrism, the projection of patterns, and its corollary, the
transfer of concepts. The observer, whether consciously or not,
formulates his problems and interprets an external reality by
basing himself on the system of values and the concepts which
his group has worked out in accordance with its own historical
experience.

In certain cases, ideology and ethnocentrism combine in the
use of concepts, such as that of "democracy" in the comparative
research by Almond and Verba on "civic culture" in five countries:
United States, Great Britain, Western Germany, Italy and Mexico.
The survey claims to be empirical. The authors try to find out
what elements of a civic culture provide the best guarantee of
democratic stability. But these elements and the questions asked in
order to assess them in each country are defined in relation to the
functioning of Anglo-American democracy: level of education and information, interest in politics and involvement with a party, subjective political competence, political co-operation and appreciation of a system. In view of the basic definitions, the result
is a foregone conclusion: the United States and Great Britain

have the best "civic culture" and "balanced democratic outlook".
This is an example of the "repressive" use of certain concepts
which are bound up with a certain conception of the world and are
used for imposing it.

Are there any universal concepts? At first sight all those
related to the fundamental activities and impulses of mankind
throughout space and time fall into this category - production,
feeding, procreation, etc. Education too, since it is inherent to
the life of any society which ensures its perpetuity through the
transmission of knowledge and values. In the same way, culture,
understood as the "system of ways of feeling, thinking and
behaving of a social group" may be considered as a universal concept. But it loses this character if we take it in the generally
accepted meaning of "system of intellectual aspects of a civilization", since this meaning imparts a greater value to written
civilizations than to oral cultures. A similar ambiguity is
inherent in the term "civilization": it has an ethnocentric and
evolutionist connotation when applied to "more developed" societies (from a moral, intellectual, artistic or technical point of
view), a connotation which it does not have if we use the term
culture in the same anthropological meaning as "the sum of the
achievements of a society".

In a branch of science such as ethnology which, by definition,
should be the scientific study of different societies, the approach
of ethnocentrism to science has been very slow: for a long time,
the anthropologist observed such societies with reference to the
standards of his own rather than in himself as cultural units
with their own significance. As Poirier wrote, two stages were
necessary for this scientific process: man recognizes the other
as a man, as somebody different, but belonging to mankind; the
other is recognized as a fellow creature. Evidence of this movement is provided by the transition from "civilization" in the
singular to "civilizations" in the plural, the recognition of the
plurality of cultures and the validity of all systems of value
(Poirier, 1974, cf. Bibliography).

A FEW PROPOSALS

How should education be conducted in order to ensure mutual
understanding of cultures? In my opinion, the main effort should
be concentrated on tenderest childhood, since this is the time
when lessons leave their deepest mark, when ways of thinking and
perceptive habits in relation to the surrounding nature and culture are learned and when the attitudes acquired are most firmly
installed. Attention should, however, also be paid to adults,
particularly in countries where different cultural, national and/
or immigrant groups co-exist.

Among the most important elements of this education, mention should be made of:

1. the training of teachers and adult educators;
2. learning foreign languages;
3. the revision of curricula and textbooks.

Before examining these elements, it would be well to speak of
the system of associated schools. The purpose of this system,
which was launched by Unesco in 1963, was to encourage certain
schools to organize special programmes in favour of international
understanding on the basis of the study of other peoples and other
cultures. It now includes about a thousand schools throughout
the world and has achieved interesting results: better adaptation
of school curricula to the objectives of international understanding (study of major world economic, social, environmental
and development problems; in dealing with the rights of man instead of sticking to abstract principles contemporary situations
bringing them into play are considered; integration of this
teaching into ordinary subjects of the curricula); production of
new teaching material; active methods implying full participation
of pupils in the choice of projects and their implementation
(constitution of files and illustrations: posters, pictures, films
transparencies, photos, recordings, etc.),surveys, group reports,
exchange of correspondence and pupils between the schools of different countries, visits by people who were born or have lived in
the country concerned, experts and officials from international
organizations, out-of-school activities with the collaboration
of Unesco and United Nations clubs and of musical and dramatic
associations.

  Education for the mutual understanding of cultures implies
in the first instance, as has already been stated, the training
of teachers and adult educators, particularly of those in charge
of multiracial classes. Since any culture is a system of ways of
thinking, feeling and behaving, it is not only a matter of
becoming initiated into the formal content of a given culture by
means of books or lectures, but also of getting to know and understand the effects in the material world (habitat, cooking), the
institutions (family, religion), the attitudes and the socio-
psychological behaviour patterns. Nor is it a matter of isolating
such and such characteristic of a culture and comparing it with
the corresponding characteristic of one's own culture, but of
seeing how the cultural whole functions, how its various elements
are articulated. Education will no longer evolve principally roun'
the teacher and be uniformly designed for an undifferentiated
public but will attempt to take into account the cultural features of each group and their respective ways of learning. Each
culture esteems and develops individual faculties in different
ways: physical (strength, skill, speed, etc.), intellectual
(oral, written, visual or spatial memory, speed of understanding,
presence of mind, etc.), artistic (dancing, music, singing,
poetry, painting, sculpture, etc.), moral (solidarity or cooperation, calmness or expressiveness, etc.). It is by knowing
the values of each group and the significance it attaches to the
various signs and symbols that the teacher, the educator, can
protect the child and the adult from the pitfalls of their training and himself from the dangers of forced acculturation and the

denial of the other, and both sides from the jamming of communication. But, an intercultural or transcultural education will be in
a position to enrich both partners mutually.

One of the most important factors in this type of education is
the learning of foreign languages. It is generally envisaged from
the point of view of the pupils, and it is certain that for them it
corresponds to the necessities of modern communication, while
at the same time providing an introduction to foreign ways of
life and civilizations. In addition, it constitutes an excellent
form of mental gymnastics, particularly when the structure of
these languages differs from that of the mother tongue, which
has the effect of clarifying a knowledge of the latter. A recent
conference on "Languages and European Co-operation" (Strasbourg,
April 1979) concluded that for both States and individuals, multi-
lingualism is the only realistic course. Today, everything should
be done to ensure that every European has an adequate knowledge
of at least two foreign languages. The effect of according a privileged place to the learning of a first foreign language would
be to reinforce the trend towards the monopoly of English and
place an obstacle in the way of communications with other Europeans.
The conference which was attended by 200 participants from about
thirty countries, rejected a "major" language, whether English,
French or German, and voted for the diversity of languages which
alone was capable of ensuring a respect for differences and a recognition of the Other.

But, for the teacher who has to deal with minority groups,
the study of their language is equally fertile, since a knowledge
of the linguistic structures provides an introduction to the methods of cognition and conceptualization. The situation is not
fundamentally different from that in which the teacher is confronted by children from working-class homes who also suffer from
difficulties in learning, since their culture is not that conveyed
by the school and their linguistic practice is not that of the
middle class which is favoured by the school. It will not be out
of place here to quote Basil Bernstein, since there are profound
analogies between the culture of the "underprivileged" and that
of immigrant workers.

As we know, Bernstein distinguishes between a "restricted
linguistic code", a descriptive and affective language of individual thought, and an "elaborated code", which is the language
of demonstration and logic providing access to universal significances. But he protests against any assimilation of the restricted code to a linguistic handicap. "This system of communication",
he writes, "provides very rich opportunities, has a considerable
metaphorical range and original aesthetic possibilities and can
engender a series of varied significances. The fact remains,
however, that the fields of knowledge and the orders of meaning-
ful relations towards which this system of communication guides
children are not in affinity with those required by the school.
If the learning situations - examples and reading books - do not
seize the imagination of the child or excite its curiosity and
do not encourage an attitude of research into its family and
social environment, the child does not feel at ease in school.

In order that the teacher's culture should become an integral
part of the child's world, it is first essential that the child's
culture should become an integral part of the teacher's world.
In order to achieve this, it may perhaps be better for the teacher
to understand the child's speech rather than make derisory attempts
to change him" (Bernstein, 1975, cf. Bibliography). This thought
also applies to relations between the teacher and the children
of foreign cultures.

One last recommendation with a view to international understanding is related to the revision of the curricula and textbooks. Allow me to reproduce as a conclusion, what I wrote in
l'Industrie de l'enseignement (1967):

"From the point of view of personal training, literary education
should concentrate less on history, criticism and the aesthetics
of genres and schools than on the human significance of the major
works of national and world literature. It is in these that the
adolescent will discover the many aspects of human nature, its
universal characteristics and variations in space and time, and
it is by a constant dialogue with them that he will deepen and
perfect his own personality. This is why thorough analysis
of a few major works is more profitable than a course of literary
history seasoned with a few morsels, no matter how well chosen
those morsels may be. The comparison of national and foreign
texts on similar subjects provides an additional enrichment: the
word "humanism" assumes its full meaning when in addition to
Shakespeare, Molière, Tolstoy, Goethe and Cervantes, the Indian
Jatakas, Lo Pen's Shores of the Lake, the Vietnamese History of
Kiêu or the oral literature of Africa are taught.

"Other approaches will be made to the plastic and musical
arts, the cinema and television, the last being used not as
teaching aids but as teaching subjects. Arts teaching is almost
totally ignored at present, and yet the emotion aroused by a
Georges de la Tour, a Ma Yuan or a Hokusai, a Dogon mask, a Khmer
torso or a statuette from the Mexican Pacific coast has an immediate power of suggestion. Sensitivity has greater difficulty
in adapting itself to various forms of music, but polyphony does
not constitute a universal point of arrival; on the contrary, it
may prove to be unsuitable for expressing the most subtle grada-
tions of human feeling. The approach to the cinema will be easier: "Potemkin", "Modern Times", and "The Tales of the Pale
Moon after the Rain" offer admirable food for thought on the
destiny of man (the Buddhist Karma), industrial civilization and
revolution.

"Literary education will also be articulated with that on
history, geography and the economic, social and political institutions which prepare the individual for insertion into his
environment and then into international society. Geography and
history will have to show the close interdependence of physical
and human phenomena, civilizations and peoples. Geography and
history will supplement one another harmoniously, for one en-
deavours to seize what is permanent in the conditions of man's
adaptation to his environment, in view of technical changes,
whereas the other relates and explains his evolution in terms

of his own creations and the contribution by other cultures.
National history develops a love of country in the child and pre-
pares him for his future duties as a citizen, but it should also
show what his country has received from the world and what it
has given. In most textbooks of all countries, national pride
predominates over historical truth: contacts between States are
reduced to war, the responsibility for which is always imputed
to the other side unless it is justified by some 'civilizing
mission', the 'inferiority'of the other people, or the 'defence
of liberty'. It is not a matter of denying the existence of wars
and international conflicts, but of explaining them as objectively as possible; and it is also a matter of showing the much
greater importance, for the life and development of peoples,
of the cultural transfers which are continually taking place.
If the child is to become aware of the common heritage of mankind, it is as well if history is represented to him in its
entirety as a coherent whole in logical order (i.e. chronological in this context) and not as the juxtaposition of individual "histories", which is the impression he gets from the organization of the curriculum."

BIBLIOGRAPHY

Almond, G. and S. Verba, The Civic Culture, Boston, 1965.

Banfield, B., "Où commence le racisme", the Unesco Courrier, March 1979.

Bernstein, B., Langage et classes sociales, Paris, Minuit, 1975.

Dague, P., Bibliographie analytique des recherches effectuées sur la psychologie de l'enfant africain francophone, Paris, Audecam, no date.

Lê Thành Khôi, l'Industrie de l'enseignement, Paris, Minuit, 1967.

Maistriaux, R., la Femme et le destin de l'Afrique. Les sources psychologiques de la mentalité dite "primitive", Brussels, 1964.

Mauviel, M., "Plaidoyer pour une éducation transculturelle", Revue française de pédagogie, Paris, October-December 1979.

Omari, I.M., "Les études transculturelles sur les aptitudes de l'enfant", in Perspectives, Unesco, Vol. VI, No. 3, 1976, pp. 392-403.

Ortega, H., "Les stéréotypes: un miroir déformant", Unesco Courrier, March 1979.

Poirier, J., Histoire de l'ethnologie, Paris, PUF, 1974.

Preiswerk, R. and D. Perret, Ethnocentrisme et histoire: l'Afrique, l'Amérique indienne et l'Asie dans les manuels occidentaux, Paris, Anthropos, 1975.

Tapia, C., "Contacts interculturels dans un quartier de Paris", Cahiers internationaux de sociologie, Vol. 54, 1973.

Unesco, "L'anthropologie et les sciences du langage au service du développement de l'éducation", Etudes et documents d'éducation, No. II, Paris, 1973.

3. *Final report*[1]

Seventeen experts met from 28 to 31 May 1979 at Unesco Headquarters, in Paris, to examine the problem of "Education for the
mutual understanding of cultures" and to make suggestions and
recommendations concerning the formulation of principles and the
undertaking of activities which would promote such education.
    Under this main theme, the agenda also included the "Assess-
ment of the first five years of publication of the journal
Cultures and the formulation, as in the preceding case, of recommendations concerning the future orientation of the journal. Its
recent return to Unesco's cultural studies programme - and consequently to the place where such studies converge - confirms its
intercultural role (2).
    The list of participants included a wide range of members
at both regional and subregional levels (3). Several participants
had already taken part in meetings previously organized by Unesco
to lay the foundations for the intercultural studies project
within which this Committee of Experts was convened: the preliminary meeting held in October 1976, in Belgrade, and the meeting
of the working group convened jointly by the ICPHS and Unesco in
Paris in March 1978, the proceedings of which were summarized
during the discussion by Mr. Alphonse Dupront, Honorary President
of the Sorbonne, who had chaired the working group of 1978.
    The Bureau elected by the participants was composed of:
Chairman: Mr. Camille Aboussouan, Ambassador, Permanent Delegate
of Lebanon to Unesco; Vice-Chairmen: Mrs. Carmen Guerrero-Nakpil
(Philippines), Mr. Vadime Elisseeff (France), Mr. Guy Kouassigan
(Togo); Rapporteur: Mrs. Pierrette Désy (Canada).
Mr. Camille Aboussouan, Mr. Guy Kouassigan and Mr.
Vadime Elisseeff succesively acted as Chairmen.

---

(1) Report drafted by Mrs. Pierrette Désy (Canada), in cooperation
    with Unesco Secretariat.
(2) The parts of the discussions and conclusions of the original
    report which pertain to the second topic of the agenda, i.e.
    the journal Cultures, have been left aside here.
(3) Cf. List of participants at the end of this volume.

Three documents or sets of guidelines were distributed to the participants:

Document No. I: Guidelines drawn up by the Secretariat with a
                      view to discussion on the theme: "Education
                      for the Mutual Understanding of Cultures -
                      Elements of Information and Conceptual Land-
                      marks" (including the Consultative Meeting's
                      Final Report, March 1978);
Document No. II: Study prepared by Mrs. Abdallah-Pretceille
                      on "Education for the Mutual Understanding
                      of Cultures, in particular at school level";
Document No. III: Study prepared by Professor Lê Thành Khôi on
                      "Education and Origins of Misunderstanding -
                      Perspectives and Practical Proposals".

After an introductory statement made by the Director General's representative, Mr. E. Pouchpa Dass, Director of the Division of Cultural Studies, the three above-mentioned documents were presented by their authors, and Mr. M. Conil Lacoste briefly commented on the guidelines drawn up by the Secretariat.

SYNOPSIS OF DISCUSSIONS

Introducing Document No. I, the Secretariat emphasized the fundamental and extremely concrete character of the topic under discussion, although it covers only part of the area on which research would be required if an in-depth study and a systematic investigation of the phenomenon and the problems of inter-cultural communication were to be undertaken.

   The discussion was directed primarily towards action, since the educational aspect of the question was central to the agenda, but before the discussion began some preliminary observations had to be made concerning the concepts and theories involved in the notion of the "intercultural", and certain key ideas had to be clarified. This initial approach, while drawing attention to such preliminary considerations, especially those concerning intercultural polarizations and deviations, at once produced valuable information about the way in which problems of cultural identity and intercultural communication arise and are experienced in certain regions. Some developing countries, owing to historical circumstances and, in particular, to their submission, over a long period, to a dominant culture, are more or less cut off from the international decision-making centres and are seriously lacking in media and in equipment. So, from the very beginning, a diversity of attitudes was revealed at the meeting, and consequently several points of view were considered.

   The first part of the discussion was focused on the documents submitted to the participants and, more exactly, on the questions raised and the ideas formulated in the Secretariat's document (No. I) and on the analyses of Documents II and III, which were further elucidated by the introductory comments made by their authors, Mrs. Abdallah-Pretceille and Professor Lê Thành Khôi.

The discussion continued on 28 and 29 May, focusing on the two principal aspects of the theme as indicated by the agenda and by the way in which the document presented by the Secretariat was set out: firstly, the psychology of intercultural communication (cf. the section of Document I on "Problematics and deviations of the intercultural relationship" and, secondly, education for intercultural communication (cf. the section entitled "Educational aspects: materials for an apprenticeship in alterity". In fact, most participants spoke on both these aspects.

The observers and members of the Education and Social Sciences Sectors of the Secretariat, whom the Chairman called upon to give an account of their studies and of the experiments and investigations with which they were associated, also spoke on one or other of these aspects.

The participants heard statements made by Mrs. Polymnia Zagefka on the methodology and the initial findings of a sampling survey, conducted by the University of Paris V, on the perception of cultural identity by foreign students and Mr. Elijah P. Lovejoy, Associate Professor of Psychology at the University of California, in Santa Barbara (U.S.A.), the object of whose studies is to identify certain ways of facilitating the integration of students attending a foreign university. Mr. Lovejoy gave a number of examples of intercultural misunderstandings that take place in daily life, which could be avoided by education designed to dispel ignorance and preconceived ideas.

In the course of this discussion the Committee of Experts was also informed about Unesco's Associated Schools Project and about certain activities of the Division of Structures, Content, Methods and Techniques of Education.

Mr. J.C. Langlois, Executive Secretary of the International Fund for the Promotion of Culture, said that the Fund (which was established by Unesco and has a considerable degree of autonomy) finances research for the purpose of evaluating, in intercultural terms, the influence of economic projects on culture and cultural values. Several projects being carried out are specifically intercultural in nature - for instance, the Intercultural Music School in Venice; the Ecole Mudra-Afrique in Dakar; audio-visual performances that show how cultures can enrich each other; or group activities or workshops for artistic creation that bring together creative artists from different cultures.

The principal points of the discussion that ensued are considered under the following headings.

The notion of cultural identity

Many participants emphasized the problem of minorities and the way in which the oppression of minorities by a dominant culture, whether it is imposed from without or is due to cultural pluralism within a nation, distorts intercultural communication. Several participants underlined, in different ways, the diachronic aspect of cultural identity. One of them said that the intercultural problem should be approached "not only in psychological terms and on one level, but also dialectically, particularly in view of the

relations of domination and the real inequalities that cause de-
viant behaviour and alienating cultural processes". Another participant, also stressing the historical dimension and the dynamics
of the meetings of cultures, suggested that the question of cultural identity should be viewed more calmly, since history fur-
nished many examples of almost imperceptible acculturation or
reciprocal borrowing, of which people were not always equally
conscious at different times and in different regions. (Several
examples pertaining to the cultural history of China were mentioned, especially in the field of music.)

Several speakers warned against the exaggerations that could
be produced by an excessively formalistic conception of cultural
identity. In this context, one participant expressed doubt about
what he called the "cultural identity card", saying that all
that remained to be done would be to authenticate it by "cultural
finger prints".

Looking at the question from the sociological standpoint,
one participant drew a distinction between several types of positive and negative cultural transformation. A culture may simply
disappear, others being indifferent; one culture may replace
another in the process of establishing national unity or through
the extinction of regional cultures under the influence of universal public education; a language or a culture may be reborn due
to the impact of tragic events upon it (e.g. the contemporary re-
vitalization of Hebrew and Syrian Aramaic); or a cultural evolution
may take place in an unchanging context, as shown by the fate of
a certain work written by a Lebanese philosopher belonging to the
Syrian Arabic culture, who died in 1933. Twenty years after its
extraordinary success in the English-speaking world, this work,
written in English but characteristically Semitic in its rhythm
and expression, which was long considered unlikely to make any
impression on the French public, attained a degree of popularity
in France which no one could have expected, in view of the literary conceptions and thought processes of the two cultures concerned.

Ethnocentrism and stereotypes

The problem of the positive and negative aspects of ethnocentrism
received particular attention. Here again, it was pointed out
that an excessively downright and radical approach to certain
ideas was undesirable. In the first place, it is not certain that
ethnocentrism and stereotypes are avoidable in our psychological
processes and attitude when we approach "other" cultures. In the
second place, it is perhaps in certain respects true that when they
get furthest away from communal traditions certain groups or individuals suffer from the lack of an already established or a new
centre to give them a sense of "belonging". Several speakers said
that the most authentic form of interculturality comes from consciousness of one's own roots. One speaker pointed out that it is
thanks to certain "centripetal" forces inherent in cultural self-
preservation that some ethnic groups have to this day preserved
their uniqueness in opposition to the centrifugal forces that can
be exerted in a context of technological aggression or political
domination: a phenomenon that can be verified both in the territorial sphere and in that of cosmogony and ideology.

This is not to deny the necessity to emphasize "human similarities" as well as differences; considerable emphasis was placed on this point by one participant, who was an expert on tension and conflicts.

None the less, the most destructive form of ethnocentrism, that which leads to the negation of the "Other", is found in all sorts of disguises and employs a variety of stratagems, as can be seen in both individual and communal behaviour. Even research in the human sciences is by no means free from deviations of this kind; in such research not only the interpretation of facts, but also the formulation of hypotheses and the gathering of data, which are never entirely objective, are too often distorted. The participants placed considerable emphasis on this point.

One participant stressed the need to "relativize" the predominance of "Western" educational structures and methods, which have been generally taken as a model. He considered that self-criticism of European education was indispensable and that non-European educational systems could make a fundamental contribution to the modes of behaviour and thinking of Western people.

In the context of these considerations, other significant questions were raised, for example, as to the existence of universal concepts and the problem of how far back a research worker should go in his analysis in order to be sufficiently free from assumptions inherent in his mental structures (in relation to those of others) for him to have a proper approach to intercultural phenomena.

General principles for an approach to the intercultural problem
One participant suggested that three levels of analysis could be distinguished:

1. Relations between man and nature; it is important to determine which types of conceptual and technological transfer are the least detrimental to the preservation of cultural identity.
2. Relations between human beings (the greatest number of insurmountable obstacles are to be found at this level).
3. Relations with "the universe or the divine (or with the 'transcendental'), in which certain ethnocentric attitudes have played the most important role in relation to the conservation of cultures".
In this connection, another participant pointed out that it is still too often the case that the concept of ethnic groups determines the concept of culture or unconsciously loads its meaning.

Several participants stressed the close relations between political power and cultural problems, urging that all action to promote the "intercultural" should "begin at the top".

Finally, it was emphasized that some regions could not be expected to benefit from intercultural communication unless they got rid of certain inferiority complexes and built up their "self-confidence".

Ways and means of promoting intercultural communication
outside the strictly educational field

Many participants stressed the prime importance of using the media, and made detailed suggestions on the matter, which are reproduced below, in the section entitled "Recommendations".

Policy, structure, educational programmes, and the various steps
to be taken in the field of education in order to promote
intercultural communication

Here again, the substance of the statements was mainly pragmatic (principles of action or specific activities). It is to be found below, in the section entitled "Recommendations".

SUGGESTIONS AND RECOMMENDATIONS

A very large number of proposals and suggestions were formulated by the participants during the discussions. Some, which were of a general nature, were essentially recommendations of principle or were very widely applicable; others were of a much more specific and concrete character. The recommendations of both kinds are reproduced below; they are classified by domain, and are accompanied by suggestions which participants in this meeting considered the most important of those made by the Consultative Meeting held in March 1978. In some cases, two recommendations which were too similar in nature to be formulated separately have been condensed into one. The following list, as it stands, includes many proposals which may be thought unlikely to be put into practice for a long time, or unrealistically ambitious in view of the difficulties met with in this field. The Rapporteur and the Secretariat have recorded these proposals as carefully as the others, so as to cover the whole range and variety of views expressed.

Teaching and educational science

Training of teachers in charge of multi-ethnic classes:
- the teacher should have an adequate knowledge of the culture of the group he is teaching, including practical knowledge (experience of field work for example) as well as information obtainable from books;
- the teacher should motivate pupils (immigrant and non-immigrant school-age children) by stimulating their desire to become acquainted with other cultures (in out-of-school and family relations, as well as in school);
- the teacher should emphasize audio-visual methods (which make a global approach to culture possible) and activity methods;
- more generally, in this field, a policy going beyond the limited framework of contemporary experience in this field should be promoted.

Teaching: languages

- It is desirable that the teacher should know the language of the minority group he is teaching;

- more generally: every effort should be made to promote the teaching of "foreign" languages, which are an excellent way of learning about the ways of life and civilizations of other people;
- every pupil, whatever his age and social level, should be encouraged to learn something, if only the rudiments, of a language belonging to another linguistic family than that of his own language; the very structure of a language gives one an insight into the mental processes of the people who speak it and provides a basis for greater understanding when one is in contact with other people;
- encouragement should be given to the teaching of languages which are discriminated against, so as to promote the principal values of the cultures to which those languages are closely linked.

Teaching: programmes and textbooks

- Literature: priority should be given to the study of great masterpieces; school libraries should be provided not only with translations but also with original texts;
- literature, miscellaneous texts: comparisons of national and foreign texts dealing with similar themes;
- literature, history, geography: textbooks should be revised; teachers and research workers from different cultural backgrounds should co-operate in this task, so that pupils are given a more balanced picture of the contributions made by different peoples to the heritage and progress of mankind;
- history: generally, the objective explanation of conflicts should be promoted, and the writing of less ethnocentric textbooks and works should be encouraged;
- history: in order to reinforce the idea of tolerance, which is of prime importance, teachers should make it a rule, whenever national deeds are mentioned, to refer where possible to events that occurred around the same time in other cultures, even if they only mention the occurrence of such events (e.g.: historical events taking place simultaneously in two different places; or, when a dynasty in a given region is being studied, mention should be made of at least the name of a contemporary sovereign in another region);
- arts: they should have a prominent place in school programmes;
- customs and practices: each National Commission should prepare a short textbook for schools on elementary politeness in each culture.

Tools, methodology and documents for intercultural education in the broad sense of the term

- An international lexicon of key notions from different cultures (synchronic and diachronic) should be prepared;
- good translations (great authors' works translated by good writers) in all cultural areas should be encouraged;
- anecdotes about inter-ethnic behaviour and the reactions of people who move from one area to another should be collected, and analytic interpretations of them should be provided;
- an intercultural documentation centre should be set up at Unesco;
- an intercultural library should be established at Unesco.

Specific studies and research
- An inventory of stereotypes (descriptive and analytic) should
be made, on the basis of clearly defined geocultural areas and
progressing from one to another in order to avoid the pitfalls
of abstraction;
- at the same time, research on the historical evolution of
certain stereotypes should be undertaken by persons belonging to
the original culture;
- a comparative and differential synchronic study of stereotypes
and ethnocentrism should be made;
- research on the phenomenon of ethnocentrism itself and its consequences in inter-ethnic relations should be carried out; it
should cover the positive and negative aspects of ethnocentrism;
- cultural relations and the problem of identity in a multinational
European village should be studied;
- the relation between "orality" (in the sense of the "oral tradition") and writing in children living in countries where oral
traditions predominate should be studied;
- the degree of possible integration of foreign students should
be studied; for example, research should be undertaken on the
cultural identity of students in socialist countries who come
from developing countries (this study should be extended to cover
different regions);
- emphasis should be given to the principle that a team of research workers with different ethnic origins or from different
cultures should study a given culture.

Exchanges
- An international inter-school correspondence network (under the
auspices of Unesco);
- intensification of international exchanges of school pupils,
university students and lecturers;
- scholarships and travel grants for students under 18 years of
age;
- extension of the Unesco Associated Schools Project;
- travelling exhibitions (on regional and ethnographic themes);
film exchanges;
- encouragement of cultural festivals.

Media
- Major newspapers and the audio-visual media should set aside
space for material on different regions;
- journalists should be encouraged to take more interest in
intercultural themes and subjects;
- every opportunity should be taken to redress the balance of
the media in favour of the developing countries;
- cultural exchanges through the media: the mechanisms of the
economic structures of communication should be examined, in
order to find out why genuine cultural exchanges are not fairly
treated by the mass media;
- the "features services" of press agencies and newspapers
should be used to promote intercultural ideas;
- pool of programmes: a recommendation should be made to the
effect that Member States should set aside 2 to 3 per cent of the

space in the press and in audio-visual transmissions for intercultural programmes, which they could select from a central pool
established at Unesco. This might be effected by formal commit-
ments deriving from acceptance of a charter;
- specific action for children: films, radio and television programmes, "picture books" that will make young people aware of
intercultural questions.

General recommendations
- Cultural pluralism: consciousness of individual bi-culturalism
in certain societies and more generally of cultural pluralism
should be encouraged, provided that this is possible in the historical, political and social conditions;
- knowledge of the different cultures within the national community and mutual appreciation between them should be encouraged,
the socio-economic, political and religious context being always
taken into consideration in all intercultural studies;
- a balance between the promotion of cultural identity and the
maintenance of national unity should be sought;
- activities that could give certain oppressed peoples the self-
confidence which could stand up against external influences
should be identified;
- the problems of the transfer or adaptation of technology should
be studied in intercultural terms; this intercultural dimension
should be introduced at the stage when economic and social development programmes and projects are being planned and prepared;
planning agencies, banks and development funds (at national,
regional and international levels) should be encouraged to include this cultural "component" in the initial pre-investment
phase of such projects. Since all cultures should be able to develop their own technology, assistance should be given to the
adoption of solutions worked out in the cultural milieux of
countries that receive technical and financial assistance.

IV. Regions and disciplines

Final report

(Extracts)

The fourth meeting took on a specific character, inasmuch as it brought together the opinions and suggestions put forward at the first three meetings and hence was primarily devoted to discussing ways and means of producing an inventory of inter-cultural research throughout the world. This is a long-range project aimed at guiding Unesco's programme of intercultural studies in terms of the world atlas of completed or on-going research that it should be possible to compile. It is likewise a project that will really start moving only when results are obtained from several pilot experiments designed to test the possibilities for implementing the project.

The technical and methodological arrangements which the Co-ordinating Group adopted in connection with this inventory – it is still at the preliminary study stage – and which are reproduced, in particular, in the last part of the Final Report, would have broken the flow of ideas forming the thread of this publication. We have therefore deleted them, together with a number of scattered references of rather administrative or pro-cedural nature, and we have, above all, retained the conceptual contribution made by the more general discussions coming outside the main scope of the agenda which the debate on the inventory was bound to spark off.

INTRODUCTION

The study group convened in March 1978 by Unesco and the
International Council for Philosophy and Humanistic Studies
(ICPHS) to determine the initial guidelines of the programme of.
intercultural studies to be implemented by the Division of
Cultural Studies recommended that an organization for
"coordinating, harmonizing and assessing" such studies should be
set up. By virtue of this recommendation, an inter-regional
group of seven specialists invited in a personal capacity met on
17th and 18th September at Unesco Headquarters in Paris under
the chairmanship of Professor A. Dupront, Président d'honneur
of the Sorbonne. (1) Unesco was represented by Messrs.
Makaminan Makagiansar, Assistant Director-General for Culture
and Communication, Emmanuel Pouchpa-Dass, Director of the
Division of Cultural Studies, and Michel Conil Lacoste, in
charge of the intercultural studies programme within the Division.
     In his opening address, Mr. M. Makagiansar emphasized the
validity of intercultural concerns. Both individually and
collectively, fundamental importance was being attached, in the
increasingly rapid movement of the contemporary world, to a vigorous promotion of open-mindedness to different cultures,
particularly those of the least developed countries, which are
sometimes related in a little known or unsuspected way to those
who may be closer to us, especially by linguistic bonds. The
Assistant Director-General, who had returned from a mission to
Pacific Islands, mentioned certain examples of the cultural
links between Africa and that area of the world, and certain
etymological similarities between the languages of Indonesia and
Polynesia.

---

(1) See the list of participants at the end of this volume.

INTRODUCTORY STATEMENT BY THE CHAIRMAN

The Chairman began by emphasizing the stake involved in the project, which corresponded to "the capital importance of a cultural
encounter at world-wide scale". By harmonious or discordant
means, sometimes as a result of wars, oppression and crimes,
"we had entered into the era of a luxuriant diversity of cultures".
The constitution and recognition of universal data should contribute to the essential establishment of a common language - a new
road by which communication is rooted in community feeling. This
was a vast task, for which learned study, though obviously
essential for an understanding of the problems, but always with
a delayed effect, would not alone suffice: analysis would have to
be accompanied by action, as had been recommended by all previous
meetings. Promotional activities should accompany research both
in the office and in the field.
     The Chairman particularly stressed on a number of essential
principles for the proper guidance of the implementation of the
project, particularly:

> - the necessity for attaching the greatest
>   importance to the historical dimension and
>   constantly allying the synchronic with the
>   diachronic;
> - the importance of never deviating - which is
>   sometimes difficult - from the specific nature
>   of the "intercultural", if we were to avoid
>   transcending an area of research which was
>   already vast.

As regarded the second point, it would be necessary for
implementing the research inventory, which was one of the essential items on the Agenda, to accept the rules governing this
distinction between what was concerned with the intercultural
proper and what was connected with the study of cultures in
general. There were at least two of these rules:

> - the "intercultural" implied that two or three
>   cultures at least were present in the phenomenon
>   or field under consideration;
> - in an analysis of the successive strata of
>   culture, all aspects of the intercultural
>   should be considered.

In short, nothing but the intercultural (so as not to run
the risk of being submerged by the quantity of material), but all
the intercultural - exclusively and exhaustively.
     The task of the Group would be to direct, coordinate and
assess the research and activities undertaken:

1. Regarding the direction of the project, the Chairman
recalled the achievements of the Study Group of March 1978
and the Committee of Experts of May 1979, both of which, as regards the purely cognitive aspect of the project and its educational dimension respectively, had outlined prospects and
suggested subjects for study and activities;
2. Coordination was obviously necessary in order to avoid
overlapping any research. But only what was known could be coordinated: hence the necessity for an inventory;
3. The assessment of an activity was particularly difficult in
the cultural field, but it would be attempted as far as possible
(though without necessarily going so far as to allot a percentage
of the budget to it, as had been proposed by a participant in
the 1979 Committee of Experts.

STATEMENTS BY THOSE RESPONSIBLE FOR THE PROJECT

The Director of the Division of Cultural Studies put forward a
number of observations regarding the way in which cultures meet.
He said that every culture sought to communicate and that
its formalization went hand in hand with its expansion and
required it. But the development of the media accentuated the
difficulties and ambiguities of communication by rendering the
cultural information put into circulation indifferent, so much so
that the older a culture became, the more it became foreign to
itself.

The Director of the Cultural Studies Division further stated
that culture only existed by virtue of its assertion, its
evolution, its openmindedness, and the interplay of universality
and singularity. The homogeneity towards which its discourse
strives is constantly encountering the stumbling block of the
special forms and experiences and the contradictory traditions
which make it up.

As far as the difficulties of communication of a culture
under the hegemony or prevalence of another were concerned, it
was generally admitted that between the two extreme cases of pure
and simple rejection of any foreign culture and disappearance
of a culture under the hegemony of another, in the majority of
cases cultural communication operated in the form of a
combinative.

The project officer in charge of the intercultural studies
then gave a more detailed history of the project and defined its
place in the Unesco programme.

It was a little more than three years ago that it had been
started in answer to the repeated wishes of Member States. The
activities pursued by the Cultural Studies Division, traditionally
organized according to geocultural areas, gave priority to the
chief regional and national cultures (African, Latin American,
etc.) or cultures and civilizations which were specific although
more widely distributed from a geographical point of view (studies
of Arab culture, Slav project, etc.).

To these cultures, which were considered, at least as a working hypothesis to be relatively homogeneous (whereas every culture, like every personality, is in fact more or less interwoven with inherited or acquired acculturations), was to be added a transverse axis to take account of the phenomena of meeting and interaction of cultures in the world of today.

From 1976 to 1979, three succesive meetings marked the main preparatory stages of the project:

1. A preliminary meeting of specialists in Belgrade in September 1976 prepared the ground. In particular, three "areas of research" or "subject zones" were defined: 1) methodology and epistemology of the intercultural (diversity of methods of recognition and representation; psycho-sociology of intercultural communication and approach through the "other" culture; individual and collective pluri-culturalism, ethnocentrism and stereotypes, etc.); 2) subjects dealing with comparisons between cultures on specific themes; 3) subjects requiring a territorial approach and dealing with regions particularly rich in cultural mixtures. With regard to the last named, it was a matter more of investigating and developing rather than innovating, since the Division had already begun some research on regions with a high degree of multi-ethnic density (Indian Ocean, Caribbean, etc.) which to some extent constituted its first inroads into the "intercultural".

2. The Study Group convened jointly by Unesco and the ICPHS at Unesco Headquarters in March 1978 had resulted in a very free discussion between more than twenty specialists from a variety of disciplines on the main aspects of encounters between cultures. The Group laid down the major guidelines for the project, drew up a rational list of research subjects and, in accordance with the provisions of the programme and budget adopted by the General Conference, recommended setting up the coordinating group now meeting for the first time.

3. Lastly, the Committee of Experts which met in May 1979, again at Unesco Headquarters, to discuss the subject of "Education for the Mutual Understanding of Cultures" emphasized the educational and promotional aspects of the project. This meeting, which was more pragmatical in character than the preceding ones, paid more attention to measures to be taken and methods to be suggested for improving cultural communication and inter-ethnic understanding in schools, universities and among the public in general, than to the direction of theoretical research. Unesco activities, even the most intellectual of them, never pursued purely clarifying objectives; in the long run their chief aim was to "change things", however modestly.

The very titles of the working documents of these three meetings, several of which were mentioned by the speaker, were a sufficient indication of the way in which a methodology had been roughed out and future prospects adjusted as the discussions progressed. These documents, as well as the final reports of the three meetings, would be the subject of a publication which was being prepared.

The speaker then pointed out how the subject was related to the objective of cultural identity which was henceforth governing all Unesco's cultural activity. In cultural studies, this objective was considered in two ways - the "awakening" of the individual, group, nation or region to its own culture (to which correspond most of the regional and national studies by geo-cultural area) and individual or collective "respect and appreciation" of the culture of others (to which corresponds that "apprenticeship of otherness" which is the aim of the intercultural studies project).

"Intercultural" will shape the future; no matter how hasty such a statement may appear at first sight, everything in the evolution of society proved it to be right. In fields as diverse as diplomacy, technical cooperation, business life and advertising, schemes to train minds along intercultural lines have been adopted almost everywhere, since certain shortcomings have shown what it costs to neglect this factor in a world where the compatibility of cultures had to correspond to the intensification of communications. Those who remained deaf to the ethical duty of pursuing a constructive dialogue among civilizations at all levels were thus reminded of the obligations imposed by world cohabitation in their daily life. The motivation of the project, therefore, was no longer merely ethical, it was also practical. The two aspects of cultural identity already mentioned, therefore, correspond to problems of the most concrete nature: while the planners themselves already recognized the fact that the people were becoming aware of their specific cultural character as a powerful catalyst for development, it was equally true that a knowledge and appreciation of the culture of others had become the key to many undertakings.

The fact remained that, so far as the implementation of the programme was concerned, the problems were proportional to the multiplicity of acceptations and approaches to which a notion as vast as the "intercultural" lent itself: historical or contemporary point of view, theoretical or psychological approach in the field, collective or individual aspects, purely cognitive aim or promotional action, the whole being imbued with interdisciplinary complexity. The officer in charge of the project concluded by pointing out that it was up to the coordinating group today, after three meetings had made a considerable contribution to isolating the objectives, to tackle the question "how?".

SUMMARY OF DISCUSSIONS

A. On the question of the inventory of intercultural research in the world

The Chairman dealt with problems related to establishing the "inventory" of intercultural research which had been deemed essential by the previous meetings.

Methods: in order to be worthwhile such an inventory should be worldwide. It would depend on the organization of an inter-

national network of informants who, at a later stage, could
become regular correspondents.

Material to be collected: the inventory should include both
diachronic and synchronic studies and research, publications,
current or projected research and accounts of meetings, intercultural experiences and pedagogical activities such as the "Major
Project on Mutual Appreciation of Eastern and Western Cultural
Values" pursued by Unesco from 1957 to 1966.

It would obviously be necessary to lay down clearly the
criteria governing what should be considered as "intercultural".
Certain activities dealing with "Cultural Policies" should not
be neglected. It would be wise to proceed by stages, beginning
with cultural areas where the data had already been collected or
could be easily. Documentation would be centralized at Unesco.
It was clear from the preceding that it would largely transcend
the context of a mere bibliography.

A discussion then took place on the two related subjects of
the inventory and the network of correspondents. One by one,
participants put forward their suggestions (1).

Dr. H.R. Abdulgani proposed as collecting areas, where
correspondents would have to be found, the "melting pot" of the
Caribbean; in Africa: the North-West (Arabs, Berbers and Europeans),
the North-East with Egypt and the Nilotic regions, the Central
Africa of the Ancient Kingdoms and, more generally, Arab, Islamic
and Persian expansion towards the East (Pakistan); in Asia: India
and China, the Sino-Japanese world (not forgetting the United
Nations University with its headquarters at Tokyo), Democratic
Kampuchea, the new Indonesian culture, Malay culture and the Philippines; the Pacific area (Polynesia, etc.).

Dr. Abdulgani put forward three principles: openminded
receptivity, flexibility and selectivity; he recommended that
various cultural strata should be taken into account and that
peaceful penetration should be taken into consideration.

Mr. E. Condurachi said that, while taking care not to succumb
to the "chauvinism of the historian", he considered that South-
Eastern Europe was perhaps one of the most appropriate areas for
starting the inventory. If the intercultural was a future rooted
in the past, South-Eastern Europe, which had "remained somewhat
backward" from certain points of view but retained certain traces
of acculturation so vividly, lent itself to a regional cultural
analysis.

----

(1) In fact, the majority of them expressed their views at this
stage, not only on the item under consideration but on their
general conception of the project. Since these background observations were often indissociable from their remarks relating
strictly to the question (inventory and network), and also
contributed to colouring the remainder of the discussion, the
editor of this report considered preferable, in the interests
of clarity, to leave them in place instead of grouping them
under another heading. Certain points of several of these
speeches were clarified or supplemented as a result of subsequent contacts with the speakers.

Certain recent activities or others planned for the near future with or without the International Association of South East European Studies (AIESEE) and covering the implantation of Western higher education and comparative literature and law in the countries under consideration, were along these lines. However, academic research of this kind eluded the middle classes; it should be made available to the cultivated general public, for example by extending the comparative method used in museums. The international journal *Cultures* could also constitute a worthwhile instrument.

In conclusion the AIESEE and its specialized committee (particularly that on the history of art and that on the history of ideas) were available to create or facilitate an interdisciplinary network of correspondents in that region.

Mr. Djibril Diallo emphasized the linguistic contribution of Africa to the culture of part of the New World. The International African Institute, to which he was attached, was at present working on survivals of African vocabulary in the Caribbean and Spanish and Portuguese America.

Mr. R. Di Piero began by tackling the problem of cultural dependence. In the case of Latin America, this phenomenon was related initially to conquest, but also to the European relay through which the recognition of Latin American literature, for example, had to pass. Cultural dependence was to a large extent related to the control of the mass media which, instead of assisting the intercultural dialogue too often operated as instruments of domination as was shown by the discussions of certain conferences organized by Unesco - particularly those of Costa Rica (1976) and Kuala-Lumpur (1979) on communication policy.

It was necessary to transcend the point of view of culture in the limited sense and consider the intercultural problem from the points of view of culture in the widest sense of the term and of the popular masses and the media. The Río carnival was originally the festival where Africans met; now it is regarded rather as a spectacle, in the restricted sense of the term culture, as we regard everything of whose original or underlying meaning we are ignorant.

Mr. Di Piero mentioned the intercultural implications of problems such as mass tourism or the "turnkey factory", a symbol (culled from the reports of previous meetings) for certain radical forms of technological transfer. He drew attention to the different ways of opening up to the culture of "others", depending on whether the psychology of "leisure time" or of "working time" was in question.

Professor W.P. Lehmann pointed to the mixed influence of African art on Picasso, relations between Indian cosmology and the European romantic movement, the spread of Japanese culture in Europe in the nineteenth century, the awakening in the United States of the Native Indians, and Creole acculturations. What happened when one culture encountered another? Professor Lehmann suggested that Unesco should have a series of half a dozen essays written on the methodology of the intercultural encounter at such and such a period.

As far as regional aspects were concerned, it would be

interesting to make a systematic study of the relations between Europe and other parts of the world.

It emerged from the exchange of views which followed that it could even be envisaged to construct acculturation "models" (in the same way that there were physical models and mathematical models), which would make it possible to study the relative "speeds" of acculturation in the various fields under consideration (music, plastic arts, literature, etc.) and the order in which these fields were affected.

Mr. A. Meddeb began by noting that the notion of a cultural identity could become a trap when it favoured an "alibi argument". It was only when Arab cultural identity - which had never ceased to exist - found itself threatened by Western expansion that it asserted itself in order to hide its own deculturation from itself.

Undoubtedly, it was very important to consider studying the mechanism of encounters between two cultures, but in fact the primordial concept is much more that of a "dominating cultural context" than that of a dominating culture. More exactly, what was at stake in cultural interaction was not so much the encounter between two individual cultures as the interaction of various cultural currents or traditions within a dominating cultural context. At each period of history there was a dominating cultural context, and it was for those who found themselves in it that openmindedness to otherness was the most natural. For example, between the eith/thirteenth centuries, Arab culture interiorized itself as the dominating cultural context; and this made possible the emergence in Arab thinking of that recognition of difference which, in certain works led to a quasi-ethnological mental analysis of which Birouni's Book of India provided the best illustration: a remarkable example of that "listening to otherness" which is to be found in noticeable literary testimonies from Goethe's openness to the East to Nerval and Flaubert, to mention only European literature.

On the other hand, as from the beginning of the nineteenth century, on the eve of the colonial night, as soon as the dominating cultural context became a Western one, the Arab countries sought to resist such a context for want of being able to assimilate its codes. And it was the resentment of the dominated which blocked the openness to Western otherness. For how could a dialogue be carried on with a supreme entity? Since in fact borrowings from Western culture became widespread, and since a breach was created between erudite and popular culture to the point of generating an acute sociological schism, the exaltations of Arab specificity could only be developed in a negative way: it did not constitute a sovereign assertion but a response incapable of holding back Western expansion.

It was only recently at the end of the 1960 s that an innovating cultural current emerged in the Arab world and sought to transcent the limits of the crisis of Arab modernity. By agreeing, implicitly or explicitly, to work in the cultural context of the epoch, such creators thought they could enrich the values borrowed by the contribution of a specific tradition and sensitivity.

Mr. J. d'Ormesson pointed out that the subject was a vast one. In a way, the intercultural was the major activity and fundamental task of Unesco. And throughout the decades during which the Secretary General of the ICPHS has been dealing with that Organization, he never seemed to have done anything else, as witness the subjects of many conferences organized by the ICPHS at Palermo, Mexico, etc. Unesco had consistently approached the problem of the diversity of cultures and the unity of culture, which included literature, tourism, communications, etc. and finally constituted the problem of our civilization.

The intercultural had positive but also negative aspects: the necessity for tolerance, regarding which everybody agreed, should not go as far as obliterating the specific and resulting in what Jean Cocteau called "visual and intellectual Esperanto". The field of research was practically unlimited, for the inter-cultural even occurred inside one and the same culture.

It was therefore necessary to introduce a certain amount of order into this lively debate by making a distinction between three major parts: 1) a general methodology of the intercultural, which could be the subject of a major publication to be entrusted to a restricted group of scholars or a single specialist; 2) a programme of concrete works: "Dictionary of Untranslatables"; a series of studies which would supplement what already existed, for trails had already been blazed through this forest; 3) and therefore the drawing up of an inventory of intercultural research which would result in a sort of atlas bringing out the "shaded zones" of which the Chairman had spoken.

The implementation of this programme would necessitate the constitution of a network of correspondents (neither too specialized nor too generalized) in permanent contact with the "power house" of the project at Unesco. It was also necessary to establish an accurate time table making generous allowance for delays.

Jean d'Ormesson also expressed his preference for a broadly interdisciplinary approach within each region, which would perhaps be more advantageous than the method of choosing three regions, for example, within which only one discipline would be tackled.

Commenting on these first speeches and expressing his own views regarding the item on the agenda, the Chairman made certain remarks during the debate, which could be grouped as follows:
- Regarding Mr. Di Piero's remarks, he alluded to the "inferiority complex" which continued to weigh on certain peoples who had remained subject for a long time, as had been stated by a par-ticipant in the May 1979 meeting. As a further dependence, the "turnkey factory" technology was in a way a form of cultural violation - a clash between universalizing technology and the "autochtonies". As for the Río carnival, mentioned by the same participant, it raised the problem of mass tourism with its intercultural implications.
- The problem of modernity, the traumatism it causes and its rejection obviously interfered with intercultural problems and with the research of which the inventory was to be drawn up.
- The writings which, in the various cultures, were dependent

on what Mr. Meddeb had called the "listening to all other-
nesses" would naturally be at the heart of the inventory,
whether the "listener" was the East or the West.
- Regarding the project generally, it was a matter of leaving
"closed research" to enter guided research, which required
exigence as much as modesty.
- Rather than theorize too hastily, it would be better to start
with case studies by "cultural pilot areas" and advance by
stages.
- The network ought not to be closely bound up with institutions;
the main thing was to find appropriate correspondents - "living
witnesses".
- In conducting the inventory, it would be necessary to take
account of two sets of priorities - by regions and by cultural
activity. It would in any case be risky to try and tackle all
disciplines at once. It might at least be possible to consider
using regions, beginning with those where the intercultural
material being inventoried existed in the largest number of disciplines.

From this exchange of views there emerged general agreement
on the principle of drawing up an inventory such as to bring out
what had been and was being achieved - and also the shortcomings -
in intercultural research throughout the world, and on the principle of setting up a network of correspondents, initially for
this purpose. Each participant indicated how he could contribute
to the survey or have contributions made to it in his region
and in such and such a field of research, the institutions which
he directed or with which he was associated. A general debate
then enabled participants to specify their attitudes regarding
the problem of the regions and disciplines to be selected for
starting the inventory and to supplement the information on the
cooperation to be expected from certain institutions.

Professor Lehmann suggested repertorying studies on cultural interactions in linguistics and their mechanism - a
discipline where the impact of external cultural contributions
could be analyzed with accuracy in terms of content, strength,
and receptivity. Jean d'Ormesson put forward aspects of the
Baroque which derive from acculturation.

Regarding the contribution by specialized committees of the
International Association of South-East European Studies proposed by Mr. Condurachi, the history of art, ethnology, the
history of ideas, linguistics and popular legends were mentioned
in priority as pilot disciplines which could be covered by the
inventory in the first stage and could give rise to a first
selective bibliography.

Referring to Brazil as a "continent inside a continent" and
to its very marked multi-ethnic character, Mr. Di Piero mentioned
a number of institutions, which could make a valuable contribution
to the inventory: particularly the Centro Nacional de Referencia
Cultural (Brasilia), which at present centralized rich documentation on intercultural phenomena and whose activities already
constituted one of the major programmes of the IPHAN (Instituto
Patrimonio Historico Artistico Nacional) and the Instituto de
Estudos Interculturales (Rio Catholic University).

Mr. Diallo spoke of the cooperation which could be expected from the International African Institute (London, Ibadan and Paris), whose work dealt with intra-African exchanges and those between Africa and the Caribbean; he emphasized the intercultural nature of Casamance in the field of linguistics from the point of view both of the working languages inherited from colonization (French-speaking Senegal, English-speaking Gambia and Portuguese-speaking Guinea-Bissau) and of the intermixture of African ethnic groups and languages. He suggested selecting Casamance as one of the pilot areas of the inventory.

Mr. R. Abdulgani mentioned the highly complex problems and linguistic phenomena connected with Indonesia and the South-East Asia and the coordinating part which could be played by certain universities and such regional institutions.

Mr. Condurachi spoke of the linguistic diaspora, of the diffusion of Venetian Italian in the Mediterranean and the Levant, of the part played by translation as a relay for the Balkanic distribution of certain classics of Western Europe.

During the debate the Director of the Division of Inter-cultural Studies intervened in order to outline the activities which Unesco was pursuing in the intercultural field at region level with the cooperation of a number of regional and national institutions (the names of which would be included in the list of organizations able to further the project). In the cultural studies division these activities were conducted in the various geo-cultural sections where they constituted the concrete application to regional cases of general studies on encounters between cultures pursued in the Intercultural Studies Section. Such is the case for example of the meetings organized recently in Mauritius, Colombo and Perth on the subject of cultural currents throughout the Indian Ocean. All these projects had already taken the form of studies which ought to be included in the inventory.

He added that the implementation of these regional inter-cultural programmes would in the future be based on the methodological directives of the coordinating group, whose recom-mendations would thus have a multiplier effect since they would also contribute to the guidance of all such undertakings. The latter, in the eyes of the Unesco authorities, had not only a scientific but a practical effect, since the definition of teaching methods and of the "universal values" in line with Unesco objectives concerned with international understanding could be derived from them.

The speaker mentioned a few of the institutions which would have a part to play for the three pilot areas which could be selected for the inventory: for example, for the Pacific Islands, the Institute of Papua New Guinea Studies (Baruka), the Institute of Pacific Studies (University of the South Pacific, Suva, Fiji) and the Pacific Islands Research Institute (Honolulu, Hawaii) and of course, for South-East Europe, the International Association of South-East European Studies, which had for a long time been in relations with Unesco through Mr. Condurachi.

B. On Priorities to be established among Research Subjects
The Chairman referred participants to the various lists of
research subjects suggested during the three meetings already
held in connection with the project, particularly those contained
in the final report of the March 1978 study group. He then announced, heading by heading, the projects contained in this list,
and asked participants to say which they were prepared to select
as priorities. The chief comments to which each of these subjects
gave rise are indicated below.

1. Instruments for an intercultural research programme
- cultural atlases (recommendation by the Belgrade meeting).
These should be both synchronic and diachronic. Certain attempts
have been made already in this field (Yugoslavia and Malasia);
- intercultural lexicon of key notions;
- vocabulary of opposition to and non-recognition of the other.
    These two subjects were taken together. The Chairman explained
that 75 per cent of these key notions were of Western origin; it
would be advantageous to discover how they had been "received" and
incorporated into the various cultures, which meaning was attributed to them by cultural autochthony, the reasons why they did not
exist in certain cultures, what were the autochthonous conceptions
which were more less equivalent to them, etc.
    A discussion began on the question of language and related
to notions of ethnocentrism and alterity. Mr. Di Piero spoke of
the "vocabulary barrier" and of the necessity for analyzing it.
    Professor Lehmann pointed out that many populations ex-
perienced the world through a language which was not their own.
Recalling that certain languages did not necessarily require a
subject or that the subject was of less importance in them, he
concluded that those who spoke them could not have the same conceptions as Europeans; this was the sense in which Nietzsche wrote
that philosophies are determined by languages.Certain notions
of a language had no equivalent in certain others. Other notions
had a very different connotation from one language to another -
for example, the word democracy in Europe and elsewhere. It was
therefore fundamental to take the conceptual structure of cultures into account.
    Participants spoke in this connection of psycho-sociological
analysis, a list of words in common use in large areas and a
parallel analysis of their meaning.
    The Chairman concluded that the "lexicon of key notions"
project suggested in March 1978 was all the more justified and
that between the two extremes - similarity of a notion between
two cultures and the pure and simple absence of such a notion in
such and such a language - there were all the intermediate cases
to be inventoried, and their analysis would be significant at
intercultural level.
    Mr. Meddeb emphasized the importance of Mr. Lehmann's re-
marks on linguistic questions and insisted on the necessity for
analysis of content going "as far as the roots". He also mentioned the "double structure of certain cultural worlds", for
example the written and vernacular tradition in the Arab world.

Mr. Diallo noted that there could be a gulf not only between two languages but between generations.

2. <u>Analysis of intercultural basic data</u>
- <u>study on the diversity of ways of achieving knowledge</u>;
- <u>the incommunicable in the intercultural</u> (for example, limits of communicability in poetic expression);
- <u>dictionary of untranslatables</u>: without specifying ways and means, participants asserted the validity of this project;
- <u>study of universal values in different pilot cultures; the archetypes of the universal</u>;
- <u>"Nation building" and the survival of autochtonous cultures</u>;
- <u>the process of cultural destruction</u>;
- <u>culture imposed and culture undergone</u>;
- <u>the process of acculturation</u>.
   In connection with this subject in particular, the problem was raised of the relative speed of acculturation according to the discipline under consideration: language, music, customs, art, etc. Andalucía and Sicily were quoted as cases of successful acculturation.
- <u>ethnocentrism</u>;
- <u>the cultural stereotypes</u> (particularly between the Northern and Southern regions of certain countries of Western Europe - and then passing to Eastern Europe).
   Regarding the last two subjects mentioned above, which were recognized as having priority, observations were made on the positive and negative aspects of ethnocentrism, on the more or less psychologically inevitable nature of the stereotypes and on attempts to go beyond ethnocentrism.
   On this latter subject, Mr. Condurachi mentioned the very great respect manifested in South-Eastern Europe, in spite of the wars and tensions of which it has been the scene, for the resistance of the concept of universal man and world citizen in the face of Ottoman domination, etc.
   Professor Lehmann spoke of research by Edward T. Hall on "proxemia" which could provide an excellent starting point for studies of cultural otherness. It was also considered from a more general point of view that the choice of Indonesia for inter-cultural research on linguistics would be excellent since, as Mr. Abdulgani had already said, the Indonesians had adopted the language of a minority.
   The Maghreb, Casamance and South-East Asia had been mentioned as regions which could be selected for certain studies of linguistics (particularly "common language and cultural identity"). Brazil could also lend itself to characteristic studies.

3. <u>Comparative or transcultural thematic studies</u>
   Under this heading (cf. list of subjects from the report of the March 1978 Study Group) could be considered a multitude of subjects applying intercultural research to concrete cases. The Secretariat had taken note of those which had particularly attracted the Committee's attention.
   Participants showed particular interest in research on conceptions and values of time and space in different cultures.

4. Applied research

The Chairman particularly mentioned in this connection:
- a systematic insertion of intercultural chronology in history books, and the revision of history books in general; this could give rise to a general recommendation or even a pilot book.

In the same way, Mr. Condurachi suggested a synchronic intercultural display in museums; this could be the subject of a recommendation to national Commissions;
- more generally: encouragement to teaching of the better knowledge of cultures at school and university.

In this connection, Professor Lehmann drew attention to the extraordinary possibilities provided by pocket computers - a domain where progress had been spectacular. Applications were immense, particularly in the teaching of languages (apprenticeship in the pronunciation of foreign languages). In Indonesia this technology could render immense service. It would also be possible to distribute to schools, for a minimum expenditure, one of those gadgets which stores in its miniaturized circuit an entire book of introduction to such and such a culture;
- studies on the integration of foreign students in the universities and activities in this sphere.

A survey being conducted at the University of Paris V was mentioned in this connection; it could produce results in proportion to the sample on which it was based, which was perhaps somewhat too restricted.
- vademecum on courtesy and polite customs in the various cultures;
- studies on cultural encounters in mass tourism.

Jean d'Ormesson spoke of the phenomenon of pilgrimage in this connection.

5. Media

Participants were invited to refer particularly to the recommendations of the final report of the meeting of the committee of experts held in May 1979 on the subject of "Education for the Mutual Understanding of Cultures".

In particular Mr. Condurachi had been particularly interested by the idea of a "programme pool" (reservations by Member States of 2 to 3 per cent of the space in their press and their audio-visual broadcasts to intercultural programmes to be chosen from a pool of programmes centralized at Unesco) and of a charter to be drawn up for this purpose; he mentioned an experiment in this direction on Rumanian television.

J. d'Ormesson emphasized the considerable dimensions of the programme suggested in May 1979, which could interest all organizations which were members of the ICPHS (linguists, anthropologists, historians, etc.) and cover all sectors of the former "major project on mutual appreciation of Eastern and Western cultural values". He suggested devoting space in Diogenes to this programme.

Although, for lack of time, the specific activities suggested in the May 1979 document had not given rise to a formal sorting out of priorities, participants manifested their support for the spirit of the recommendations.

Appendix

In order to retain in their entirety the ideas and thoughts expressed during the Consultative Meeting of March 1978, essential directions and findings of which are reflected in the final report (see earlier part II), President A. Dupront felt it appropriate to investigate further the themes thus established. We are here reproducing this substantial text, which, in a less conventional form than that allowed by the restrictions of the final report, has permitted more personal emphasis while widening the scope for interpretation of the intentions and perspectives.

1. The intercultural:
approaches and prospects

Alphonse Dupront

The foregoing report, being intended as a synthesis, expresses
as briefly as possible the general features of the discussions
which took place; it therefore suffers from two obvious defects -
first, it conveys little of the "brain-storming" atmosphere of
the debates, and second it ignores many of the enlightening suggestions put forward during the symposium. The following pages
constitute an attempt to make up for these shortcomings, for
everything which was contributed, in an unanimous desire for efficacity and a keen feeling of co-responsibility for an essential
task, is worth retaining as an introduction to a research and
teaching policy promoting world-wide realization of the supreme
importance of intercultural communication for an order of peace
and justice.

Some of the ideas here presented might appear to have been
given already in the report. If repetition there be, it is just
another way of bearing witness to a joint awareness of the
essential, this time by means of a more direct approach to the
experience of the debates which took place - for such is the
purpose of the pages which follow.

The atmosphere of the meeting can be conveyed more clearly
by a few generalities.

1. First of all, regarding its composition. The list of participants published in the present volume will bear witness to the
fact that most major cultural areas and even continents were
represented by some of the most authoritative voices. It was unanimously regretted that, only in the European context, owing to
a variety of circumstances, the participation of the Socialist
countries was limited to one representative. As was quite rightly
pointed out, the processes of thought, the problems and even the
ways of tackling intercultural problems in Socialist countries
are somewhat different from those in non-Socialist countries.
Fortunately, the working party possessed, among its preparatory
documents, an extremely voluminous report full of clarifying
points of view, drawn up by Professor Arutiunov, which is included
in the present volume. There was general agreement regarding the
extremely high quality of the participants and of the working
documents which had been prepared.

2. From the beginning, it was obvious that participants were fully
aware of the importance of the problem. The size of the task
before the symposium was very soon defined as the result of a

few speeches. This was no longer a matter of experts meeting to
draw up a working programme in their various individual specialities; they were directing a task useful for mankind. Hence the
concern, very firmly expressed, that there should be a prior
analysis of the various targets of intercultural studies, and
that they should be clearly defined with the three following
objectives: constituting the means of reciprocal knowledge; explaining, by a collective effort of thought, the phenomena of
cultural change and above all making people aware of them; seeking
practical applications of them, and thus providing service.
Another speech called for a prospective demand for our work and
the ambition - or the duty - of defining a policy. A policy for
organizing research but also for conveying its results well beyond
the necessarily narrow confines of research proper. In other
words a demand that our work should be useful: the words "im-
perious necessity" were even used.
3. After the objectives, the limits of research, or more exactly,
the specific nature of the intercultural. By all accounts, the
analyses of the internal dynamisms of cultures or of the syn-
theses established within them are a source of material for intercultural studies; from this point of view it may be worth while
to list them, or at least to recognize them. But a deliberately
exhaustive inventory, previous or parallel to the development of
intercultural studies, would not only compromise them but also be
a source of possible confusion. In the same way, proceeding from
a cultural study methodology to an intercultural one would affect
the specific nature of the latter. Undoubtedly, the two are
closely bound up together; all the more reason for distinguishing
between them. In other words, intercultural research would very
soon become a sort of isolated exploration of the very interior
of a culture. There would be a risk that the means of communication or reciprocal influence might very soon disappear, together
with the language of intercommunication which alone can act as
the basis of the pedagogics of positive knowledge between peoples and cultures - an even greater loss.
    The endeavour by the working party to insist essentially
on the prefix <u>inter</u> rather than <u>intra</u> was therefore as sustained
as it was praiseworthy.
    The fundamental choice was expressed by the philosophical
question: would there still be any culture at all if there were
only one culture? This question is not by any means a school hypothesis or a debating epigram; it is the essentially lucid
point of view that culture and the intercultural are organically
related and that in truth - even though such absolutisms might
suffer from it - culture cannot be defined or developed except
in the consciousness of other cultures. Hence the intercultural
is a guarantee of the existence of cultures and, in a way, the
key to them.
4. One of the primary concerns of the working party was the problem of methodology. But it very soon appeared that, by dealing
with methodology alone, there was a considerable danger of
remaining at the discourse level, which often conceals passions
and ideologies without attaining more concrete results, although

these are essential for the human efficacity of a world-wide
policy of intercultural relations.

Two channels therefore asserted themselves for joint consideration as fundamental to the real fecundity of intercultural
research.

One was the parallel development of methodological definitions based on existing and future experiments and the implementation of a programme of case studies. This consideration of
actual cases, the realization of the difficulties of approaching
the subject, the revelation of what is inaccessible or untranslatable, the assessment of the quality of the material and the
various ways of processing it, and any confrontations as a
result of cross-checking in the field are all sources for constituting a corpus of information which would comprise the most
enlightening of methodologies, that of a multi-form experience
carried on in space and time. The establishment of this corpus
on the basis of the close examination of a great number of case
studies could be one of the leading priorities in the development of intercultural studies; obviously, it is up to Unesco to
promote its implementation.

A few general guidelines are necessary regarding the choice
of cases for study. While generally speaking any well-defined
case, located in space and time and dealt with as both specific
and anthropologically significant, provides material for analysis
and knowledge, the economics of research and its subsequent use
imposes priorities. What emerged from a number of contributions
to the debate, thus assuming the value of evidence regarding the
most urgent necessities in the contemporary world, was the importance attached, for intercultural studies, to phenomena of
change; in other words, the priority of the dynamic over the
static in a world of accelerated change.

This correspondence with the epoch, which is profound participation, actually favours cultural change - at the level of
the major State and national formations, political, economic or
social changes, changes affecting urban and rural societies, of
traditional and modern or ultra-modern cultures such as that of
the "electronic age", of stable and mobile societies, and of
traditional to periodical nomadism, which latter has become a
collective impulse to go "elsewhere", acts of the present but
also of the past, with crystallized or stratified results for
our cultures. Thus, acculturation and deculturation appear to be
the two realities to be rendered conscious in a development of
intercultural studies conducted, as was emphasized on a number
of occasions, not only diachronically but also, and sometimes
above all, synchronically. This may, in the progress of exchanges
between cultures, be both a measure and an assertion of a more
acute knowledge of the authenticities and an acceptance of the
relations now recognized, or even the mutual feeling of a greater
richness, and therefore a common avocation, in the force of experienced fact, to serve the new world of intercultural communication lucidly and confidently. Particularly as a profound analysis of the phenomena of change obviously discovers specific or
common values, the only authentic material which leads to practical achievements concerning any cultural policy at State or

country level and concerning intercultural policy at the various
area levels.

But the greater the cause, the more essential are even the
most elementary rules, great or small, gradually to impart life
to it.

The second channel is therefore proposed in the formulation
of a research deontology: in other words, what we often harden
into a method, with rules too mechanically applied, without taking
into account the "fluctuating and miscellaneous" which are the
very essence of the intercultural phenomenon, and translate into
concrete attitudes of knowledge, providing research with the most
reliable opportunities of an actual approach to the material.

The problem had already been raised, by the light of a very
wide experience, in Professor Bazin's report. The contrast of
two "reports on evidence" immediately revealed its importance to
the working party. One established the necessity for studies on
Africa to be conducted by Africans, if they were to be well-
founded, since the approach to the essential part of a culture
could only be validly undertaken by natives imbued with the deep-
lying meaning and roots of their language.

Even in the autochthonous area, incidentally, the signs of
language could have very different connotations according to the
circles or age-groups using them. The internal knowledge of a
culture therefore is rightly the privilege of those who live with
it. The other report, while emphasizing the supreme importance
of the language as an instrument and sign of cultural unity,
chiefly noticed a change in the quality of the "evidence" of inter
cultural knowledge. In comparatively recent times, western
scientists and researchers used to stay for long periods in
African countries, where they learnt the local languages and sometimes knew them even better than the Africans themselves. Today,
the westerner passes through too quickly to notice and extend
his knowledge of the essential realities: contact remains superficial, and the result is all too often an unfortunate misunderstanding. But nothing in the field of intercultural relations is
so important as the endeavour, made by him who wants to find out,
to attain the essential values of the culture under consideration:
this makes the dignity of the "other" manifest.

Thus, at the very core of intercultural knowledge, we have
either an unavoidable bottleneck bearing witness to an inevitably
partial communication of the most essential values of a necessarily treacherous culture, or a common realization of the possibilities of extending the limits of the apparently impossible.
Manifestly, the working party decided for the second alternative,
and thus the formulation of a deontology of intercultural studies
for the acquisition of knowledge. Particularly since, it was
pointed out, the work of foreign scientists on a given culture
is often more enlightening. Hence the guidelines of this deontology, first the endeavour to approach the other culture: a
personal endeavour through a knowledge of the language and through
work in the field, through an increasing openness to the various,
and even the strange, slowly recognized, accepted and situated
according to the vital rule that any cultural unity lives on
organic cohesions and an order of existence; next, the acceptance

and practice of this evidence of the very act of knowing that the "foreigner" remains essential to it, for the attitude of "another you" is inherent to it. Translated into concrete terms, this basic reality constitutes intercultural research as an act of general knowledge in which differences and meeting points in the common awareness of the specific and of the respect demanded of it are explained alternately. Many translations procured by nationals - it was pointed out - are often far from being the best. The foreigner's attitude not only coincides with that of the native but, in an exchange of "spirit and truth", complements it to such an extent that it enlightens the unsuspecting one regarding his cultural identity. At this point intercultural research becomes a reciprocal discovery and thus actual communication. The study of intercultural knowledge is therefore evidence of an authentic reality for those who, for various reasons, are subsequently called upon to use it.

In the discipline of the material provided by case studies, in the demands of knowledge as it has just been defined, a methodology of intercultural studies transcending formal rules is being organized: it is the commitment of the whole man not only to the discovery of what is not himself but above all to the respectful acknowledgement of the other as an enrichment of oneself. A phrase that was used in the discussions was: the investigator should be investigated in his turn. This is not a case of mistrust or outward protest but the implementation of a deontology of knowledge in order to attain a common threshold of truth.

5. The implementation of this deontology raises first, quite naturally, the problem of Eurocentrism. All those who spoke were in favour of denouncing its belittling limitations, its oppressive and illusory universalism and even its misdeeds. The analysis of it was lucid but not vengeful. No purpose would have been served, in fact, by contesting a historical fact. What was important was to recognize the damage and also the connotations rightly imposed for a history - that of a spirit of Enlightenment reducing the diversity of cultures to "universal" data, the mental comfort of a West in its possession of the world; and above all the association between colonialism and Eurocentrism indelibly imprinted on the sensitivity of all those who had to suffer from them. Even more profoundly, it was as well to discover the paralyzing penetration of such cultural imperialism.

This was submitted in the proceedings of the working party in a particularly acute manner in the analysis of the paradoxical consequences of the more or less consciously tyrannical reign of European man in the heart of the movements of our time. In the expansion of the values and forms of Western thought over two and a half centuries (roughly the eighteenth and nineteenth), many of the elite of non-western cultures participated in the outlook and mental universe of the dominating or conquering power: to this extent, they were responsible, within their cultures of origin, for mutilation, and too often for the destruction of entire sectors. In self-defence against their elite, the autochthonous cultures withdrew into their shells with the result that, just as frescoes retain their brilliance under whitewash, the destructive action protected and conserved the essential,

the living sources of the cultural genius, or in other words the
traditions.

In many Third World countries, there came the time of political independence, which is today an accomplished fact: interior
decolonization normally rediscovers traditional values. Thus with
the Arab world: throughout successive occupations it had carefully
retained its identity as a result of a sort of passive resistance.
There resulted a kind of fixedness, from which it only liberated
itself slowly several years after a political independence which
had been acquired with difficulty. The same process of liberation,
whether it takes place through a recognition of the original
latencies and an up-dating of profound "sources", or whether it
is defined by new structures, is developed in a violent contrast
with the values of the West which was but recently still dominant.
But contrasts and rejections give proof of just so many attach-
ments. To the extent that a serious dissociation and even rifts
become manifest, even affecting cultural equilibria, between autochthonous cultures and the foreign culture whose fascination it
remains difficult not to undergo, often at the expense of another
mutilation. "Let the look, both admired and reviled, of the one
fall with a certain irony or a damning repudiation on the values
of the other, and it will vastly complicate everything," it was
stated with lucid fervour. Particularly as patience and a trusting
benevolence in the very recognition of diversity and its justice
are unusual virtues and attitudes in international relations.
And here is one of the major services which Unesco could render:
creating the conditions and teaching the exercise not only of increasing tolerance but of a mutual respect of reciprocal autochthonies.

Thus is beginning to take shape an authentic spirituality of
intercultural duties, so as to avoid what might become the impoverishment of all, consisting of that withdrawal of threatened
national cultures into their shells, in the pattern of what happened in the assertion of political independence - a withdrawal
in which the wounds of yesteryear are buried alive, becoming un-
atonable crystallizations. An analysis which, in the moving elo-
quence of a personal witness, terminated with this lesson: "It
takes much wisdom and patience to get somebody who has been
forced to sing in a given key to sing in chorus". This was, in
the manner of the wise men, to discover the reliable therapy, un-
tiring and strong in the hope of communication between cultures,
the only one which can today found a human order in the world to
the greatest benefit of all. Also the only one which, recognizing
the reality of Eurocentrism as a historical fact, enables it to
transcend itself, free itself in depth from its belittling effects
and liberate itself from all the others in a positive manner, so
as to render to Europe its true position, not as the centre but
as part and servant of the world order - no longer reducing itself to a pattern impoverishing all but exuberating in the diversity of the other.

To this end nothing would be more useful than what was proposed: the inversion of rôles in intercultural knowledge. Although
the usual mechanism of the discovery of the world in modern times

has consisted essentially of a European approach to the knowledge of others by means of the self-sufficient equipment of its own categories (1), why should the West not be subjected to a discovery of itself by others? In this way, the investigator would become the investigated. The eyes of the other, which are always particularly revealing, would be the mirror of Europe, the discoverer of the obvious limits and of unsuspected wealth, as well as the humane liberator from paralyzing, hidebound schemes, mutilating stereotypes, a belittling, unjust assessment of oneself in communication with others, all the more enslaving for oneself than it was for others. A wide-open policy, increasing the number of studies carried out by scientists and researchers from the other major cultural areas and the regular establishment of a dialogue of self-discovery by others would restore the necessary order, while at the same time freeing Europe from its universal narcissism. The human basis of such a policy is that everybody should grow out of the attitude, so productive of mistrust and conflicts, of concerning oneself with others in order to mould them to one's own pattern. It is obvious that nothing would better serve the discovery of an authentic Europe than to get rid of the habit of investigating the Other in order to reduce him to one's own measure, with which we have been imbued for about three centuries. Instead of casting the Imperial regard on the other - paralyzing for all concerned and an inexhaustible source of avowed or dangerously hidden aggressiveness - let the European receive the clarity of the coolness of the other's look. That such an opinion was expressed during the discussions, is striking evidence of a return of that youthfulness so beneficial to Europe.

"What astonished me in the West," said one participant, "is what no longer astonishes the Westerner". For example, the sanctification of the limits of private property, or at least the absolute character so deeply attached to it. Even under socialist collectivism, the West remains individualist, whereas the African enjoys a communal society. Without any reciprocal tyranny of pattern, the clarity of the other's look illuminates a relative order, concisely defined in a narrow domain between Spain and France by the wisdom of Montaigne - wisdom obstinately rejected by a dominating western spirit, determined, in spite of adventurous discoverers, not to recognize anyone but itself in others. It has taken, therefore, three centuries and two world wars for this order of the relative no longer to be incriminated as a source of scepticism and to appear as a principle of true

---

(1) It has been rightly and most lucidly said that everything happened as if European contact with other cultures was a sufficient condition for the other peoples to be considered historical. For example, the recognition of a history, the sovereign privilege of the West, but also its fragile secularization. This raises the major problem of the consciousness of the historical in intercultural encounters and thus the multiplicity of historical times in the diversity of cultures.

interknowledge. The consequence has been to re-establish Europe as a full partner in the concert of cultures, whereas, by one of time's revenges, there might have been a considerable temptation to leave her in the lurch.

The resumed debate was concentrated on three essential items.

One, obviously, was to determine the concept of culture, although without getting bogged down in a definition of the word. From the start of the discussions, a firm decision had been taken that at least, now that we were getting down to work, we knew enough about the subject to know what we were talking about. This was by no means to invalidate what followed; however, in the fulsomeness of the debate a number of more or less pronounced accentuations were made. It is worth while repeating them here, since such a swelling of the content can only better serve the awaited establishment of the operational concept of culture. Whether, in the methodological considerations, an account is given of the general approach, or whether emphasis is placed on the phenomena of change, culture appears to be a unit expressing an entire collective system and experienced by it, both in the present (state or synchrony) and in the past (evolutive forms or successive diachronic states). The notion of culture may thus be considered as "functional", i.e. covering in a single word both the collective creation of a system of signs expressing an individuality and a way of experiencing the world and the existence of the specific coherencies signified by such a system. Culture then is both the definition of oneself or liberation through the constitution of a mental equipment and the use of that equipment as principle, source or pattern of collective life. A collective individuality of this sort is as such an assertion in relation to others and thus, in its most positive element, a natural constraint of relations with other cultural systems - relations which will assume different characters according to the diversity of historical situations.

For here it is that things become complicated. Two problems posed many times by participants made this abundantly clear - first that of what might be called internal interculturality, and second that of cultural identity - a term much in vogue at present. As regards the first, almost everything was included in the forcefully put question: Is any culture not intercultural? In the geo-cultural area of the Caribbeans, two languages exist side by side - that of the men and that of the women. To take the example of Hungary, interculturality within one and the same society was again emphasized in the coexistence of an urban, intellectual culture with a peasant culture, which is still vigorous. Thus was broughtout the complexity of the cultural fact in the more or less unifying context of a political society and the wider one of a geo-political area.

At least two aspects appear to call for analysis: in the present or historical stage of building of national States, in which each nation tends to define itself on the basis of a more

or less homogeneous cultural unity, what are the consequences
for the different cultures assembled within that State and condemned to discover unitary foundations? What forms of coexistence
or reciprocal intra-influences are there between the elite
culture (very felicitously described as "cult culture") and a
popular culture, the freshness and creative spontaneity of which,
to quote Gramsci, very often remain intact, even when they are
found to be buried in the venerability or customs of a corpus of
traditions; and therefore what is the reality of cultural levels
within a given society?

With regard to the first aspect, emphasis was chiefly placed
on the relations between the dominant and the dominated culture.
Hence the importance of establishing the problematics of cultural
discrimination within States - a de facto situation for which the
notion of "culturism" was suggested - defined as "the attitude
of oppression or discrimination exerted on one culture by another".
In the cultural area of Latin America, for example, concrete
research ought to be pursued into the relations established
between social groups in one and the same State. Thus, within the
context of a forced coexistence, there would appear asymmetrical
relations essentially of a conflictual nature, and therefore reducing or mutilating the dominated culture, sometimes to the point
of total destruction (1). At the same time, studies were necessary
regarding the constraints in respect of the insertion of immigrant
workers into industrialized countries. Or an entire chapter, considerable where research and politico-human service are concerned,
on acculturation and deculturation in Western Africa, South America and the western countries, with the ethnic consequences related to the collective, irrational, epidemic and segregating phenomena of xenophobia or racism. Such is the weighty dominant of
factual data, lucidly considered in the joint discussion. This,
from the point of view of aggressive dynamism, is still actual or
henceforth extinct but seeking resurrection.

From a more or less synchronic point of view, it is - second
aspect - the evidence of cultural levels which is necessary. In
it the intra-social dynamism may perhaps find its fecundity and
source of common richness, providing the specific nature of such
levels is recognized as valid. At least, it was forcefully stated
that it was essential to distinguish the existence of levels for
any intercultural research. Practically no society is monolithic
and even if class cultures prove to be different and even antagonistic, many common features are established on the basis of
similarity and difference. To be sure, the existence of a certain degree of similarity should not dissimulate or gradually
confuse an essential diversity. It was therefore possible to propose the criterion that, for a discrimination of cultural levels
to be valid, they should be situated in direct, and even conditioning, relation with the political and economic condition of the

---

(1) One of the forms, a verbal one to be sure but negating in
     depth, is the current confusion of "indigenous" culture with
     folklore, which merely has the right to exist for show
     business or as a subject of study for specialists.

society under consideration. Such an enlightenment, fortified by the convergence of other analytical methods relating to mentalities, values and myths, may make it possible to compensate for antagonisms, or the memory of them, profoundly engraved in dominated or crushed cultures, by a growing ambition for what is today called "cultural pluralism". Both the words and the thing were fortunately mentioned, with a very penetrating recommendation regarding the method, of taking peripheral cultures fully into account, so as to prevent any constraint within a State, nation or people. This properly "situated" the matter, as well as emphasizing connections between the intercultural of the political community and that of the world.

The notion of "cultural pluralism" is quite recent, like a promise or a hope. That of "cultural identity" dates from a few decades earlier. For some factions this is a notion redolent of a demand for liberation; better far, it is a fair recognition of a worthiness to exist. Its "operational" value, however, was disputed in our very open discussion. What cultural identity, it was asked. That of the peasants or that of the intellectuals? (1) What is homogeneous and standardized about the expression "identity" may well have appeared to tinge the concept with a certain lack of reality, or at least of partiality, for there are two levels to the definition of the content of the notion: one which covers merely the fundamental elements of the cultural identity and the other, more demanding and also more concrete, which considers the cultural identity as the overall expression of a cultural system, with its methods of production, forms of distribution and trade, the technological machinery and - at the heart of Third World cultures today - the use of imported technology, whether merely side by side with the traditional culture or slowly assimilated by it. There is another possible danger in using the notion: it may nourish aggressive nationalist passions and sometimes crystallize them: which is the irrational fruit of excessively cautious or rigid limitations. In fact, as a result of intermingled reactions, one thing has become obvious - the difficulty of using, without numerous ambiguities, the same vocabulary for analyzing the intrasocial intercultural and the intercultural in the broad, international sense. Or at least the necessity, for the proper management of intercultural research, of a well-defined vocabulary if not a generally accepted one - which may be asking too much at present - at least in the use of key-notions with an obvious clarity of content. This is not always easy, so charged with passion, agony and sometimes exasperation is the expression "cultural identity" owing to the historical situations which have engendered it. One of the wisest and surest methods may therefore be not to define "cultural identity", even case by case, as such, but to decide what realities it expresses, or in other words, what it comprises|

_____

(1) To put things into their context, the participant, in developing his argument, suggested carrying out parallel research into societies and cultures of the East-European world and those of the Third World.

Seven factors appear to be essential to it: language, history, mental structures, forms of production, ways of living, biologico-social organization and religion, each to a different degree, but language, apparently the most immediately distinguishable on account of its circulation, its roots and its "untranslatables", seems to be its most manifest expression. However that may be, breaking the cultural identity down into its constituent parts brings us to the genetics of autochthony. To tell the truth, a very long method, but the only one making it possible to achieve an exact consciousness of oneself and to bear witness of it to others. Chain reflections which lead to two practical conclusions, very different in context but basically expressing an essential element of intercultural knowledge. One is that, in intercultural communication the notion of identity should be used cautiously and explained wherever possible. The other, the mental attitude essential to any real exchange, confirms that there is no valid evidence about oneself without a lucid knowledge of oneself. The discipline of the conscious identity therefore may be the consciousness of the other. In this reciprocal ascesis of truth, the intercultural becomes indispensable for us to experience our identity (1).

Facing the diversity of cultures, is the fact of the universal. Expressing the fundamental aspects of the latter is first a historical situation, second, developments in the contemporary world, and third, existential research into the human race. The last is all the more important, inspiring and liberating, in that the factual data will be lucidly manifest. While the working party paid less attention to them than to the perception and proper defence of specific cultural features, a few participants strongly emphasized the handicaps which weigh upon us in dealing with this universal notion. Since we receive it at the end of its historical development, it has in fact been the sovereign instrument of "Eurocentrism". The values of a European civilization, liberated by the Enlightenment of the eighteenth century and its "system", have been spread throughout the world, while the latter has been assimilated or had its essential diversities reduced to the European "pattern". A phenomenon both of European origin, but completely sterilizing for the cultural wealth of the planet and all the more fallacious in that for at least two centuries the West, intoxicated with itself, remained unconscious of it, and of the establishment of intercultural relations in such an assymetrical way that the result of it could only be reciprocal non-recognition and thus the crystallization of passions of stereotypes or rejections. Thus Europe was responsible for blinding both sides and for reducing the world to its own measure. Are we really free from the mental attitudes which have been aroused in us by this blindness, of which we are now aware? Nothing is more tenacious than the convenience of the "ready-made" in the act of pretended

---

(1) One of the ways of recognizing it would be the establishment of a "cultural inventory" covering an entire culture, as was suggested for the African cultures.

acknowledgement. An entire work of reversal, therefore, needs
to be carried out with perseverance in order to recognize and
laboriously expurgate the imperialist patterns which turn our
knowledge of the world into a smug ignorance.

A similar necessity - if not, a pious recommendation - calls
for an entire programme of research applied to the analysis of
the mental forms, vocabulary, collective representations, and
consciousness, the structural and historical elements of other
cultures, in contemporary developments of western knowledge
regarding the diversity of cultures. Moreover, to consider
things on a world-wide basis, while the task of mental expurga-
tion of the traditional schemes of the universe may make an
enormous contribution to liberating westerners from their Eurocentrism, ethnocentrism is not exclusively an attribute of the
West. Making a sort of absolute rule of the diversity of cultures,
it was pertinently remarked, might confirm other ethnocentrisms
- even older than that of Europe. Through the diversity of
cultures as a principle and duty of inter-knowledge, therefore,
should be sought and established an equilibrium both certain and
subtle and with universal values, fundamental for communication
between cultures.

Particularly as it must be acknowledged that, in the contemporary world, universal forms are taking shape which can all be
the means of unity, while at the same time reinforcing reciprocal
misunderstandings. Three of these at least appeared in the
working party's discussions. The first, which is undoubtedly the
most insidious and the most difficult to grasp results from the
partitioning of cultures in the context of what is called a
"national" State with the result that culture is considered to
be a different entity from the State or the nation. Since the
image of unity becomes dominant and at the same time a simplifi-
cation of the diversity of cultures, resulting in the convenience
of knowledge and of the development of inter-relations, there is
a great temptation to simplify matters at a time when there is
a general trend towards the constitution of major assemblies of
States. What may be a stage towards the establishment of an easier
system of relations presents the other danger of being merely an
internal imperialism and thus providing an artificially rooted
foundation for consciousness of the universal.

The second is the epidermically irresistible establishment
of a technology of universal expansion. Nobody would dream of
disputing the benefits it brings and to what extent it can, in
certain proportions, serve to develop the sense of human community.
But a community by standardization - that "coca-colafication" of
the world referred to with serious humour and the force of a
rejection! There is no doubt that technological transfers, essential to a right claimed by all, involve serious consequences in
many cultural fields. A case-by-case study is called for, therefore, of the material and psychical conditions for the introduction of these new and extremely powerful tools into cultures
which are centred in quite a different world order, and which
have often been in a state of balance for thousands of years. In
this case we are dealing with something quite different from the
relation between tradition and modernity, but with a shock and

violence all the more. uprooting the greater the power of the tool.
In such circumstances what would be the value, for the human race
and its well-being, of a universal which causes a strain or
break between man and his natural, human environment? In the face
of real communication, merely a new snare. The question was put
like a cry of alarm: will not the industrialization and robot-
ization of the world achieve imperialism in another form, or at
least a homogenization which will spell out death to all cultural
authenticities?

There should also be an urgent, extensive and profound
analysis with the aim of directing the universal technology of
the future, today unbridled and levelling, to the service of
world unity, organically defined by cultural diversity. A system of universal communication can always be used for human encounters, providing its limitations, its exact value and its
dangerous partialities are well known. Does the same apply to
the third form, which is particularly prevalent today and which
was denounced in our discussion as an "electronic civilization"?
There are two problems in fact - that of electronics as such;
but above all that of the media. As for the first aspect, we
are quite right to consider it as an increasingly dominating
factor of the technological universe: languages in binary form
are establishing themselves in world-wide circulation. In the
mental structures of totally different cultural areas, what are
the virtues or shortcomings of such languages, sometimes completely foreign to the autochthonous systems of consciousness
of the world and to the existing cultural balances? Not to undertake profound research into this problem would be to increase
even further the apparently calm indifference underlying the
lightning expansion of contemporary technology, even though the
electronic civilization remains the privileged instrument of the
few in our present-day society.

The same cannot be said of "box culture" - the felicitous
expression which emerged during our discussions. For we do not
sufficiently realize how omnipresent the media are, and the time
appears to be ripe to study their conditioning effect on the
development of intercultural relations, if we are not to be considered guilty of deliberate blindness. Such a powerful instrument may well be used either to develop an awareness of the
universal or to block its channels, perhaps for ever. Two aspects,
therefore, which will be recognized as essential, were suggested
for research in the service of intercultural communications. On
the one hand, clarifying the capital fact of the creation by the
media of another, specific reality - the obsessive proliferation
of the image insidiously substituting itself for the concrete
environment; it establishes a fiction of the real truth. It was
stated that young people cannot remember two years after the
screening of a big match whether they were at the stadium or
watched it on television. And this enclosed world of vision has
a curious orientation; it is dominated by brutal competition,
violence, crisis and war. Mankind generally appears in perpetual
aggressiveness, and the pictures mainly exploit passion, fear,
and the irrational passivities and impulses of life. Hence the
urgent necessity for revealing the conditioning imposed by the

media and dismantling its mechanisms, unless we are prepared
to allow a world of fiction to insert itself between reality
and life and make communications among men a source of perpetual
misunderstanding, in the generally accepted disguise of valid
information. The danger is all the greater in that, in the
present world situation, inequality in the power of the media
makes the possession of them an instrument of cultural imperialism.
What could be a means of intercultural knowledge and of the
possible discovery of common links between cultures becomes, as
if naturally, owing to the enormous bulk of information launched
through space, an attack on autochthonous cultures - and sometimes a traumatizing one. Thus, the Third World becomes a victim
of invasion by European and American media.

Such are the distinguishable dangers in the spread of these
forms of the universal, very different in truth but all tending
towards the achievement of a homogeneous world, naturally antagonistic to the diversity of cultures. That being so, what is
important is to start research as a warning against a kind of
mechanical unconsciousness in the adoption or propagation of
"patterns" or forms each of which has the redoubtable ambivalence,
in a human universe of autochthonous cultures, of being either
destructive, sometimes irremediably, or of being the means of an
elementary awareness of the unity of the human race, the true
and healthy form of all universal ambition. The awakening of
consciousness thus acts as a measurement of the limitations of
the instrument, of the dangers it may involve and therefore the
ways of using it properly. In other words, the foundation of a
policy on resolute, enlightened research.

On the subject of the universal, two other suggestions are
worth mentioning here: one, regarding a method research; the
other, on the definition of a psychology of culture; both equally
demanding on the fundamental but conducting research into consciousness and manifestation by totally differing methods. The
first, already outlined by the IUED (University Institute for the
Study of Development) of Geneva, starts with the problematics
bound up with development, with that so often checked conclusion
that the industrialized societies are often the last to know what
direction they are taking. Apart from this quasi-mechanical and
acultural - if not anti-cultural - restriction, studies of the
realities of the universal which are discernable and usable in
the service of international communication - communication of the
soul rather than of discourse, always abstract and making for
partiality - should formulate a sort of spectrography of the
basic requirements of the human race. To start with, there is
the discernment of these requirements: whether on the basis of a
more or less theoretical typological analysis or by way of empirical methods of inventory; perhaps it does not matter which.
What is important is to establish the most reliable methods of
replying to the following two essential questions: are the fundamental requirements the same in all parts of the world, and at
what levels of requirement or only of consciousness; how are they
satisfied in the both inevitable and necessary diversity of
cultural systems? Thus, in the very living soul of cultures and
with the strength of meaning based on a discipline of equally

strict studies, would be formulated a consciousness of the
"universal" incarnate in the collective being of the peoples.
Making it manifest would be to render signal service to a dynamism of unity, this time respecting all the specific languages
by means of which cultures affirm their irreplaceable and unique
originality.

The second method grasps the intercultural as a fundamental
ontological reality. In it, peoples and nations find themselves
close, equal and related. For we have arrived at a moment in
history when the intercultural, in its full, organic sense, pro-
duces a common culture. Today, it was forcefully stated, when
technology, although triumphant, is beginning to discover its
limitations and sometimes its excesses and dangers - at the
start then of a post-technological period - the requirements and
fundamental values become, even in the etymological sense of the
word, metaphysical; culture imposes itself as the supreme means
of achieving the discovery and life of a plenitude of existence.
That being so, culture can be defined as a methodology leading
from the personal to the impersonal, the rules and stages of
which it would be as well to determine. There are manifestly two
orders of cultural development. One, horizontal, humanistic, historical and ideological, would appear to be that of the present-
day West; but the need to get ahead which becomes increasingly
evident in it discovers the other order, which is even more fundamental and which, being vertical, attains to the cosmological.
It is the vision and the wisdom of the traditional East, where the
cosmological is the figure and the possible reading of the ontological. In being is unity: this moment of our epoch is henceforth
capital, when the East and the West must meet one another in
pooling their loftiest spiritual experiences. At this point, which
is that of the cultural flowering of the human race, there can be
neither opposition nor rejection, but only the development of a
double approach in the continuing life of each, based on two
certainties: the horizontal, carried to its furthest possible
limits (i.e. the inventory of the existential data) leads to an
exhaustive demand and should attain the vertical, or in other
words, the common existence; the vertical, organic consciousness
of the world or cosmology, an ontological transcendency, imparts
both necessity and meaning to the diversity of the horizontal.
Plato and Aristotle reconciled, if you like, to speak in western
terms, as was suggested during this both enlightening and demanding
speech (1).

So many ideas and mental approaches towards a liberating
analysis of an abstract "universal" and the concrete discovery
of the "intercultural" in flesh and blood, after which so many
things will become possible, from the basic anthropological data
regarding human conditions to the necessary multiplicity of

---

(1) Research into the subject of destiny (conceptions, traditions,
     survivals, transfers, etc.) in various cultures, the importance
     of which was specially emphasized, converges quite naturally
     on to the cultural ontological.

autochthonous cultural universes. The liveliness of the debate
attested, as a result of the convergencies recognized by all,
and the sometimes crushing, or at least traumatizing, handicap,
for both victims and users, of a fiction of the universal which
impoverished the world and the sequels of which still weigh
heavily on the reciprocal recognition of cultural authenticities
and the increasingly pressing need, the more cultural diversity
confirms its indefensible singularity, of evidence, if not of
similarity then at least of correspondence: an anthropology in
fact, but without dogmatic pronouncements, without premature
and incorrect classifications, more concerned with emphasizing
diversity than recognizing the identical, thus slowly creating
a harmony in which is expressed, with the slowly acquired cer-
titude of common requirements, the supreme multiplicity of
cultural experiences, visions and consciousness of the world -
the incommensurable richness of the human race in its quest
for the fullness of life.

     Thus, the discussions of the working party resulted less
in a definition of the intercultural - which resulted, if it
was required, from the preceding analyses - than in the im-
perious consciousness that living it was much more important
than defining it - as one of the most urgent requirements of the
contemporary world. It was therefore a matter of putting, in
the midst of our present-day life, the requirements of the
"intercultural" actually and in the tenacious developments of
its polymorphous achievement, of discerning the attitudes imposed by its lucid recognition and of sketching a plan or policy
for a more widespread and more profound awareness, at the same
time as its practical methods. Much of this has been reported
and emphasized in the summary report; the preceding pages can
only, it seems, add emphasis to its most striking features. It
appeared, nevertheless, to be essential to record a few important
items of it at the end of this analysis.

     First of all, regarding the attitudes required for develop-
ing studies on intercultural relations. With a reliable vigilance,
such a consideration has remarkably rooted the research to be
undertaken in experience, recalling that culture is what its
creators made it and not the result of the academecian who
studies it. Differences in outlook and difference in spirit, it
is as well to remember, if we want to avoid a situation in which
our studies become isolated in the enclosure of specialists,
usually university men and therefore more or less participating
in the partitioning of disciplines; already, by insisting on the
necessity of an overall approach to the knowledge of a culture,
the question of an honest approach had been fortunately raised.
Now the researcher raises the question, with as essential consequences, research as participation and therefore as a bi- or
poly-cultural interdiscipline, and also checked against the facts.

     Research is no longer narrowly linked to the office; basic
and applied research are intimately linked together: this is the
very dynamism of the humanities which are today seeking in certain cultural areas, both the best ways of attaining the totality
of experience and also their utility.

     In the same movement, an overall discipline appears increasingly indispensable for the progress of intercultural research. During the meeting, the large number of studies which may already be concerned with intercultural relations was mentioned; but the majority of them all suffer from the same drawback - fragmentation, that fragmentation which is inherent to the possibilities of individual research. While there is no question of disputing its value as an "awakener" and, in certain particular cases, the eminent quality of penetration into the evidence to the point of establishing a privileged and sometimes inspired communication between the researcher and the culture studied, the conditions of present-day research make increasingly necessary the assistance of inter-disciplinary teams, or at least, so as to avoid a fragmentation which may prevent the stage of "curiosity" from being passed, the establishment of general programmes on basic subjects suitable for immediate use. Here the rôle of Unesco becomes apparent, particularly at the essential level of sponsoring and guidance, but assistance as well and, once the inventory of knowledge acquired is under way, the services of the working party, whose setting up on a permanent basis was requested at the conclusion of our proceedings.

In further relation to attitudes, there is one fact and one discipline. The fact honestly attests what subjective impregnation there is in any objective approach to intercultural realities. It is certain that, things being what they are, the chief reaction should be to recognize or take into account what is in conflict with the principle of intercultural relations and that other established fact, the contemporary mental processes of which tend excessively to make us forget its quasi-mechanical property - that all cultural homogenization implies a degree of violence: the deeper are their roots, the more the autochthonies are bruised. Thus, not without melancholy or courage, the real present-day difficulty has been expressed in a concise formula, which is also the definition of a vast, essential task: undoing by discussion what was done by the sword. But there are also states of pacific coexistence and equilibria which have existed for centuries: in this sense, both the open analysis of neighbourhood relations and an attentive look at history will make it possible to increase the number of methods of studying the phenomenon in its entirety - a study in which any excessively uniform interpretation would provide food for antagonism.

This deliberate increase in the number of methods is the first article in a discipline of the knowledge of intercultural relations, which if not sound, is at least impartial. There is another, which demands the most thorough analysis. Thus, it was pointed out that, for any significant analysis of relations, it was necessary to distinguish most clearly between the behaviour of those conveying the culture and those who are subjected to it, or even receive it or sometimes violently or tacitly reject it. Thus, in the sustained rigour of an ascesis of knowledge it would be possible to advance "in spirit and in truth" into the heart of a vast, essential problem and attempt to "take the heat out of it": which would be reciprocal lucidity for all concerned, and therefore beneficial. And the general exercise of the virtue, so often mentioned during our discussions, of tolerance,

undoubtedly a complex reality and difficult to achieve, but so
necessary that the study of the way it is exercised between
cultures was suggested and unanimously agreed to.

But such research cannot be confined to offices and labora-
tories. Their natural and necessary consequence is to lead,
through a knowledge of the forms of interculturality, to another,
profound communication between cultures, in a concourse demanding
dignity from all. This transition to an activity fecund for a
better or truer world was fervently and unanimously requested
by the working party. The features of a general policy governing
this activity were laid down in the final report.

The present report will undoubtedly reflect most reliably
the spirit common to all members of the working party by making
a cluster of suggestions and reflections all converging on the
request or expectation of achievements with the strength of
exemplary efficacity. This need for immediate commitment was
expressed first of all in the wish that Unesco, at present
anxious to formulate a declaration condemning racism and all its
consequences in the face of the world, should consider doing the
same for "culturism", particularly that whose violence is
exerted in the context of the nation-State, all the more blame-
worthy in that it is less noticeable from outside or is legitimi-
zed for a reason of State, which is always invoked as the
sovereign reason. Next the vital task - the forms of education
in the knowledge of other cultures and in the development of
communications between them. In this vast field, constituted at
world scale by the fact that so many widely varying cultures co-
exist, exchanges are unceasingly taking place without any close
analysis of their elementary, mechanical expressions, their
respective attitudes, their collective mental crystallizations,
their stereotypes and often the misunderstandings and the fatal
injustices, which it is subsequently very difficult and sometimes impossible to undo, being pursued in the vital areas where
they meet. Such studies would clarify the constitution of a
pedagogical system essential for a "collective" consciousness
of the "other" - that "other" who would be neither foreign nor
inferior, but a companion for a life together in the world of men.

These studies must be conducted in places where encounters
take place, either for young people in the universities where
practically everything is still to be done both in regard to the
enlightened presentation of the host culture and to the understanding, without traumatic reaction, of the astonishments, the
rejections, or the "ill-at-ease" feelings of the students
received, or, in these days of mass culture and great human mobility, in the places frequented by tourists. Tourism, of which
it was penetratingly remarked that it had effects not only on
the search for the cultures of other countries but also on the
tourist's knowledge of his own country, causes, in both cases,
not only the attenuation or hardening of centuries-old stereotypes, but also the creation of new collective images, a "shake-
up" of the image of the "other", which may become an extraordinary
laboratory of common knowledge, providing that observers, inter-
preters and guides are available: the intercultural studies
should make it possible to recruit them. For just as in the

analysis of the cultural fact the existence of levels of
culture has been brought to light, in just the same way we
all considered that one of the first objectives of research
into the "intercultural" should be to associate, in a receptive
attitude towards different cultures and a knowledge of them
as free of prejudice, bias and summary condemnations as possible, the widest possible circles and the masses in the certainty of mutual enrichment. Internal and external interculturality should reinforce one another in the interest of a collective education for communication, accepted as the essential
foundation for a new world.

The preceding pages represent an attempt at fidelity.
This is the justification for their length. Transcending the
summary report, my desire was to report our exchanges of views
and preserve their results as much as possible. It was also to
offer to those who want to read them, together with the sincere and lucid memorandum of a joint research, reduced to its
essentials, reflections, judgments and problematics all carrying
the mark of experience; such a concourse of evidence expresses
more intensely than a discourse or a study of principle, the
intensity of our expectations and a number of ways of fulfilling
them; it remains to reconnoitre them resolutely.

2. List of participants

	1976[1]	1978[2]	May 1979[3]	Sept 1979[4]
Martine ABDALLAH-PRETCEILLE (Mrs), inspectrice de l'éducation nationale, Paris			*	
H. Roeslan ABDULGANI, Chairman, "Advisory Group to the President on State Ideology", Jakarta.				*
Camille ABOUSSOUAN, Ambassador, Permanent Delegate of Lebanon to Unesco, editor and writer, Paris.			*	
Serghei AROUTIUNOV, Institute of Ethnography, Academy of Sciences of USSR, Moscow.	*			
John C. BARTHOLOMEW, Director, The Geographical Institute, John Bartholomew & Son Ltd., Edinburgh	*			
Ola BALOGUN writer, film maker, Lagos.			*	
Ruben BAREIRO-SAGUIER, writer; University of Paris VIII, Paris.			*	

(1) Meeting on preliminary aspects of a project of intercultural studies (Belgrade, 5-7 October 1976)
(2) Consultative meeting to draw up a Programme of Intercultural Studies, arranged jointly by Unesco and ICPHS (Unesco, Paris, 21-22 March 1978)
(3) Committee of Experts on "Education for the Mutual Understanding of Cultures" (Unesco, Paris, 28-31 May 1979)
(4) Coordination Group on Intercultural Studies, first meeting, (Unesco, Paris 17-18 September 1979)

	1976	1978	May 1979	Sept. 1979
Louis BAZIN, Secretary-General, International Union for Oriental and Asian Studies, Paris.		*		
Jacques BERTIN Director, Laboratoire de graphique, Ecole des hautes études en sciences sociales, Paris.	*			
Ivan BOLDIZSAR, Chief Editor, "The New Hungarian Quarterly", Budapest.		*	*	
Wadi BOUZAR, Sociologist, University of Algiers, Algiers.			*	
Aleksa CELEBONOVIC, painter and critic, professor at the Faculty of Applied Arts, Belgrade.	*			
Emile CONDURACHI, Academy of the S.R. of Roumania, Secretary-General of the Association internationale d'études du Sud-Est européen, Bucarest.				*
Rafael CONTE, writer and literary critic; Director of the weekly cultural supplement of "El Pais", Madrid.			*	
Milan DAMJANOVIC, Faculty of Drama, Belgrade.	*			
Pierrette DESY (Mrs), Ethnologist, specialist in North American Indians, Sainte-Foy, Québec			*	
Djibril DIALLO, Assistant Director, External Relations, International African Institute, London.				*
Germaine DIETERLEN (Mrs), Vice-President, Société des africanistes; Ecole des hautes études, Paris.	*			

	1976	1978	May 1979	Sept. 1979
Cheikh Anta DIOP Historian; Physicist; Director, Laboratoire de radiocarbone, I.F.A.N. Université, Dakar.		*		
Alphonse DUPRONT, président d'honneur de la Sorbonne, Paris.		*	*	*
Vadime ELISSEEFF, Historian; Chief Curator, Musée Cernuschi, Paris.		*	*	
Bozidar FELDBAUER, Geographer, cartographer, Institute of Lexicography of Yugoslavia, Zagreb.	*			
Claude FELL, literary critic, specialist in Latin American literature, Univer- sité de Haute Bretagne, Rennes (France).			*	
H.A. FISCHER-BARNICOL, philosopher, Professor, Director of the Institute of Intercultural Research, Heidelberg.			*	
Bozidar GAGRO, Director, Institut de recherches culturelles de Croatie, Zagreb.	*		*	
Carmen GUERRERO-NAKPIL (Mrs), writer and journalist, Commis- sioner, National Commission on the Rôle of Women, Manila.			*	
James HAMILTON, member of the Bureau of the Inter- national Union for Oriental and Asian Studies, Paris.		*		
Heikki KIRKINEN, University of Joensuu, Joensuu (Finland).	*	*		
Otto KLINEBERG, Socio-psychologist, ethnologist; Director, Centre international d'études sur les relations entre groupes ethniques (CIERGE), Ecole des hautes études en sciences sociales, Paris.			*	

	1976	1978	May 1979	Sept. 1979
Guy A. KOUASSIGAN, Researcher, Secretariat of the International Year of the Child; Professor, Institut universitaire d'études du développement, Genève			*	
Seydou B. KOUYATE, former Minister of Education and Culture of Mali, Argenteuil.		*		
Christian LALIVE D'EPINAY, Institut universitaire d'études du développement, Genève.	*			
Graciela de LA LAMA (Mrs), Vice-President of the International Union for Oriental and Asian Studies; Secretary-General of the Asociación latinoamericana de estudios afroasiáticos; Director of the Center of Arab and Asian Studies of the Colegio de Mexico, Mexico.		*		
Napoléon LEBLANC, vice-recteur de l'Université Laval, Québec.		*		
W.P. LEHMANN, The University of Texas, College of Social and Behavioural Sciences, Department of Linguistics, Austin (Texas).				*
LE THANH KHOI, Professor, Université René Descartes (Sciences humaines), U.E.R. de Sciences de l'éducation, Paris.			*	
Svetozar LUKIC, writer, Belgrade.	*			
Stevan MAJSTOROVIC, Director, Institut de recherches du développement culturel, Belgrade.	*			
Abdelwahab MEDDEB, writer, Paris.				*

	1976	1978	May 1979	Sept. 1979
Louis NECKER, Institut universitaire d'études du développement, Genève.	*			
Jean d'ORMESSON, de l'Académie française; Secretary-General of the International Council for Philosophy and Humanistic Studies (ICPHS), Paris.		*	*	*
Mohd. Taib OSMAN, Faculty of Arts, University of Malaya, Kuala-Lumpur.	*			
Antun PETAK, University of Zagreb, Institute of Social Research, Zagreb.	*			
Reginaldo DI PIERO, Ecole des hautes études (Sociologie de la littérature), Paris.				*
Roy PREISWERK, Director of the Institut universitaire d'études du développement, Genève.		*		
Sandor RADO, Dr. h.c. Dr.Sc.Dr.Econ.F.R.G.S. National Office of Lands and mapping, Budapest.	*			
Raja RAO, Central Institute of English and Foreign Languages, Hyderabad.		*		
Asesela RAVUVU, Co-ordinator in Pacific Studies University of the South Pacific, Suva (Fidji).			*	
Estavão de REZENDE MARTINS, Professor of Philosophy and History at the University of Brasilia, Charenton-le-Pont (France).		*		
Arthur SEYMOUR, poet, critic; Chairman, National Commission for Research on the Material on Guyana; Deputy-Chairman, Guyana National Trust, Georgetown, Guyana.			*	

	1976	1978	May 1979	Sept. 1979
Rodolfo STAVENHAGEN sociologist; Director of the Center of Social Studies, Colegio de Mexico, Mexico.		*		
Ronald SYME, Wolfson College, Oxford.	*			
Zeljko SKALAMERA, National Library of the S.R. of Serbia, Belgrade.	*			
Salah STETIE, writer and poet; Deputy Permanent Delegate of Lebanon to Unesco, Paris.		*		
Tatsuro YAMAMOTO, Academy of Japan; President of the ICPHS; Vice-President of the International Union for Oriental and Asian Studies, Tokyo. (1)		*		

Unesco

Makaminan MAKAGIANSAR, Assistant Director-General for Culture and Communication.

Emmanuel POUCHPA DASS, Director of the Division of Cultural Studies.

Michel CONIL LACOSTE, in charge of the Project in the Division of Cultural Studies.

---

(1) For each participant, the titles, functions and residences indicated are those which applied at the date of the meetings in which they participated.